DEAN KOONTZ

FEAR NOTHING

volume one

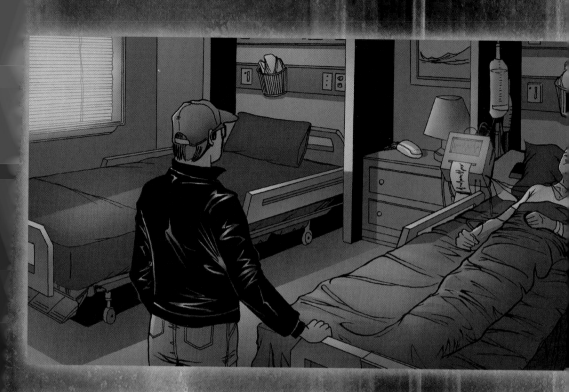

ENTERTAINMENT

WWW.DYNAMITEENTERTAINMENT.COM

NICK BARRUCCI	•	PRESIDENT
JUAN COLLADO	•	CHIEF OPERATING OFFICER
JOSEPH RYBANDT	•	EDITOR
JOSH JOHNSON	•	CREATIVE DIRECTOR
RICH YOUNG	•	DIRECTOR OF BUSINESS DEVELOPMENT
JASON ULLMEYER	•	GRAPHIC DESIGNER

First Printing   10 9 8 7 6 5 4 3 2 1   ISBN-10: 1-60690-168-0   ISBN-13: 978-1-60690-168-7

DEAN KOONTZ

FEAR NOTHING

written by
DEAN KOONTZ

adapted by
GRANT ALTER &
DEREK RUIZ

artwork by
ROBERT GILL

coloring by
MOHAN

lettering & design by
BILL TORTOLINI

consultants
LES DABEL &
ERNST DABEL

Inspiration is a stranger animal than people think. Readers tend to suppose that ideas for novels come to me in bad dreams. In fact, I've never gotten an idea from a nightmare. Well, except that once in a while I have urgent water dreams of tsunamis and burst dams--from which I always awake to discover that I need to pee. But story ideas --no.

For the most part, ideas don't come from reading newspapers and magazines, either. By the time something's in the press-- some curious true story or perhaps a new scientific development--it's either old news to the community of writers, which is always striving to be ahead of the curve, or a gajillion and a half other novelists see it in the same magazine and sit down at once to write a story around that same kernel.

In the case of Fear Nothing, however, a magazine article did have something to do with my inspiration. People ran a story about children with xeroderma pigmentosum (XP), an inherited disorder in which the body is unable to repair damage to the skin and eyes caused by exposure to the sun and other sources of light. Cumulative damage can lead to terminal cancer. People with XP have to live by night and candlelight, always in the shadows.

Before coming across this article, I had wanted to write a novel in which surfing played a major role. At that time, we owned a house on Balboa Peninsula Point, in Newport Beach, less than a leisurely five-minute walk to the Wedge, which is one of the most famous surfing locations in the world. I found surfing culture fascinating, and its lingo was singularly rich. I knew I wanted to set the story in a California coastal town that was sort of a cross between Carmel and Morro Bay, and I figured that something weird would be going on in that town. Something related to genetic engineering. This wouldn't just be a story about surfing and XP but also about aggressive lab monkeys on the loose, dogs and cats that seem strangely intelligent, people becoming eerily animalistic, flocks of birds behaving in a peculiar fashion, immense secret underground research facilities.... I am not a minimalist.

I was also fascinated by the vast military bases that were being closed following the end of the cold war, some of them like entire little cities with shops and theaters and on-base housing for thousands, which became ghost towns. I knew one such base would exist adjacent to the town--which became Moonlight Bay--that it would be called Fort Wyvern, and that the source of the weirdness in the town would arise from some experiment that had been--and might still be-- conducted on the base.

Halfway through the article on xeroderma pigmentosum, I whooped out loud, realizing that my lead character, who became Christopher Snow, would suffer from this condition. He would be tragic and yet hugely romantic, a night surfer who knew the night better than anyone had ever known it, who was at home in the night as no other human being could ever be. His mother- -deceased--had been a scientist who worked on the closed base. Chris loved her, missed her--but as he began to realize that the end of the world had begun in Moonlight Bay, he also began to suspect that his mother might have been a driving force behind research that went badly wrong. Yep, his mom might have inadvertently become the destroyer of the world as we know it. Now, there's a little emotional quandary that would make even Hamlet grateful for his family situation.

I have promised to write the third Chris Snow, and I will. In fact, I have begun it. Meanwhile, I am delighted with this graphic novel, and I think Derek Ruiz, Grant Alter, and Robert Gill have produced a brilliant adaptation. So hang on and hang ten through this apocalypse with monkeys.

Dean Koontz

chapter one

RIIINNG RING

I AM **NOT** PSYCHIC. I DO NOT SEE SIGNS AND PORTENTS IN THE SKY.

I DON'T HAVE A GYPSY'S ABILITY TO DISCERN THE PATTERNS OF FATE IN WET TEA LEAVES.

BUT I KNEW THE RINGING TELEPHONE MEANT THAT A **TERRIBLE** CHANGE WAS COMING.

MY FATHER HAD BEEN DYING FOR DAYS. I HAD SPENT THE PREVIOUS NIGHT MOPPING SWEAT FROM HIS FOREHEAD AND LISTENING TO HIS LABORED BREATHING.

RIIINNG RING

I DREADED LOSING HIM AND, FOR THE FIRST TIME IN MY 28 YEARS, OF BEING ALONE. I HAD LOST MY MOTHER TWO YEARS EARLIER AND NOW I WAS TO LOSE MY FATHER.

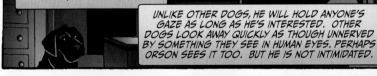

ORSON ALSO KNEW WHAT THE RINGING MEANT.

HE'S A **STRANGE** DOG. BUT HE'S MY DOG, MY STEADFAST FRIEND, AND I LOVE HIM.

UNLIKE OTHER DOGS, HE WILL HOLD ANYONE'S GAZE AS LONG AS HE'S INTERESTED. OTHER DOGS LOOK AWAY QUICKLY AS THOUGH UNNERVED BY SOMETHING THEY SEE IN HUMAN EYES. PERHAPS ORSON SEES IT TOO. BUT HE IS NOT INTIMIDATED.

HELLO?

CHRIS, IT'S ANGELA. IT'S NOT LOOKING GOOD. YOU BETTER COME DOWN TO THE HOSPITAL.

I UNDERSTAND. THANK YOU.

RIIINNG

SASHA. I HAD TO CALL SASHA.

AT NIGHT, I WOULD BE ABLE TO WALK TO THE HOSPITAL ON MY OWN. BUT AT THIS TIME OF DAY, IT WOULD MAKE ME TOO MUCH OF A SPECTACLE AND PUT ME AT TOO GREAT A RISK.

CHRIS, I'M SO SORRY.

SASHA GOODALL SPUN MUSIC FROM MIDNIGHT UNTIL SIX AM ON **KBAY**, THE ONLY STATION IN MOONLIGHT BAY. SO AT A FEW MINUTES PAST FIVE, SHE WAS MOST LIKELY SLEEPING AND I REGRETTED HAVING TO WAKE HER. BUT I NEEDED A RIDE TO THE HOSPITAL.

IT WAS AS THOUGH SHE'D BEEN WAITING FOR THIS CALL, AS IF SHE'D HEARD THE SAME OMINOUS TONE IN THE RING OF HER PHONE THAT ORSON AND I HAD HEARD IN MINE.

I HAD HELD OUT HOPE THAT EVEN AT THE ELEVENTH HOUR, THE CANCER WOULD GO INTO REMISSION.

I'LL BE THERE IN FIVE MINUTES.

NO. DRIVE CAREFULLY. I'LL PROBABLY TAKE TEN MINUTES OR MORE TO GET READY.

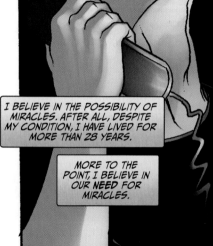

I BELIEVE IN THE POSSIBILITY OF MIRACLES. AFTER ALL, DESPITE MY CONDITION, I HAVE LIVED FOR MORE THAN 28 YEARS.

MORE TO THE POINT, I BELIEVE IN OUR **NEED** FOR MIRACLES.

LOVE YOU, SNOWMAN.

LOVE YOU TOO.

I HAVE **XERODERMA PIGMENTOSUM**, XP FOR SHORT, A RARE AND FREQUENTLY FATAL GENETIC DISORDER.

EVERYONE INCURS SUNLIGHT DAMAGE TO THEIR DNA.

HEALTHY PEOPLE'S CELLULAR REPAIR SYSTEMS NATURALLY MEND THIS DAMAGE.

THIS IS NOT THE CASE FOR US XPERS.

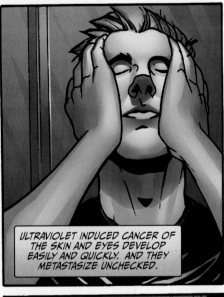

ULTRAVIOLET INDUCED CANCER OF THE SKIN AND EYES DEVELOP EASILY AND QUICKLY. AND THEY METASTASIZE UNCHECKED.

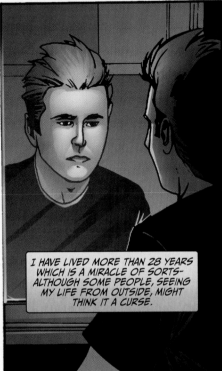

I HAVE LIVED MORE THAN 28 YEARS WHICH IS A MIRACLE OF SORTS- ALTHOUGH SOME PEOPLE, SEEING MY LIFE FROM OUTSIDE, MIGHT THINK IT A CURSE.

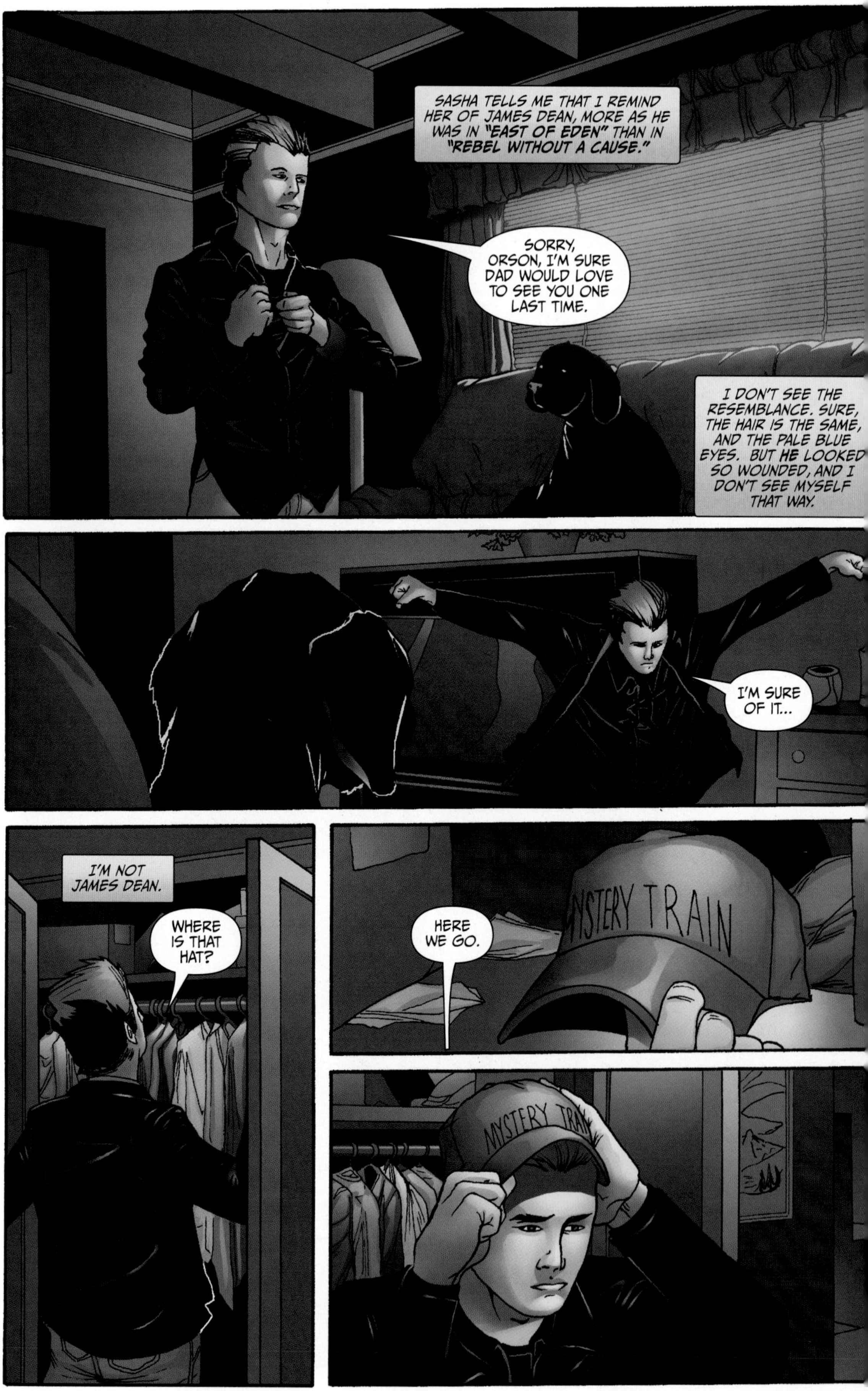
SASHA TELLS ME THAT I REMIND HER OF JAMES DEAN, MORE AS HE WAS IN "EAST OF EDEN" THAN IN "REBEL WITHOUT A CAUSE."
SORRY, ORSON, I'M SURE DAD WOULD LOVE TO SEE YOU ONE LAST TIME.
I DON'T SEE THE RESEMBLANCE. SURE, THE HAIR IS THE SAME, AND THE PALE BLUE EYES. BUT HE LOOKED SO WOUNDED, AND I DON'T SEE MYSELF THAT WAY.
I'M SURE OF IT...
I'M NOT JAMES DEAN.
WHERE IS THAT HAT?
HERE WE GO.
MYSTERY TRAIN
MYSTERY TRAIN

I AM NO ONE BUT ME, CHRISTOPHER SNOW, AND I CAN LIVE WITH THAT.

I COULD'VE SWORN HIS GAZE BRIMMED WITH GRIEF AND SYMPATHY. PERHAPS IT WAS BECAUSE I WAS LOOKING AT HIM THROUGH REPRESSED TEARS OF MY OWN.

MY FRIEND BOBBY SAYS THAT I TEND TO ANTHROPOMORPHIZE ANIMALS. GIVING THEM HUMAN ATTRIBUTES AND ATTITUDES THAT THEY DON'T, IN FACT, POSSESS.

PERHAPS IT'S BECAUSE ANIMALS, UNLIKE PEOPLE, HAVE ACCEPTED ME FOR WHAT I AM.

WE'LL BE ALL RIGHT, BOY.

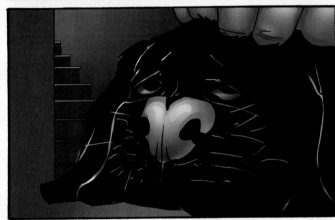

THESE FOUR-LEGGED CITIZENS OF MOONLIGHT BAY SEEM TO POSSESS A MORE COMPLEX UNDERSTANDING OF LIFE AND KINDNESS THAN AT LEAST SOME OF MY NEIGHBORS.

HONK HONK

BOBBY TELLS ME THAT ANTHROPOMORPHIZING ANIMALS, REGARDLESS OF MY EXPERIENCES WITH THEM, IS A SIGN OF IMMATURITY.

I TELL BOBBY TO GO COPULATE WITH HIMSELF.

WE'LL BE ALL RIGHT. I PROMISE.

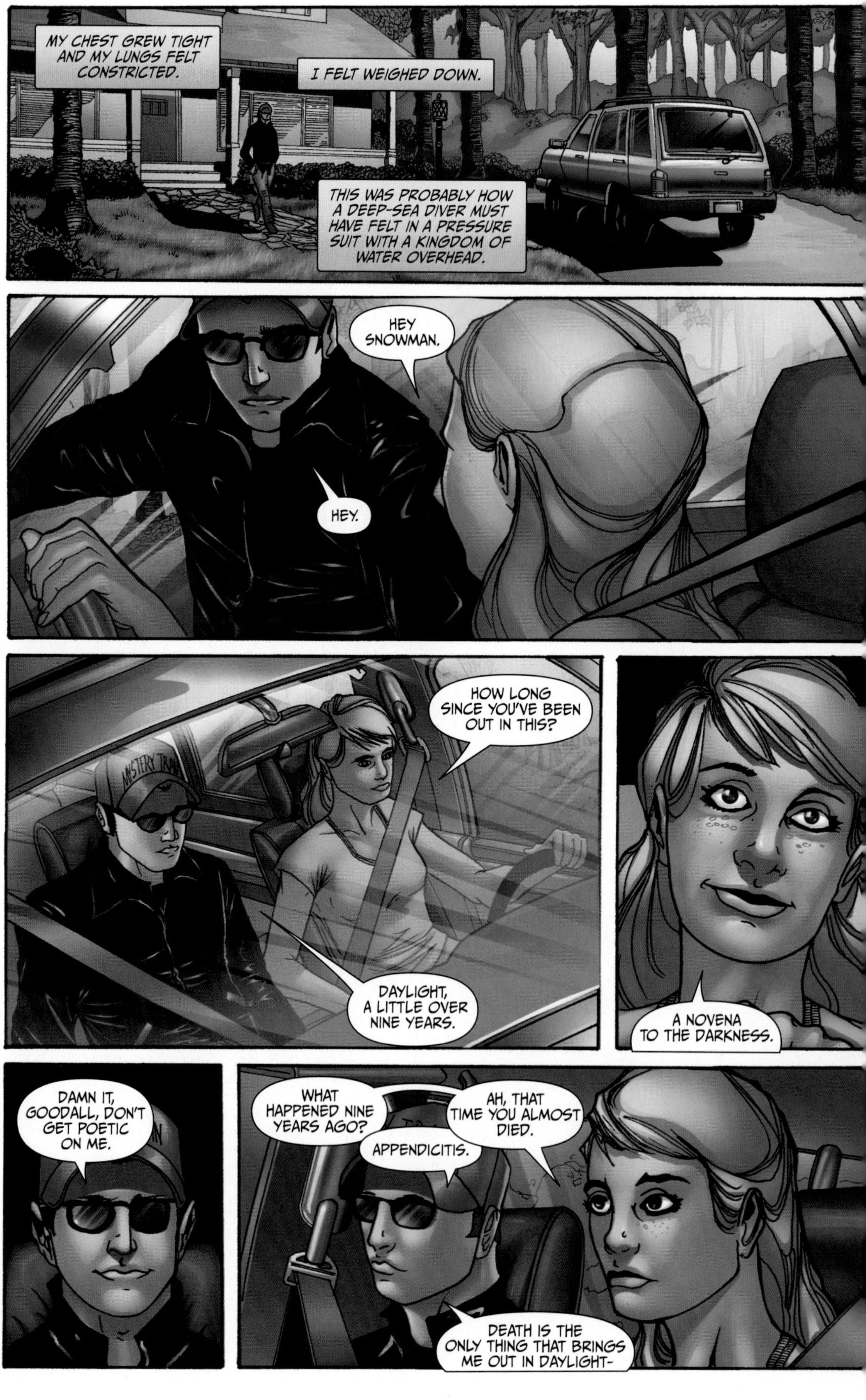
MY CHEST GREW TIGHT AND MY LUNGS FELT CONSTRICTED.
I FELT WEIGHED DOWN.
THIS WAS PROBABLY HOW A DEEP-SEA DIVER MUST HAVE FELT IN A PRESSURE SUIT WITH A KINGDOM OF WATER OVERHEAD.
HEY SNOWMAN.
HEY.
HOW LONG SINCE YOU'VE BEEN OUT IN THIS?
DAYLIGHT, A LITTLE OVER NINE YEARS.
A NOVENA TO THE DARKNESS.
DAMN IT, GOODALL, DON'T GET POETIC ON ME.
WHAT HAPPENED NINE YEARS AGO?
APPENDICITIS.
AH, THAT TIME YOU ALMOST DIED.
DEATH IS THE ONLY THING THAT BRINGS ME OUT IN DAYLIGHT-

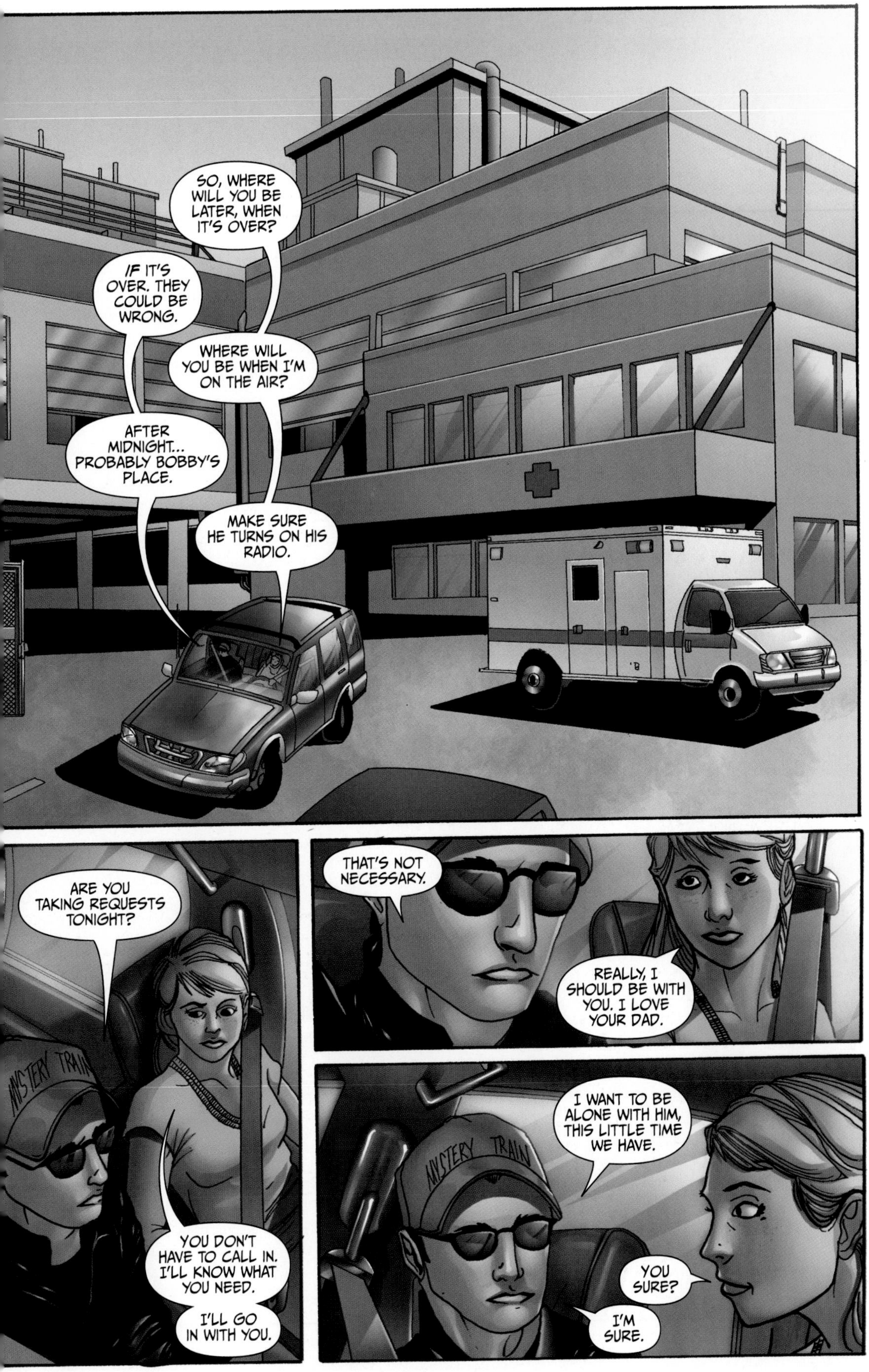
SO, WHERE WILL YOU BE LATER, WHEN IT'S OVER?
IF IT'S OVER. THEY COULD BE WRONG.
WHERE WILL YOU BE WHEN I'M ON THE AIR?
AFTER MIDNIGHT... PROBABLY BOBBY'S PLACE.
MAKE SURE HE TURNS ON HIS RADIO.
ARE YOU TAKING REQUESTS TONIGHT?
YOU DON'T HAVE TO CALL IN. I'LL KNOW WHAT YOU NEED.
I'LL GO IN WITH YOU.
THAT'S NOT NECESSARY.
REALLY, I SHOULD BE WITH YOU. I LOVE YOUR DAD.
I WANT TO BE ALONE WITH HIM, THIS LITTLE TIME WE HAVE.
YOU SURE?
I'M SURE.

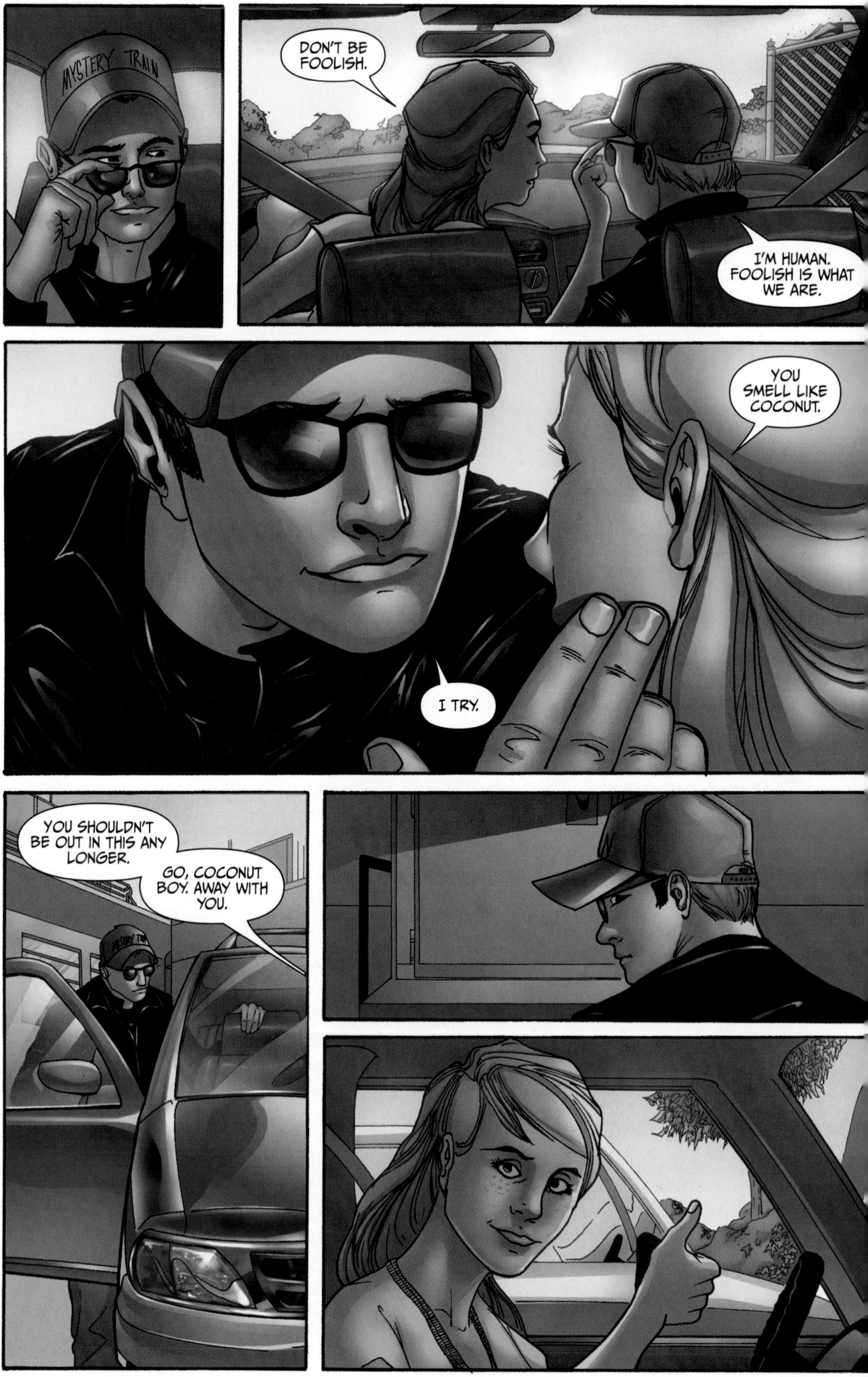
MYSTERY TRAIN
DON'T BE FOOLISH.
I'M HUMAN. FOOLISH IS WHAT WE ARE.
YOU SMELL LIKE COCONUT.
I TRY.
YOU SHOULDN'T BE OUT IN THIS ANY LONGER.
GO, COCONUT BOY. AWAY WITH YOU.

CHRIS... I'M GLAD YOU'RE HERE.

ANGELA FERRYMAN WAS WORKING THE EVENING SHIFT ON THE THIRD FLOOR. SHE HAD COME DOWNSTAIRS TO WAIT FOR ME.

SHE WAS A SWEET WOMAN AND WHEN I GOT THE CHICKEN POX OR THE MUMPS AS A BOY, SHE WOULD BE THE ONE TO COME SEE ME AT HOME.

IS HE?

IS HE ALRIGHT, CHRIS. HE'S HOLDING ON... FOR YOU, I THINK.

SINCE I COULDN'T BE TREATED OUTSIDE THE HOUSE, ANGELA WAS A GODSEND...A COMFORT. BUT THIS HUG WAS MORE FRIGHTENING THAN COMFORTING.

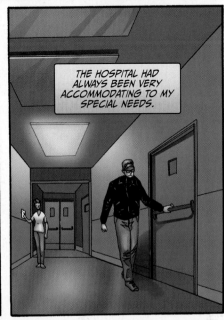

THE HOSPITAL HAD ALWAYS BEEN VERY ACCOMMODATING TO MY SPECIAL NEEDS.

WE'RE MEDICATING HIM FOR PAIN, SO HE'S BEEN DRIFTING IN AND OUT. BUT EVERY TIME HE COMES TO, HE ASKS TO SEE YOU.

SETH CLEVELAND WAS NOT JUST MY FATHER'S DOCTOR. HE WAS ONE OF MINE AS WELL.

THESE PEOPLE WERE NOT ATTRACTED TO ME BECAUSE OF ANYTHING ESPECIALLY WINNING ABOUT MY PERSONALITY OR SPECIAL LOVE FOR MY FATHER. EVERYONE WHO KNEW HIM LOVED HIM. BUT TO THESE DEDICATED HEALERS, I REPRESENT THAT THING...BEYOND THEIR ABILITY TO CURE.

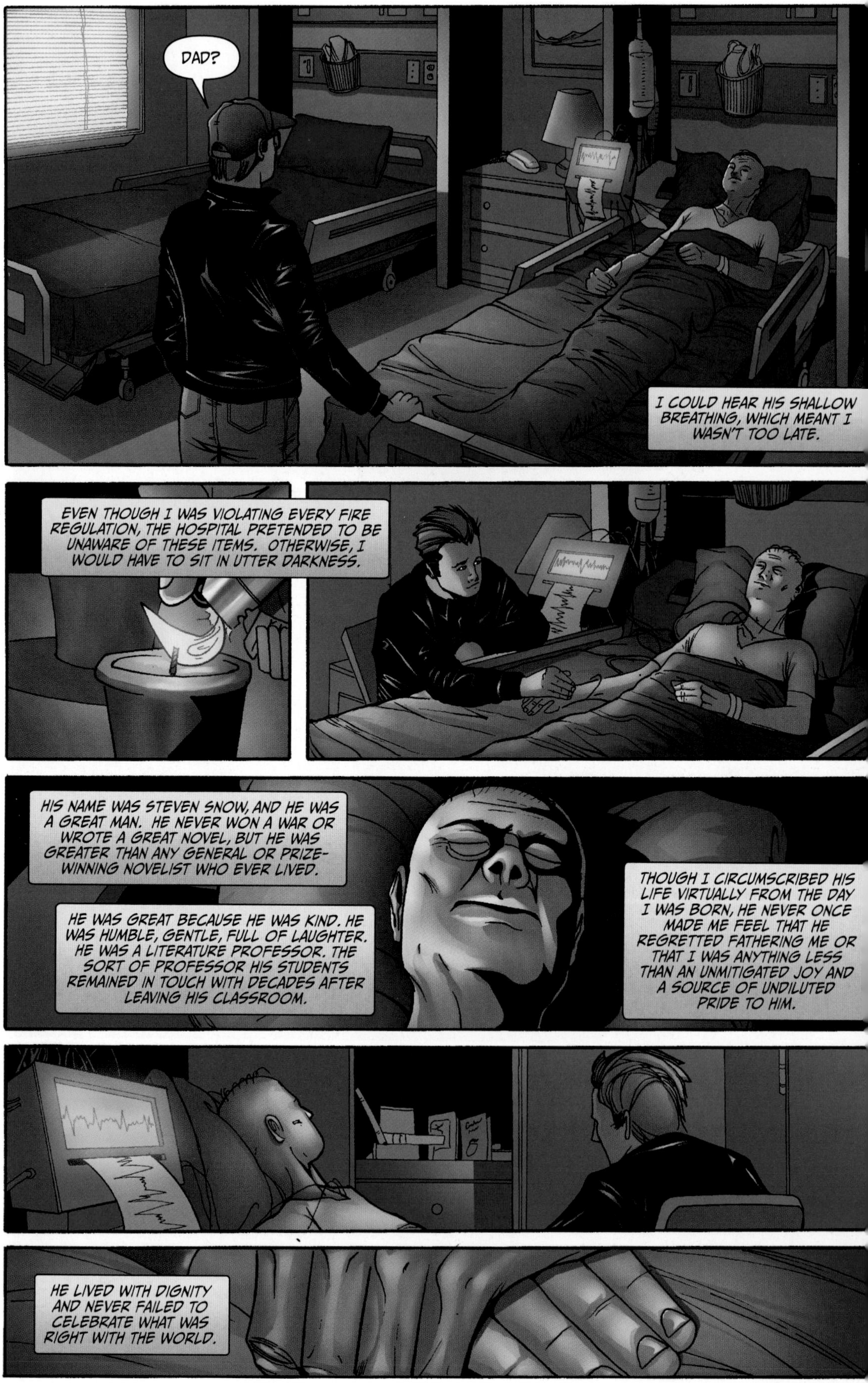
DAD?
I COULD HEAR HIS SHALLOW BREATHING, WHICH MEANT I WASN'T TOO LATE.
EVEN THOUGH I WAS VIOLATING EVERY FIRE REGULATION, THE HOSPITAL PRETENDED TO BE UNAWARE OF THESE ITEMS. OTHERWISE, I WOULD HAVE TO SIT IN UTTER DARKNESS.
HIS NAME WAS STEVEN SNOW, AND HE WAS A GREAT MAN. HE NEVER WON A WAR OR WROTE A GREAT NOVEL, BUT HE WAS GREATER THAN ANY GENERAL OR PRIZE-WINNING NOVELIST WHO EVER LIVED.
HE WAS GREAT BECAUSE HE WAS KIND. HE WAS HUMBLE, GENTLE, FULL OF LAUGHTER. HE WAS A LITERATURE PROFESSOR. THE SORT OF PROFESSOR HIS STUDENTS REMAINED IN TOUCH WITH DECADES AFTER LEAVING HIS CLASSROOM.
THOUGH I CIRCUMSCRIBED HIS LIFE VIRTUALLY FROM THE DAY I WAS BORN, HE NEVER ONCE MADE ME FEEL THAT HE REGRETTED FATHERING ME OR THAT I WAS ANYTHING LESS THAN AN UNMITIGATED JOY AND A SOURCE OF UNDILUTED PRIDE TO HIM.
HE LIVED WITH DIGNITY AND NEVER FAILED TO CELEBRATE WHAT WAS RIGHT WITH THE WORLD.

THE CANCER HAD SPREAD FROM HIS LIVER TO HIS LYMPHATIC SYSTEM, THEN TO OTHER ORGANS UNTIL HIS BODY WAS RIDDLED WITH IT.

WATER?

NO, I'M ALRIGHT.

I'M SORRY, CHRIS. SO *DAMN* SORRY.

YOU HAVE NOTHING TO BE SORRY ABOUT.

SORRY ABOUT THE INHERITANCE, SON.

IT WILL BE OKAY. I CAN TAKE CARE OF MYSELF.

NOT MONEY. THERE'LL BE ENOUGH OF THAT. THE OTHER INHERITANCE. THE XP.

DAD, NO. YOU COULDN'T HAVE KNOWN.

I'M SO SORRY...

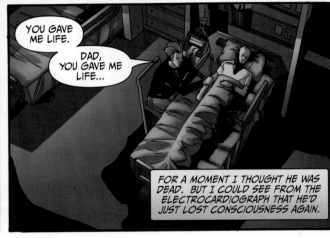

YOU GAVE ME LIFE.

DAD, YOU GAVE ME LIFE...

FOR A MOMENT I THOUGHT HE WAS DEAD. BUT I COULD SEE FROM THE ELECTROCARDIOGRAPH THAT HE'D JUST LOST CONSCIOUSNESS AGAIN.

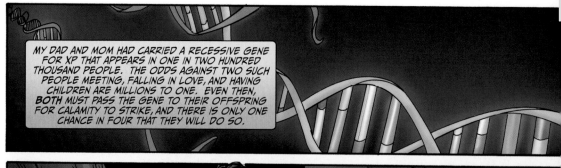

MY DAD AND MOM HAD CARRIED A RECESSIVE GENE FOR XP THAT APPEARS IN ONE IN TWO HUNDRED THOUSAND PEOPLE. THE ODDS AGAINST TWO SUCH PEOPLE MEETING, FALLING IN LOVE, AND HAVING CHILDREN ARE MILLIONS TO ONE. EVEN THEN, *BOTH* MUST PASS THE GENE TO THEIR OFFSPRING FOR CALAMITY TO STRIKE, AND THERE IS ONLY ONE CHANCE IN FOUR THAT THEY WILL DO SO.

THEY HIT THAT JACKPOT.

ALL MY LIFE, OUR HOUSE HAD BEEN FILLED WITH CONVERSATION.

MY DAD, MOM, AND I TALKED ABOUT NOVELS, OLD MOVIES, POLITICIANS, POETRY, MUSIC, HISTORY, SCIENCE, RELIGION, OWLS AND RACCOONS AND BATS AND OTHER CREATURES THAT SHARED THE NIGHT WITH ME.

WE DISCUSSED EVERYTHING. NO PROGRAM OF PHYSICAL EXERCISE WAS COMPLETE IN OUR HOUSE IF IT DIDN'T INCLUDE A DAILY WORKOUT OF THE TONGUE.

YET NOW, WHEN I MOST DESPERATELY NEEDED TO OPEN MY HEART TO MY FATHER, I WAS SPEECHLESS.

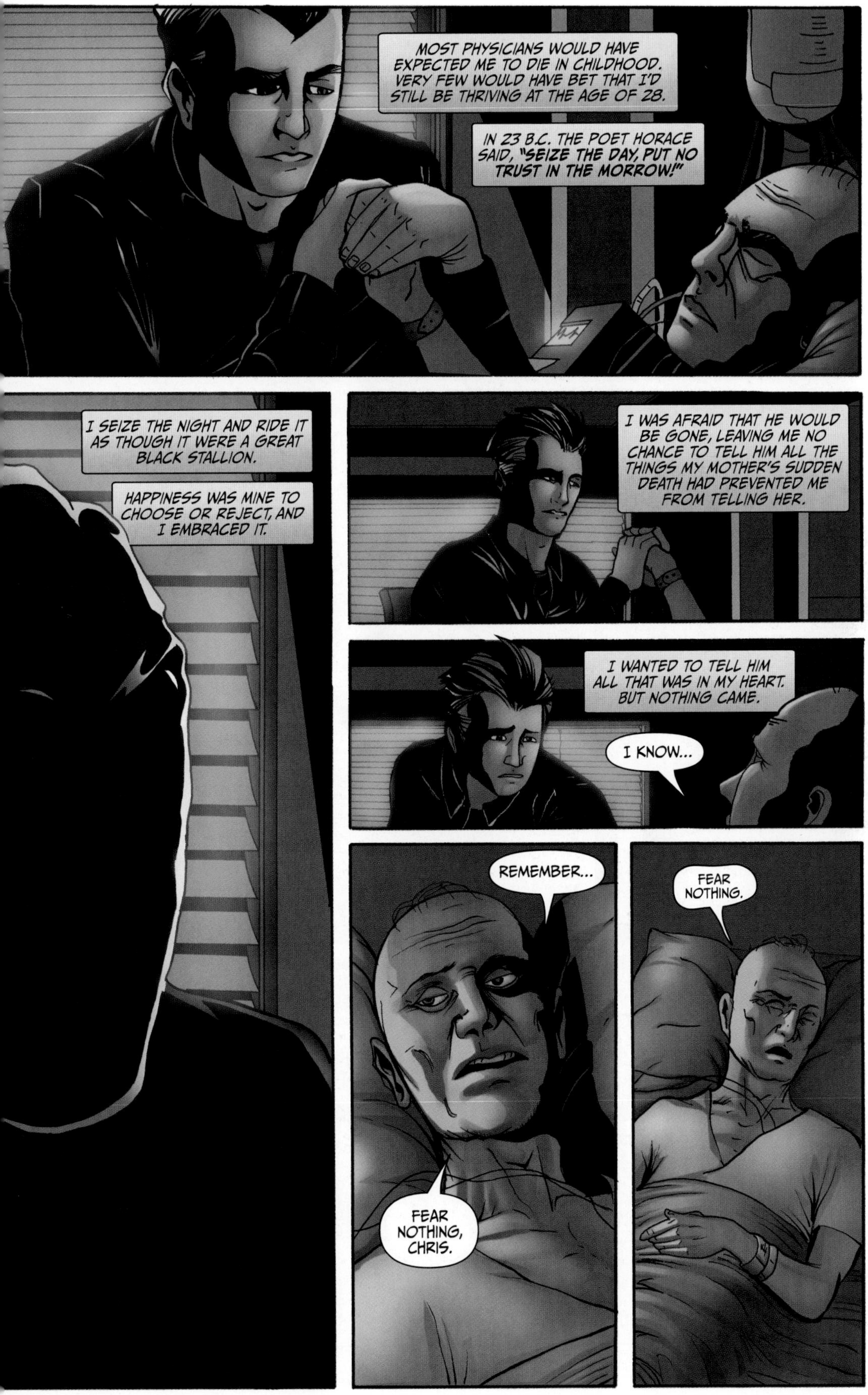
MOST PHYSICIANS WOULD HAVE EXPECTED ME TO DIE IN CHILDHOOD. VERY FEW WOULD HAVE BET THAT I'D STILL BE THRIVING AT THE AGE OF 28.
IN 23 B.C. THE POET HORACE SAID, "SEIZE THE DAY, PUT NO TRUST IN THE MORROW!"
I SEIZE THE NIGHT AND RIDE IT AS THOUGH IT WERE A GREAT BLACK STALLION.
HAPPINESS WAS MINE TO CHOOSE OR REJECT, AND I EMBRACED IT.
I WAS AFRAID THAT HE WOULD BE GONE, LEAVING ME NO CHANCE TO TELL HIM ALL THE THINGS MY MOTHER'S SUDDEN DEATH HAD PREVENTED ME FROM TELLING HER.
I WANTED TO TELL HIM ALL THAT WAS IN MY HEART. BUT NOTHING CAME.
I KNOW...
REMEMBER...
FEAR NOTHING, CHRIS.
FEAR NOTHING.

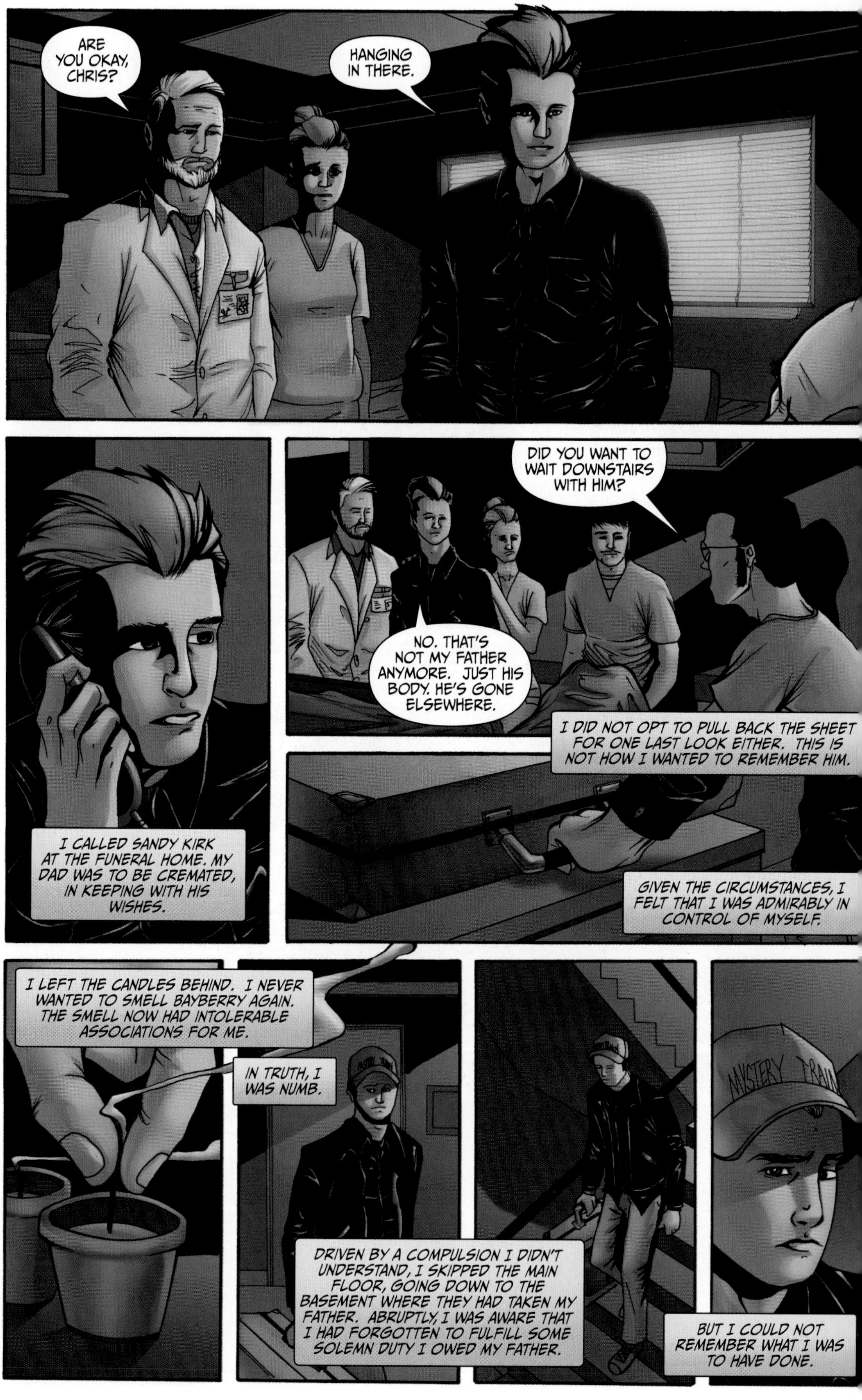
ARE YOU OKAY, CHRIS?
HANGING IN THERE.
I CALLED SANDY KIRK AT THE FUNERAL HOME. MY DAD WAS TO BE CREMATED, IN KEEPING WITH HIS WISHES.
DID YOU WANT TO WAIT DOWNSTAIRS WITH HIM?
NO. THAT'S NOT MY FATHER ANYMORE. JUST HIS BODY. HE'S GONE ELSEWHERE.
I DID NOT OPT TO PULL BACK THE SHEET FOR ONE LAST LOOK EITHER. THIS IS NOT HOW I WANTED TO REMEMBER HIM.
GIVEN THE CIRCUMSTANCES, I FELT THAT I WAS ADMIRABLY IN CONTROL OF MYSELF.
I LEFT THE CANDLES BEHIND. I NEVER WANTED TO SMELL BAYBERRY AGAIN. THE SMELL NOW HAD INTOLERABLE ASSOCIATIONS FOR ME.
IN TRUTH, I WAS NUMB.
DRIVEN BY A COMPULSION I DIDN'T UNDERSTAND, I SKIPPED THE MAIN FLOOR, GOING DOWN TO THE BASEMENT WHERE THEY HAD TAKEN MY FATHER. ABRUPTLY, I WAS AWARE THAT I HAD FORGOTTEN TO FULFILL SOME SOLEMN DUTY I OWED MY FATHER.
MYSTERY TRAIN
BUT I COULD NOT REMEMBER WHAT I WAS TO HAVE DONE.

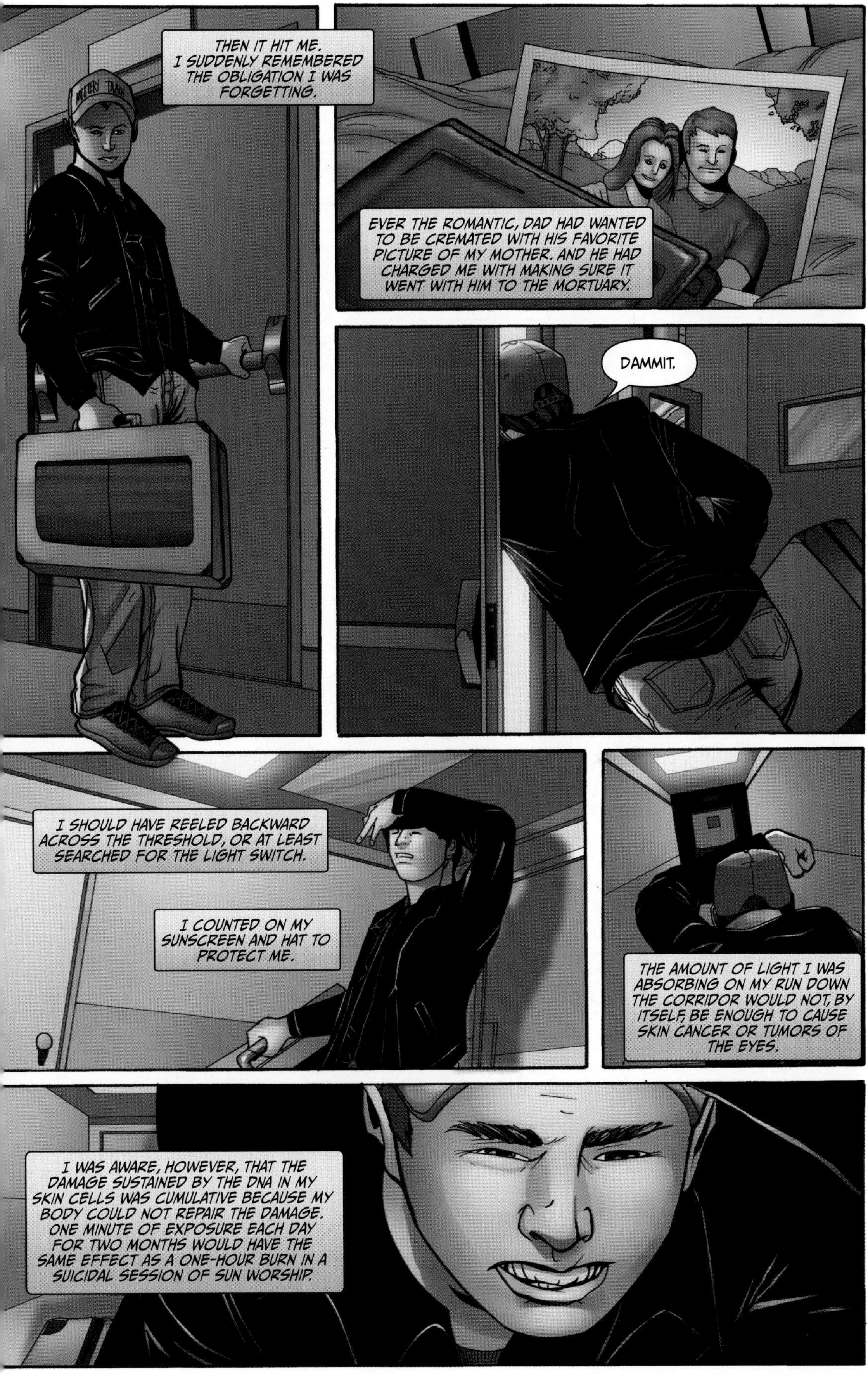
THEN IT HIT ME. I SUDDENLY REMEMBERED THE OBLIGATION I WAS FORGETTING.
EVER THE ROMANTIC, DAD HAD WANTED TO BE CREMATED WITH HIS FAVORITE PICTURE OF MY MOTHER. AND HE HAD CHARGED ME WITH MAKING SURE IT WENT WITH HIM TO THE MORTUARY.
DAMMIT.
I SHOULD HAVE REELED BACKWARD ACROSS THE THRESHOLD, OR AT LEAST SEARCHED FOR THE LIGHT SWITCH.
I COUNTED ON MY SUNSCREEN AND HAT TO PROTECT ME.
THE AMOUNT OF LIGHT I WAS ABSORBING ON MY RUN DOWN THE CORRIDOR WOULD NOT, BY ITSELF, BE ENOUGH TO CAUSE SKIN CANCER OR TUMORS OF THE EYES.
I WAS AWARE, HOWEVER, THAT THE DAMAGE SUSTAINED BY THE DNA IN MY SKIN CELLS WAS CUMULATIVE BECAUSE MY BODY COULD NOT REPAIR THE DAMAGE. ONE MINUTE OF EXPOSURE EACH DAY FOR TWO MONTHS WOULD HAVE THE SAME EFFECT AS A ONE-HOUR BURN IN A SUICIDAL SESSION OF SUN WORSHIP.

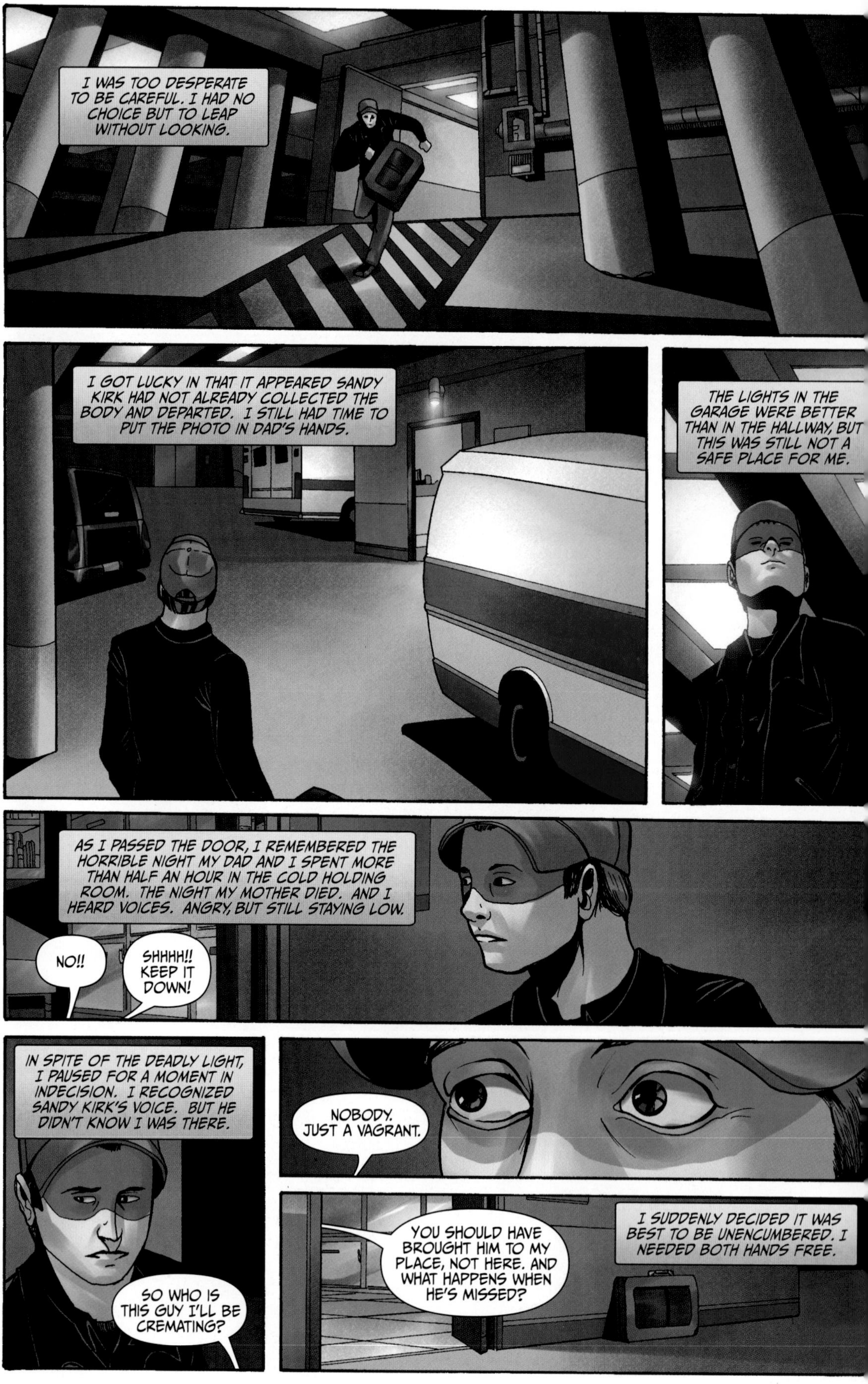
I WAS TOO DESPERATE TO BE CAREFUL. I HAD NO CHOICE BUT TO LEAP WITHOUT LOOKING.
I GOT LUCKY IN THAT IT APPEARED SANDY KIRK HAD NOT ALREADY COLLECTED THE BODY AND DEPARTED. I STILL HAD TIME TO PUT THE PHOTO IN DAD'S HANDS.
THE LIGHTS IN THE GARAGE WERE BETTER THAN IN THE HALLWAY, BUT THIS WAS STILL NOT A SAFE PLACE FOR ME.
AS I PASSED THE DOOR, I REMEMBERED THE HORRIBLE NIGHT MY DAD AND I SPENT MORE THAN HALF AN HOUR IN THE COLD HOLDING ROOM. THE NIGHT MY MOTHER DIED. AND I HEARD VOICES. ANGRY, BUT STILL STAYING LOW.
NO!!
SHHHH!! KEEP IT DOWN!
IN SPITE OF THE DEADLY LIGHT, I PAUSED FOR A MOMENT IN INDECISION. I RECOGNIZED SANDY KIRK'S VOICE. BUT HE DIDN'T KNOW I WAS THERE.
SO WHO IS THIS GUY I'LL BE CREMATING?
NOBODY. JUST A VAGRANT.
YOU SHOULD HAVE BROUGHT HIM TO MY PLACE, NOT HERE. AND WHAT HAPPENS WHEN HE'S MISSED?
I SUDDENLY DECIDED IT WAS BEST TO BE UNENCUMBERED. I NEEDED BOTH HANDS FREE.

I TOLD YOU HE WAS A VAGRANT. EVERYTHING HE OWNED IS IN HIS BACKPACK. HE DISAPPEARS, WHO'LL KNOW OR CARE?

WHAT ABOUT HIS MEDICAL RECORDS?

HE DIDN'T DIE HERE. I PICKED HIM UP EARLIER, HITCHHIKING ON THE HIGHWAY.

I'M TAKING A BIG RISK.

YOU'RE UNTOUCHABLE.

I WONDER.

WORRY ON YOUR OWN TIME.

I HAD CAUGHT THEM IN SOME UNKNOWN SCHEME THAT CLEARLY INVOLVED ILLEGALITIES. THEY WOULD CERTAINLY WANT TO KEEP IT SECRET FROM ME, OF ALL PEOPLE.

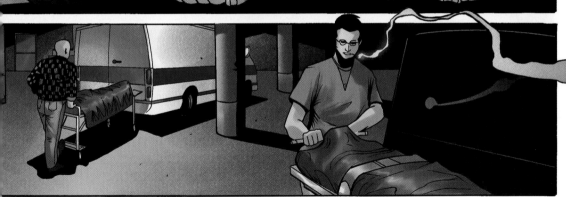

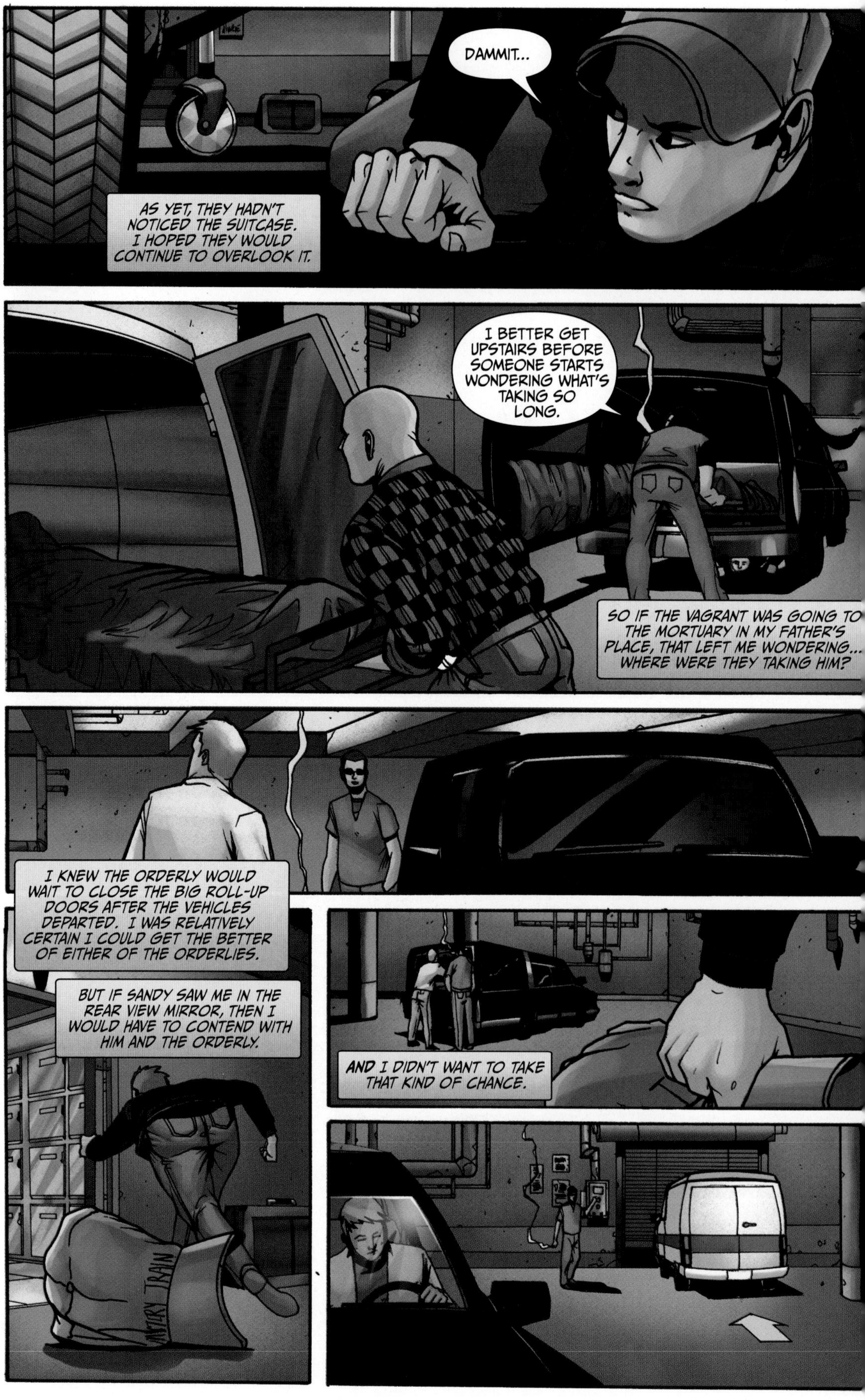
DAMMIT...
AS YET, THEY HADN'T NOTICED THE SUITCASE. I HOPED THEY WOULD CONTINUE TO OVERLOOK IT.
I BETTER GET UPSTAIRS BEFORE SOMEONE STARTS WONDERING WHAT'S TAKING SO LONG.
SO IF THE VAGRANT WAS GOING TO THE MORTUARY IN MY FATHER'S PLACE, THAT LEFT ME WONDERING... WHERE WERE THEY TAKING HIM?
I KNEW THE ORDERLY WOULD WAIT TO CLOSE THE BIG ROLL-UP DOORS AFTER THE VEHICLES DEPARTED. I WAS RELATIVELY CERTAIN I COULD GET THE BETTER OF EITHER OF THE ORDERLIES.
BUT IF SANDY SAW ME IN THE REAR VIEW MIRROR, THEN I WOULD HAVE TO CONTEND WITH HIM AND THE ORDERLY.
AND I DIDN'T WANT TO TAKE THAT KIND OF CHANCE.

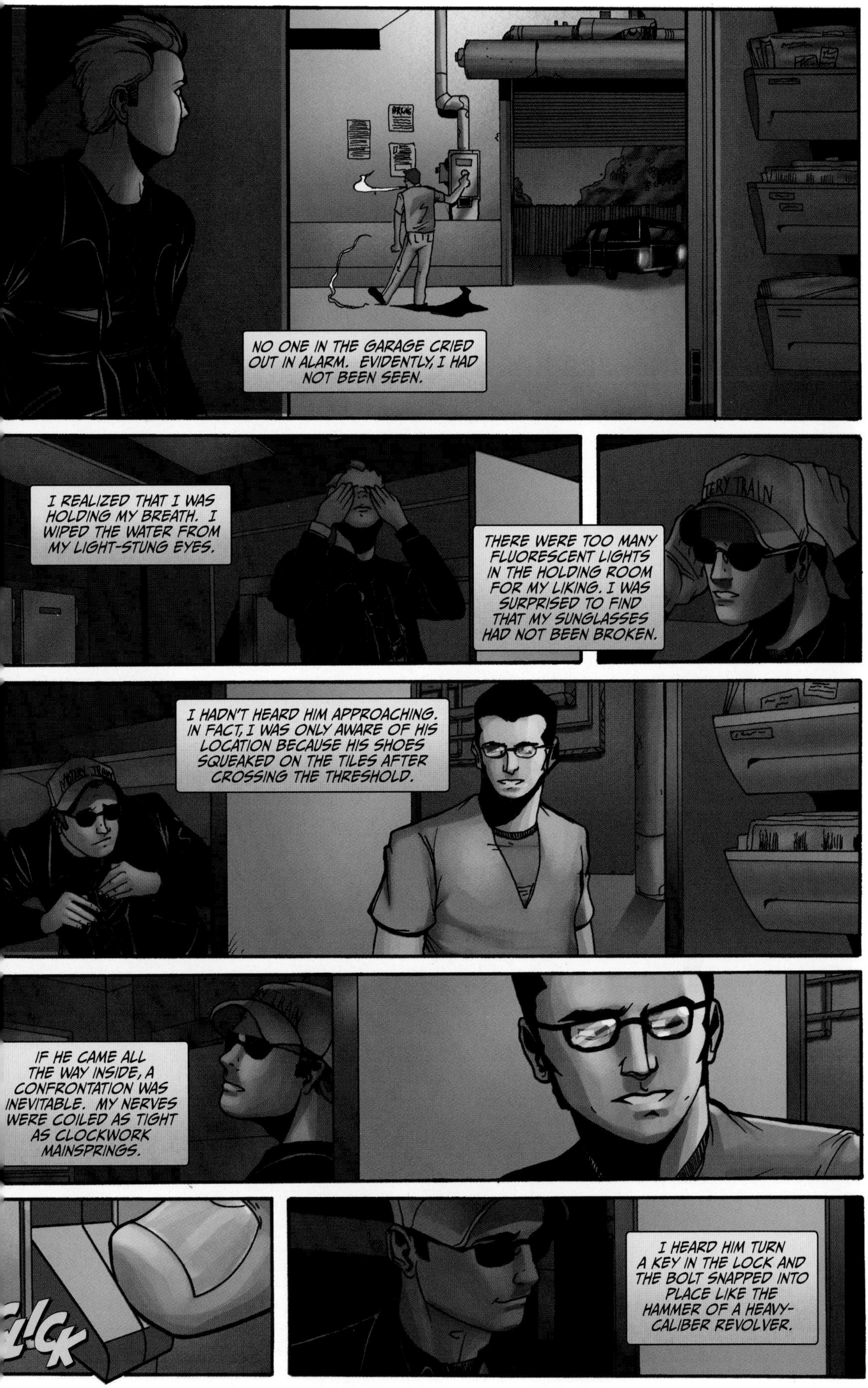
NO ONE IN THE GARAGE CRIED OUT IN ALARM. EVIDENTLY, I HAD NOT BEEN SEEN.
I REALIZED THAT I WAS HOLDING MY BREATH. I WIPED THE WATER FROM MY LIGHT-STUNG EYES.
THERE WERE TOO MANY FLUORESCENT LIGHTS IN THE HOLDING ROOM FOR MY LIKING. I WAS SURPRISED TO FIND THAT MY SUNGLASSES HAD NOT BEEN BROKEN.
I HADN'T HEARD HIM APPROACHING. IN FACT, I WAS ONLY AWARE OF HIS LOCATION BECAUSE HIS SHOES SQUEAKED ON THE TILES AFTER CROSSING THE THRESHOLD.
IF HE CAME ALL THE WAY INSIDE, A CONFRONTATION WAS INEVITABLE. MY NERVES WERE COILED AS TIGHT AS CLOCKWORK MAINSPRINGS.
I HEARD HIM TURN A KEY IN THE LOCK AND THE BOLT SNAPPED INTO PLACE LIKE THE HAMMER OF A HEAVY-CALIBER REVOLVER.

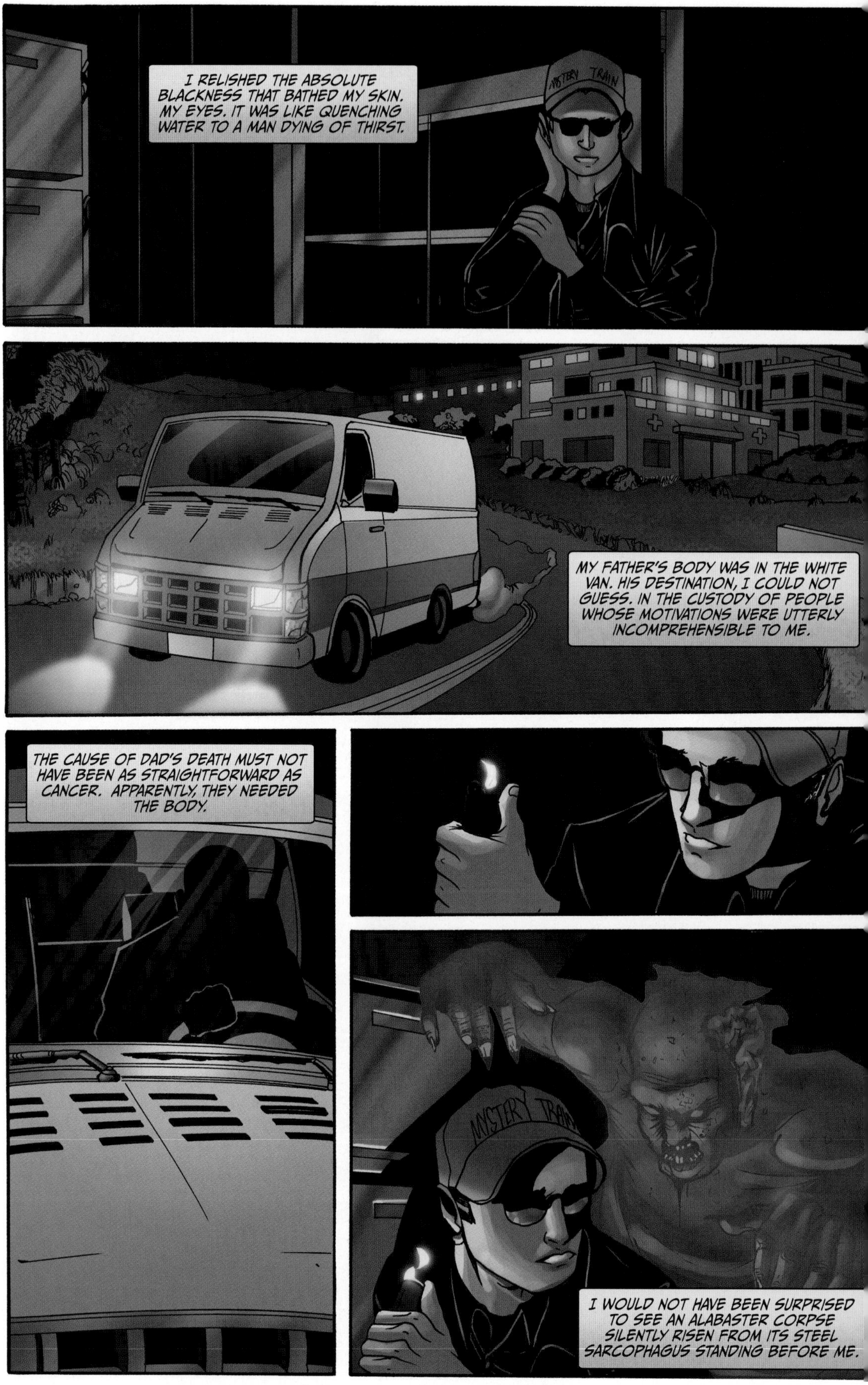
I RELISHED THE ABSOLUTE BLACKNESS THAT BATHED MY SKIN. MY EYES. IT WAS LIKE QUENCHING WATER TO A MAN DYING OF THIRST.
MYSTERY TRAIN
MY FATHER'S BODY WAS IN THE WHITE VAN. HIS DESTINATION, I COULD NOT GUESS. IN THE CUSTODY OF PEOPLE WHOSE MOTIVATIONS WERE UTTERLY INCOMPREHENSIBLE TO ME.
THE CAUSE OF DAD'S DEATH MUST NOT HAVE BEEN AS STRAIGHTFORWARD AS CANCER. APPARENTLY, THEY NEEDED THE BODY.
MYSTERY TRAIN
I WOULD NOT HAVE BEEN SURPRISED TO SEE AN ALABASTER CORPSE SILENTLY RISEN FROM ITS STEEL SARCOPHAGUS STANDING BEFORE ME.

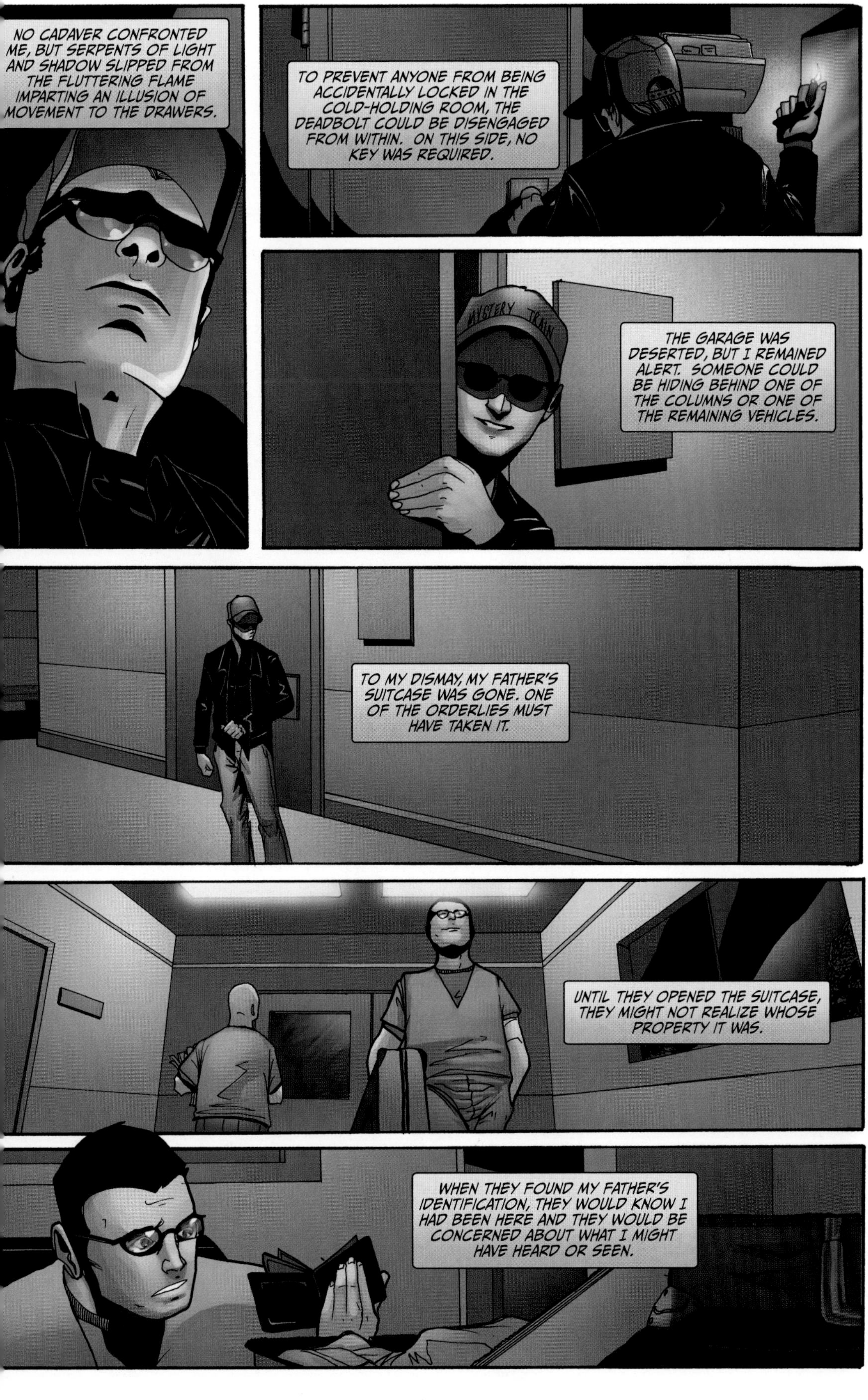
NO CADAVER CONFRONTED ME, BUT SERPENTS OF LIGHT AND SHADOW SLIPPED FROM THE FLUTTERING FLAME IMPARTING AN ILLUSION OF MOVEMENT TO THE DRAWERS.
TO PREVENT ANYONE FROM BEING ACCIDENTALLY LOCKED IN THE COLD-HOLDING ROOM, THE DEADBOLT COULD BE DISENGAGED FROM WITHIN. ON THIS SIDE, NO KEY WAS REQUIRED.
MYSTERY TRAIN
THE GARAGE WAS DESERTED, BUT I REMAINED ALERT. SOMEONE COULD BE HIDING BEHIND ONE OF THE COLUMNS OR ONE OF THE REMAINING VEHICLES.
TO MY DISMAY, MY FATHER'S SUITCASE WAS GONE. ONE OF THE ORDERLIES MUST HAVE TAKEN IT.
UNTIL THEY OPENED THE SUITCASE, THEY MIGHT NOT REALIZE WHOSE PROPERTY IT WAS.
WHEN THEY FOUND MY FATHER'S IDENTIFICATION, THEY WOULD KNOW I HAD BEEN HERE AND THEY WOULD BE CONCERNED ABOUT WHAT I MIGHT HAVE HEARD OR SEEN.

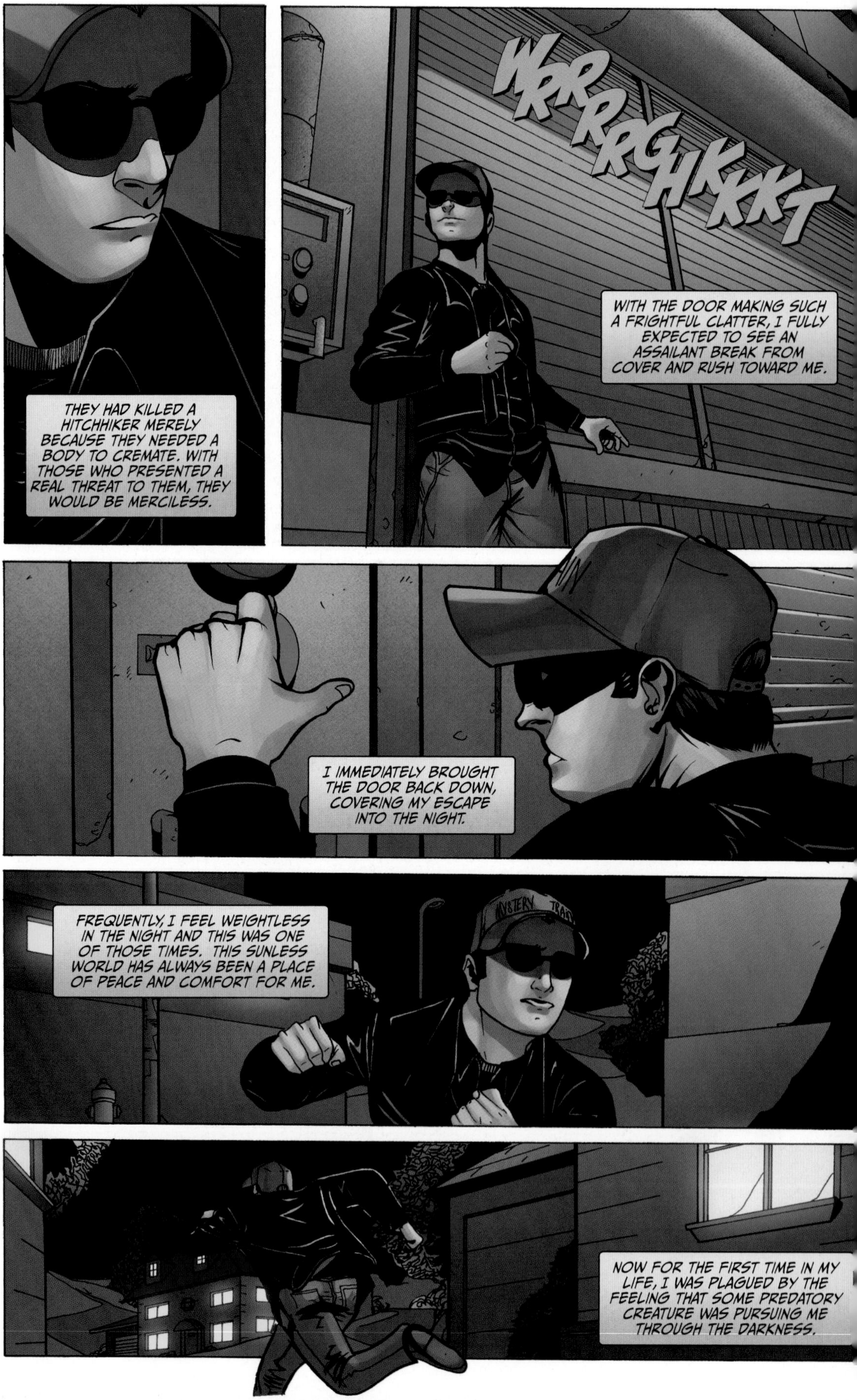
THEY HAD KILLED A HITCHHIKER MERELY BECAUSE THEY NEEDED A BODY TO CREMATE. WITH THOSE WHO PRESENTED A REAL THREAT TO THEM, THEY WOULD BE MERCILESS.
WRRRRGHKKKT
WITH THE DOOR MAKING SUCH A FRIGHTFUL CLATTER, I FULLY EXPECTED TO SEE AN ASSAILANT BREAK FROM COVER AND RUSH TOWARD ME.
I IMMEDIATELY BROUGHT THE DOOR BACK DOWN, COVERING MY ESCAPE INTO THE NIGHT.
FREQUENTLY, I FEEL WEIGHTLESS IN THE NIGHT AND THIS WAS ONE OF THOSE TIMES. THIS SUNLESS WORLD HAS ALWAYS BEEN A PLACE OF PEACE AND COMFORT FOR ME.
NOW FOR THE FIRST TIME IN MY LIFE, I WAS PLAGUED BY THE FEELING THAT SOME PREDATORY CREATURE WAS PURSUING ME THROUGH THE DARKNESS.

chapter two

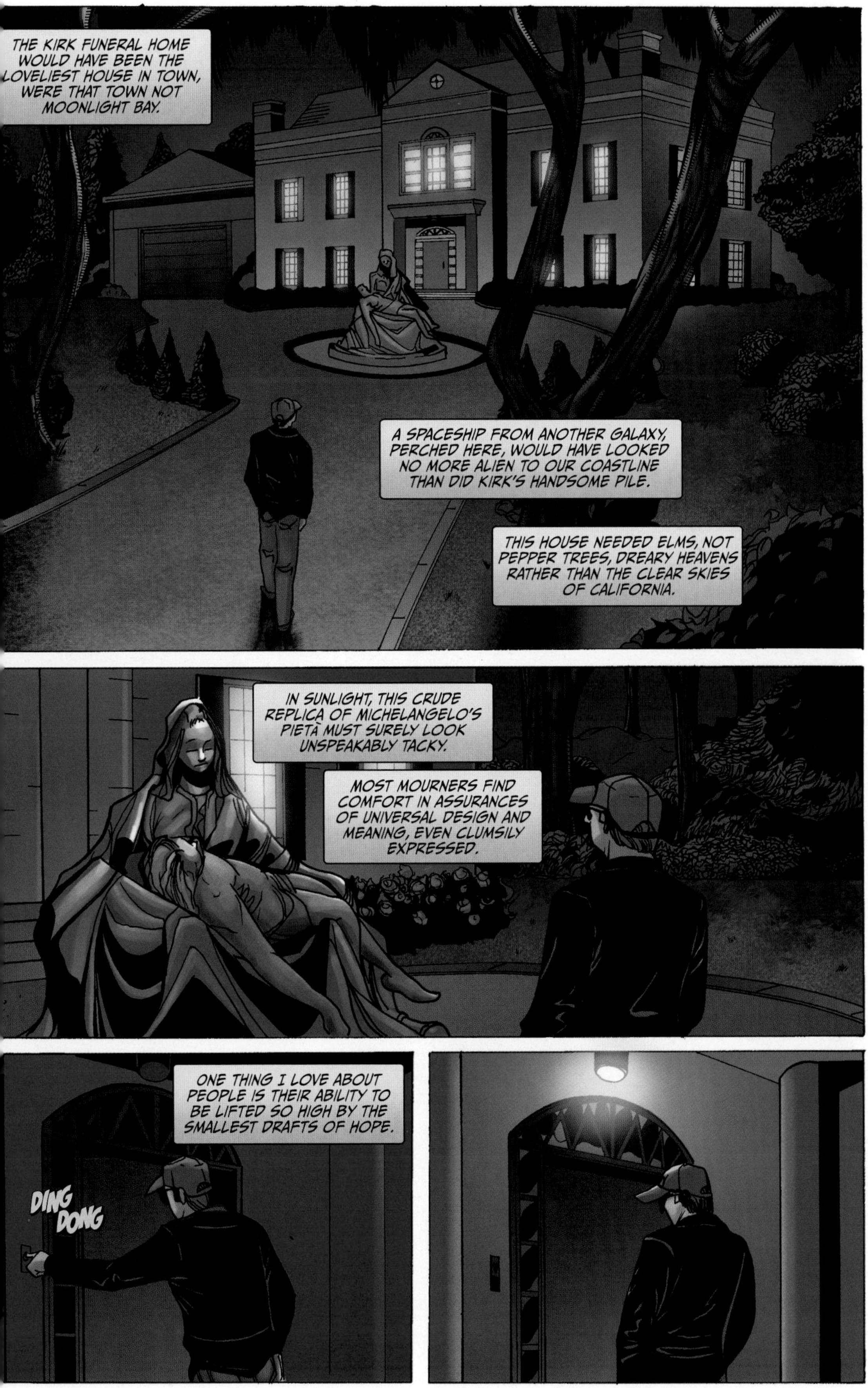

THE KIRK FUNERAL HOME WOULD HAVE BEEN THE LOVELIEST HOUSE IN TOWN, WERE THAT TOWN NOT MOONLIGHT BAY.
A SPACESHIP FROM ANOTHER GALAXY, PERCHED HERE, WOULD HAVE LOOKED NO MORE ALIEN TO OUR COASTLINE THAN DID KIRK'S HANDSOME PILE.
THIS HOUSE NEEDED ELMS, NOT PEPPER TREES, DREARY HEAVENS RATHER THAN THE CLEAR SKIES OF CALIFORNIA.
IN SUNLIGHT, THIS CRUDE REPLICA OF MICHELANGELO'S PIETÀ MUST SURELY LOOK UNSPEAKABLY TACKY.
MOST MOURNERS FIND COMFORT IN ASSURANCES OF UNIVERSAL DESIGN AND MEANING, EVEN CLUMSILY EXPRESSED.
ONE THING I LOVE ABOUT PEOPLE IS THEIR ABILITY TO BE LIFTED SO HIGH BY THE SMALLEST DRAFTS OF HOPE.
DING DONG

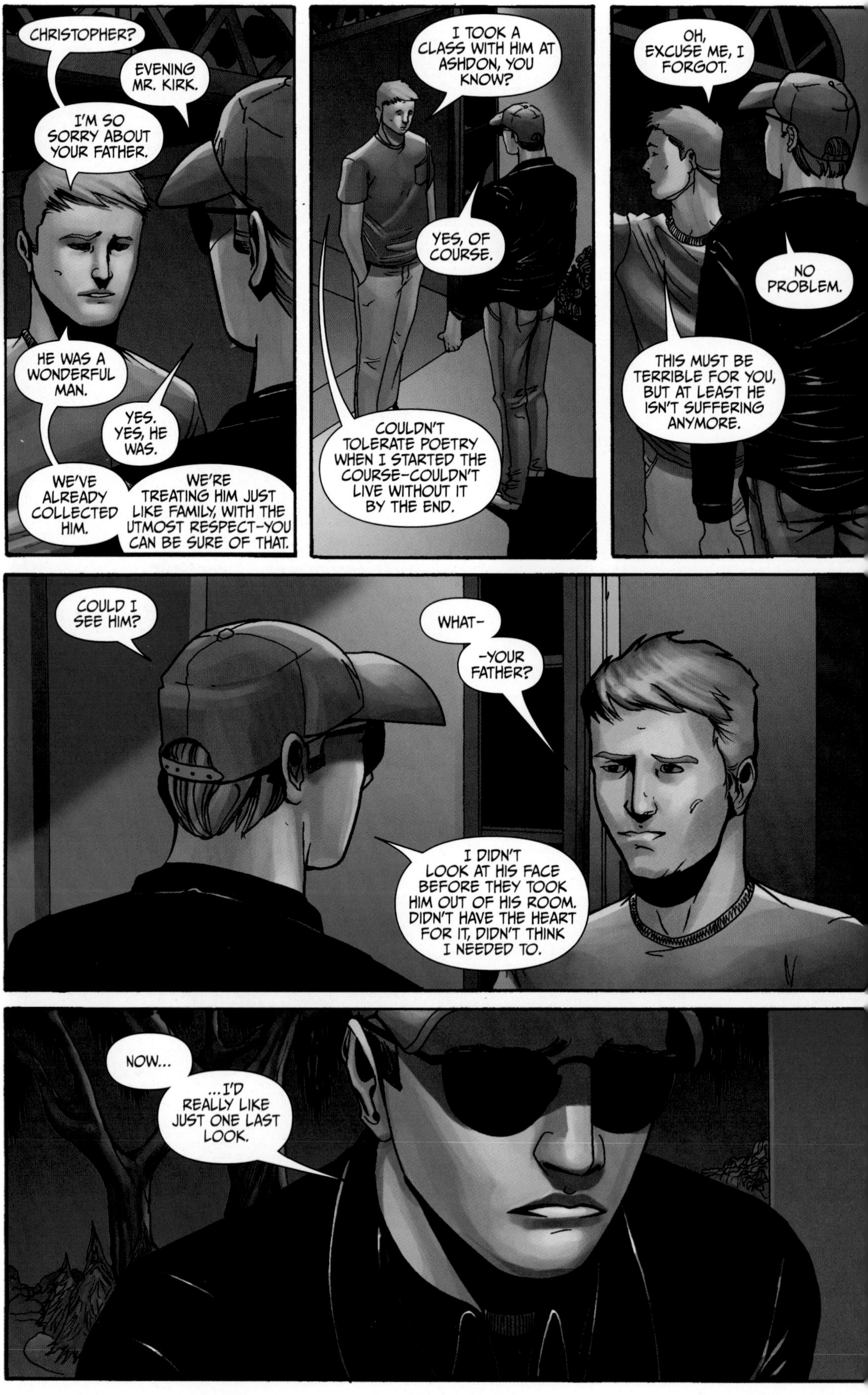
CHRISTOPHER?
EVENING MR. KIRK.
I'M SO SORRY ABOUT YOUR FATHER.
HE WAS A WONDERFUL MAN.
YES. YES, HE WAS.
WE'VE ALREADY COLLECTED HIM.
WE'RE TREATING HIM JUST LIKE FAMILY, WITH THE UTMOST RESPECT–YOU CAN BE SURE OF THAT.
I TOOK A CLASS WITH HIM AT ASHDON, YOU KNOW?
YES, OF COURSE.
COULDN'T TOLERATE POETRY WHEN I STARTED THE COURSE–COULDN'T LIVE WITHOUT IT BY THE END.
OH, EXCUSE ME, I FORGOT.
NO PROBLEM.
THIS MUST BE TERRIBLE FOR YOU, BUT AT LEAST HE ISN'T SUFFERING ANYMORE.
COULD I SEE HIM?
WHAT-
-YOUR FATHER?
I DIDN'T LOOK AT HIS FACE BEFORE THEY TOOK HIM OUT OF HIS ROOM. DIDN'T HAVE THE HEART FOR IT, DIDN'T THINK I NEEDED TO.
NOW...
...I'D REALLY LIKE JUST ONE LAST LOOK.

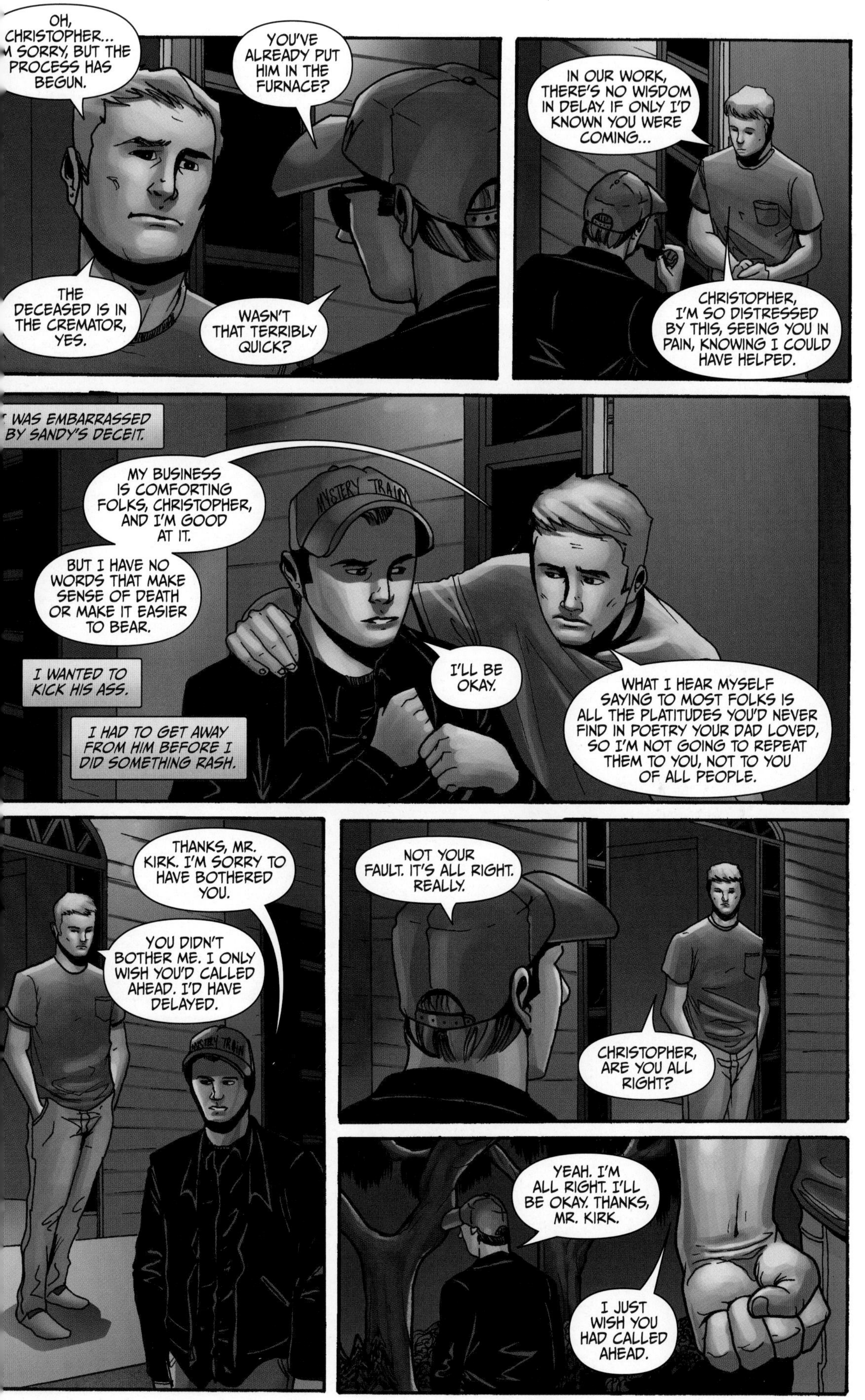
OH, CHRISTOPHER... 'M SORRY, BUT THE PROCESS HAS BEGUN.
YOU'VE ALREADY PUT HIM IN THE FURNACE?
THE DECEASED IS IN THE CREMATOR, YES.
WASN'T THAT TERRIBLY QUICK?
IN OUR WORK, THERE'S NO WISDOM IN DELAY. IF ONLY I'D KNOWN YOU WERE COMING...
CHRISTOPHER, I'M SO DISTRESSED BY THIS, SEEING YOU IN PAIN, KNOWING I COULD HAVE HELPED.
' WAS EMBARRASSED BY SANDY'S DECEIT.
MY BUSINESS IS COMFORTING FOLKS, CHRISTOPHER, AND I'M GOOD AT IT.
BUT I HAVE NO WORDS THAT MAKE SENSE OF DEATH OR MAKE IT EASIER TO BEAR.
MYSTERY TRAIN
I WANTED TO KICK HIS ASS.
I HAD TO GET AWAY FROM HIM BEFORE I DID SOMETHING RASH.
I'LL BE OKAY.
WHAT I HEAR MYSELF SAYING TO MOST FOLKS IS ALL THE PLATITUDES YOU'D NEVER FIND IN POETRY YOUR DAD LOVED, SO I'M NOT GOING TO REPEAT THEM TO YOU, NOT TO YOU OF ALL PEOPLE.
THANKS, MR. KIRK. I'M SORRY TO HAVE BOTHERED YOU.
YOU DIDN'T BOTHER ME. I ONLY WISH YOU'D CALLED AHEAD. I'D HAVE DELAYED.
MYSTERY TRAIN
NOT YOUR FAULT. IT'S ALL RIGHT. REALLY.
CHRISTOPHER, ARE YOU ALL RIGHT?
YEAH. I'M ALL RIGHT. I'LL BE OKAY. THANKS, MR. KIRK.
I JUST WISH YOU HAD CALLED AHEAD.

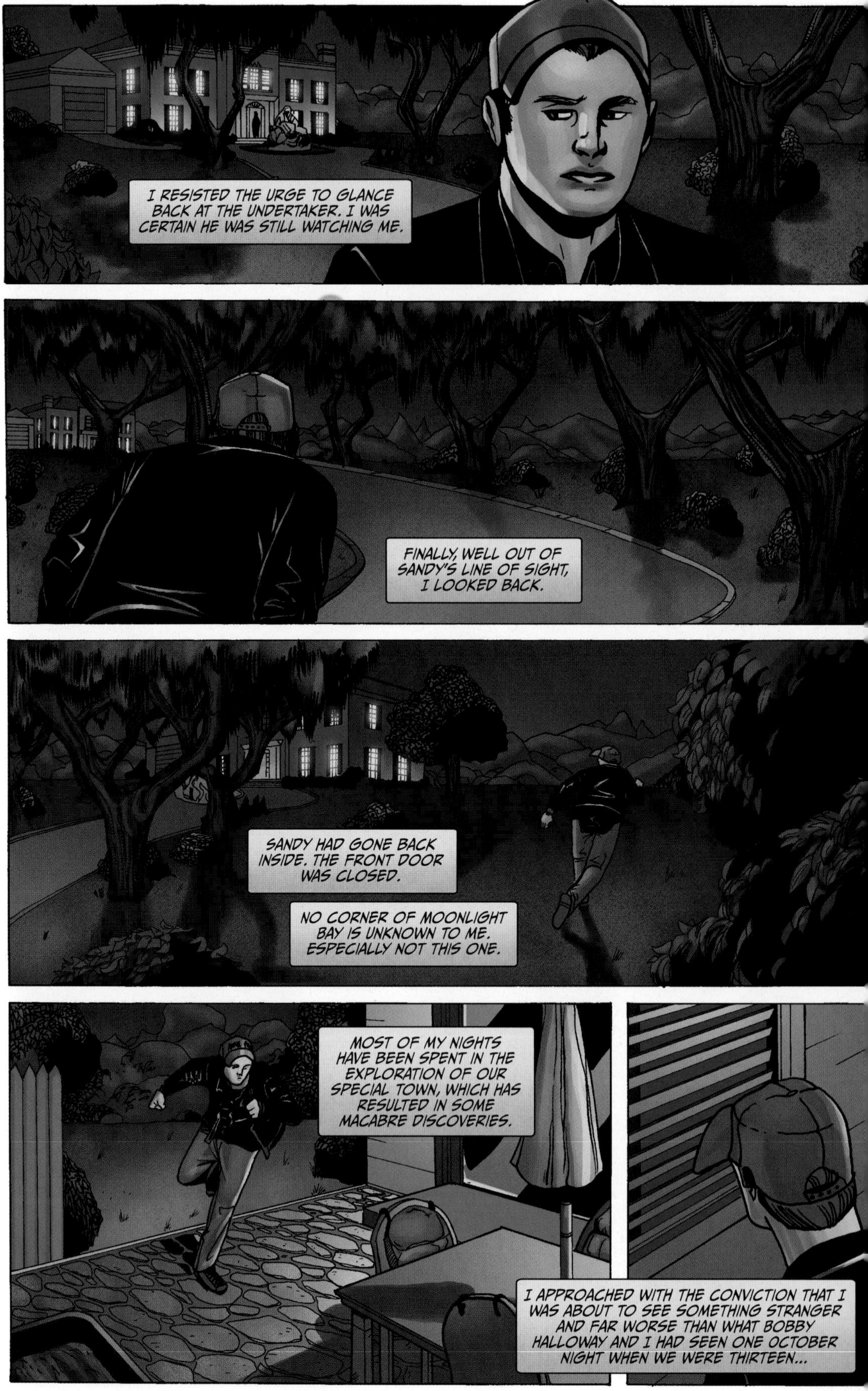

I RESISTED THE URGE TO GLANCE BACK AT THE UNDERTAKER. I WAS CERTAIN HE WAS STILL WATCHING ME.
FINALLY, WELL OUT OF SANDY'S LINE OF SIGHT, I LOOKED BACK.
SANDY HAD GONE BACK INSIDE. THE FRONT DOOR WAS CLOSED.
NO CORNER OF MOONLIGHT BAY IS UNKNOWN TO ME. ESPECIALLY NOT THIS ONE.
MOST OF MY NIGHTS HAVE BEEN SPENT IN THE EXPLORATION OF OUR SPECIAL TOWN, WHICH HAS RESULTED IN SOME MACABRE DISCOVERIES.
I APPROACHED WITH THE CONVICTION THAT I WAS ABOUT TO SEE SOMETHING STRANGER AND FAR WORSE THAN WHAT BOBBY HALLOWAY AND I HAD SEEN ONE OCTOBER NIGHT WHEN WE WERE THIRTEEN...

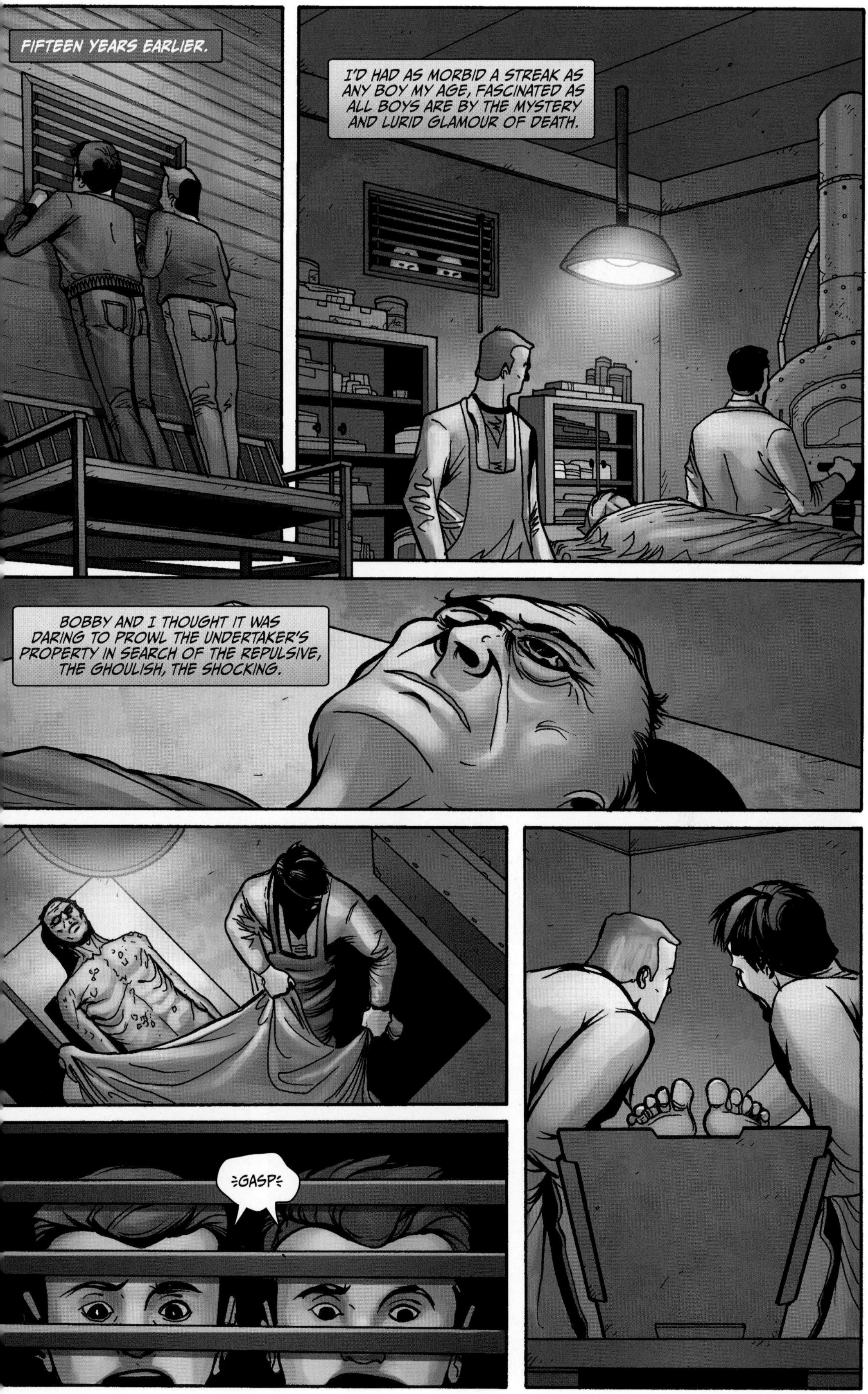
FIFTEEN YEARS EARLIER.
I'D HAD AS MORBID A STREAK AS ANY BOY MY AGE, FASCINATED AS ALL BOYS ARE BY THE MYSTERY AND LURID GLAMOUR OF DEATH.
BOBBY AND I THOUGHT IT WAS DARING TO PROWL THE UNDERTAKER'S PROPERTY IN SEARCH OF THE REPULSIVE, THE GHOULISH, THE SHOCKING.
GASP

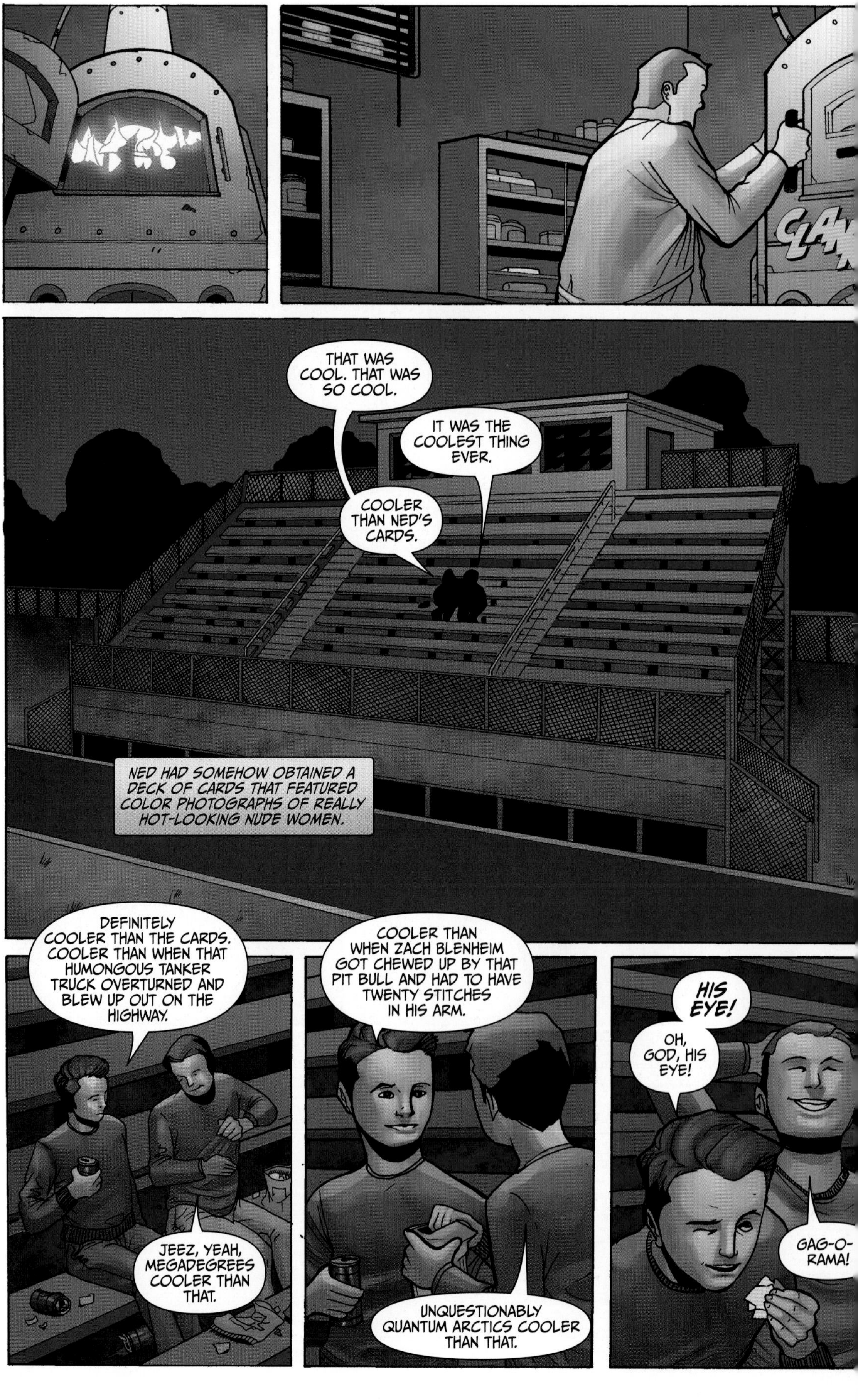

CLANK
THAT WAS COOL. THAT WAS SO COOL.
IT WAS THE COOLEST THING EVER.
COOLER THAN NED'S CARDS.
NED HAD SOMEHOW OBTAINED A DECK OF CARDS THAT FEATURED COLOR PHOTOGRAPHS OF REALLY HOT-LOOKING NUDE WOMEN.
DEFINITELY COOLER THAN THE CARDS. COOLER THAN WHEN THAT HUMONGOUS TANKER TRUCK OVERTURNED AND BLEW UP OUT ON THE HIGHWAY.
JEEZ, YEAH, MEGADEGREES COOLER THAN THAT.
COOLER THAN WHEN ZACH BLENHEIM GOT CHEWED UP BY THAT PIT BULL AND HAD TO HAVE TWENTY STITCHES IN HIS ARM.
UNQUESTIONABLY QUANTUM ARCTICS COOLER THAN THAT.
HIS EYE!
OH, GOD, HIS EYE!
GAG-O-RAMA!

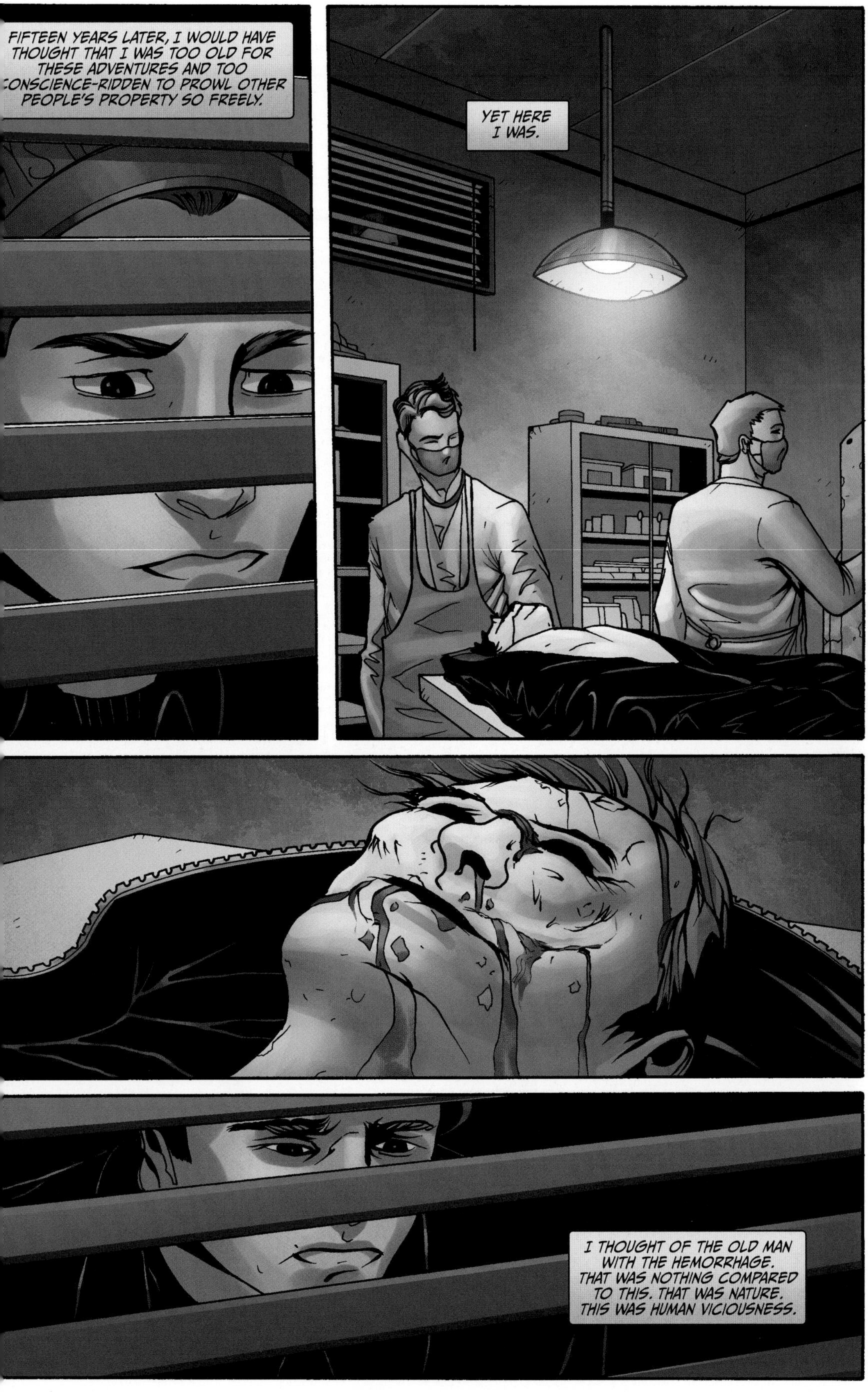
FIFTEEN YEARS LATER, I WOULD HAVE THOUGHT THAT I WAS TOO OLD FOR THESE ADVENTURES AND TOO CONSCIENCE-RIDDEN TO PROWL OTHER PEOPLE'S PROPERTY SO FREELY.
YET HERE I WAS.
I THOUGHT OF THE OLD MAN WITH THE HEMORRHAGE. THAT WAS NOTHING COMPARED TO THIS. THAT WAS NATURE. THIS WAS HUMAN VICIOUSNESS.

THAT WINTER, BOBBY HALLOWAY AND I PERIODICALLY RETURNED TO THE CREMATORIUM WINDOW.

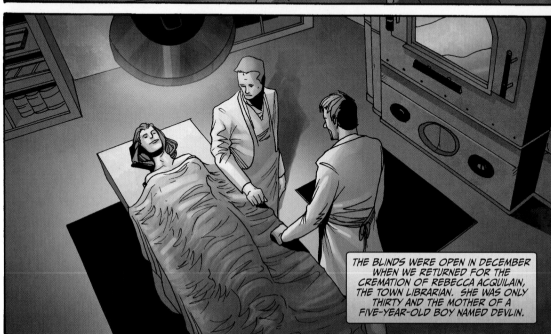

THE BLINDS WERE OPEN IN DECEMBER WHEN WE RETURNED FOR THE CREMATION OF REBECCA ACQUILAIN, THE TOWN LIBRARIAN. SHE WAS ONLY THIRTY AND THE MOTHER OF A FIVE-YEAR-OLD BOY NAMED DEVLIN.

LYING UPON THE GURNEY, SHE WAS SO BEAUTIFUL THAT SHE WAS MORE THAN A VISION ON OUR EYES. SHE WAS A WEIGHT ON OUR CHESTS. WE COULD NOT BREATHE.

DEATH HAD NOT RAVAGED HER, FOR SHE HAD DIED QUICKLY.

WE HAD REALIZED, I SUPPOSE, THAT SHE WAS PRETTY, BUT WE HAD NEVER MOONED OVER HER.

A FLAW IN AN ARTERY WALL, CONGENITAL NO DOUBT, SWELLED AND BURST. SHE WAS GONE IN HOURS.

SHE LOOKED LIKE SHE WAS SLEEPING. SO YOUNG. SHE LOOKED IMMORTAL.

OTHER NIGHTS, FRANK KIRK AND HIS ASSISTANTS CHATTED ALMOST CONTINUOUSLY. THIS NIGHT THEY HARDLY SPOKE AT ALL. WE WERE SILENT TOO.

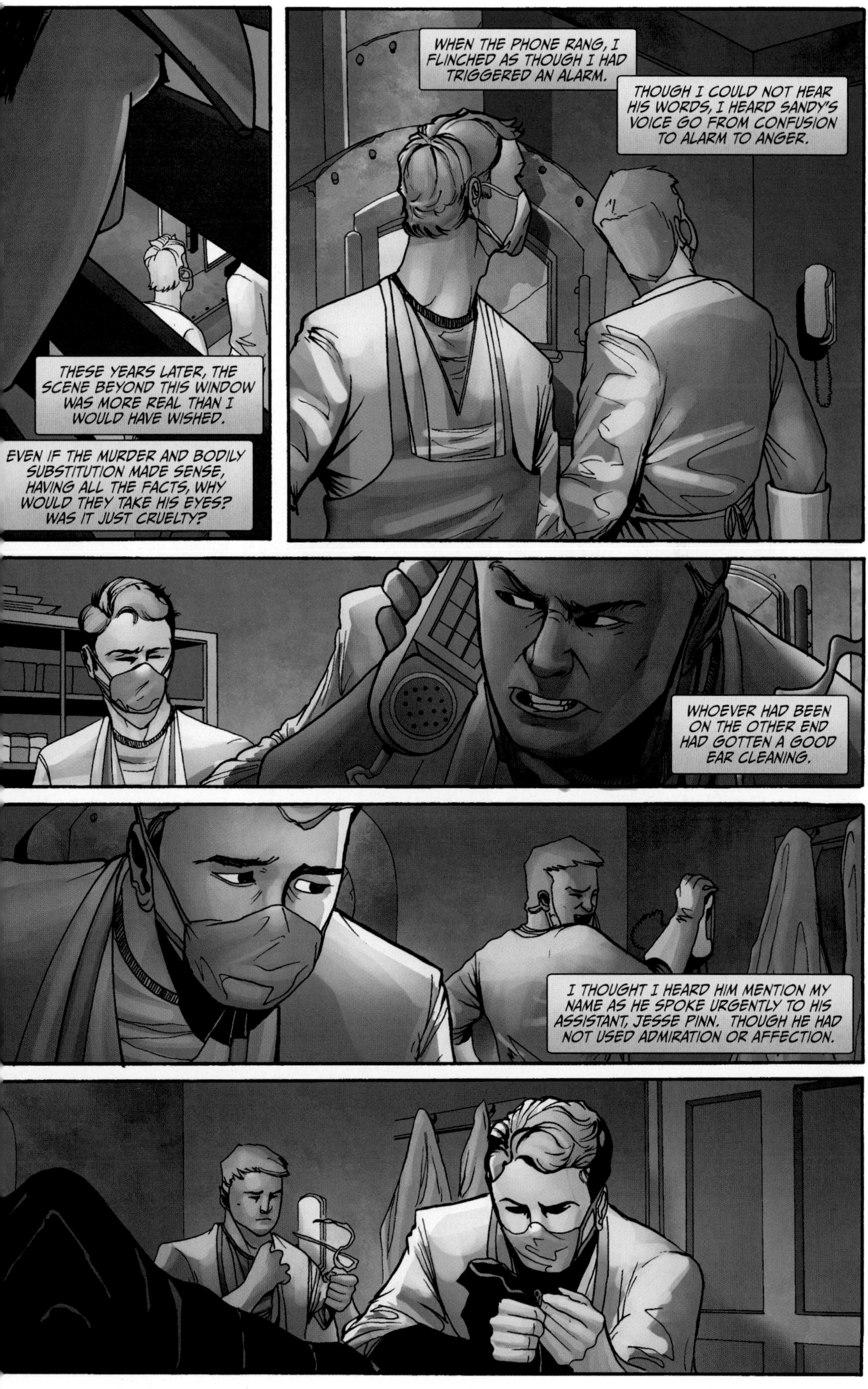
THESE YEARS LATER, THE SCENE BEYOND THIS WINDOW WAS MORE REAL THAN I WOULD HAVE WISHED.
EVEN IF THE MURDER AND BODILY SUBSTITUTION MADE SENSE, HAVING ALL THE FACTS, WHY WOULD THEY TAKE HIS EYES? WAS IT JUST CRUELTY?
WHEN THE PHONE RANG, I FLINCHED AS THOUGH I HAD TRIGGERED AN ALARM.
THOUGH I COULD NOT HEAR HIS WORDS, I HEARD SANDY'S VOICE GO FROM CONFUSION TO ALARM TO ANGER.
WHOEVER HAD BEEN ON THE OTHER END HAD GOTTEN A GOOD EAR CLEANING.
I THOUGHT I HEARD HIM MENTION MY NAME AS HE SPOKE URGENTLY TO HIS ASSISTANT, JESSE PINN. THOUGH HE HAD NOT USED ADMIRATION OR AFFECTION.

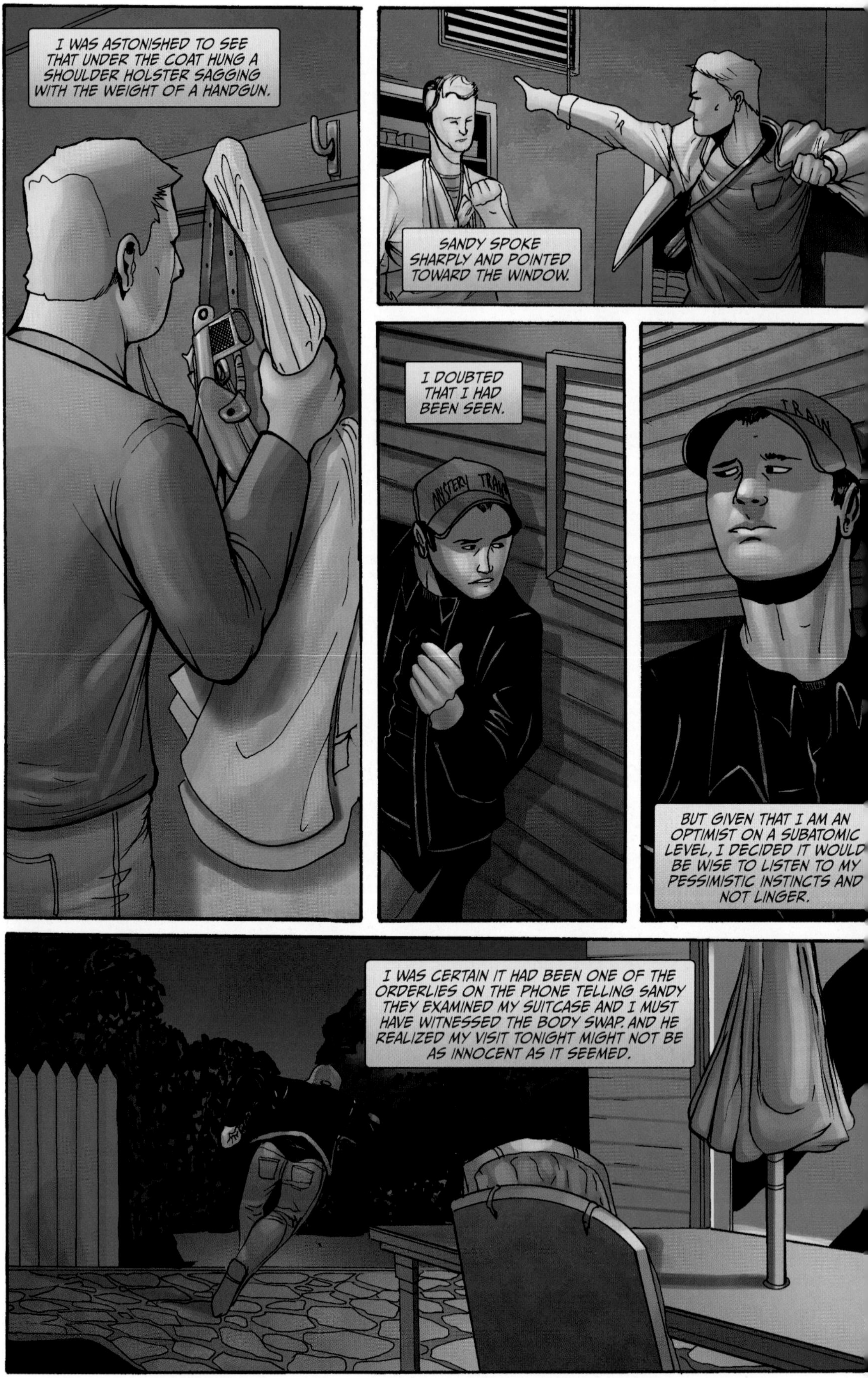
I WAS ASTONISHED TO SEE THAT UNDER THE COAT HUNG A SHOULDER HOLSTER SAGGING WITH THE WEIGHT OF A HANDGUN.
SANDY SPOKE SHARPLY AND POINTED TOWARD THE WINDOW.
I DOUBTED THAT I HAD BEEN SEEN.
MYSTERY TRAIN
BUT GIVEN THAT I AM AN OPTIMIST ON A SUBATOMIC LEVEL, I DECIDED IT WOULD BE WISE TO LISTEN TO MY PESSIMISTIC INSTINCTS AND NOT LINGER.
I WAS CERTAIN IT HAD BEEN ONE OF THE ORDERLIES ON THE PHONE TELLING SANDY THEY EXAMINED MY SUITCASE AND I MUST HAVE WITNESSED THE BODY SWAP. AND HE REALIZED MY VISIT TONIGHT MIGHT NOT BE AS INNOCENT AS IT SEEMED.

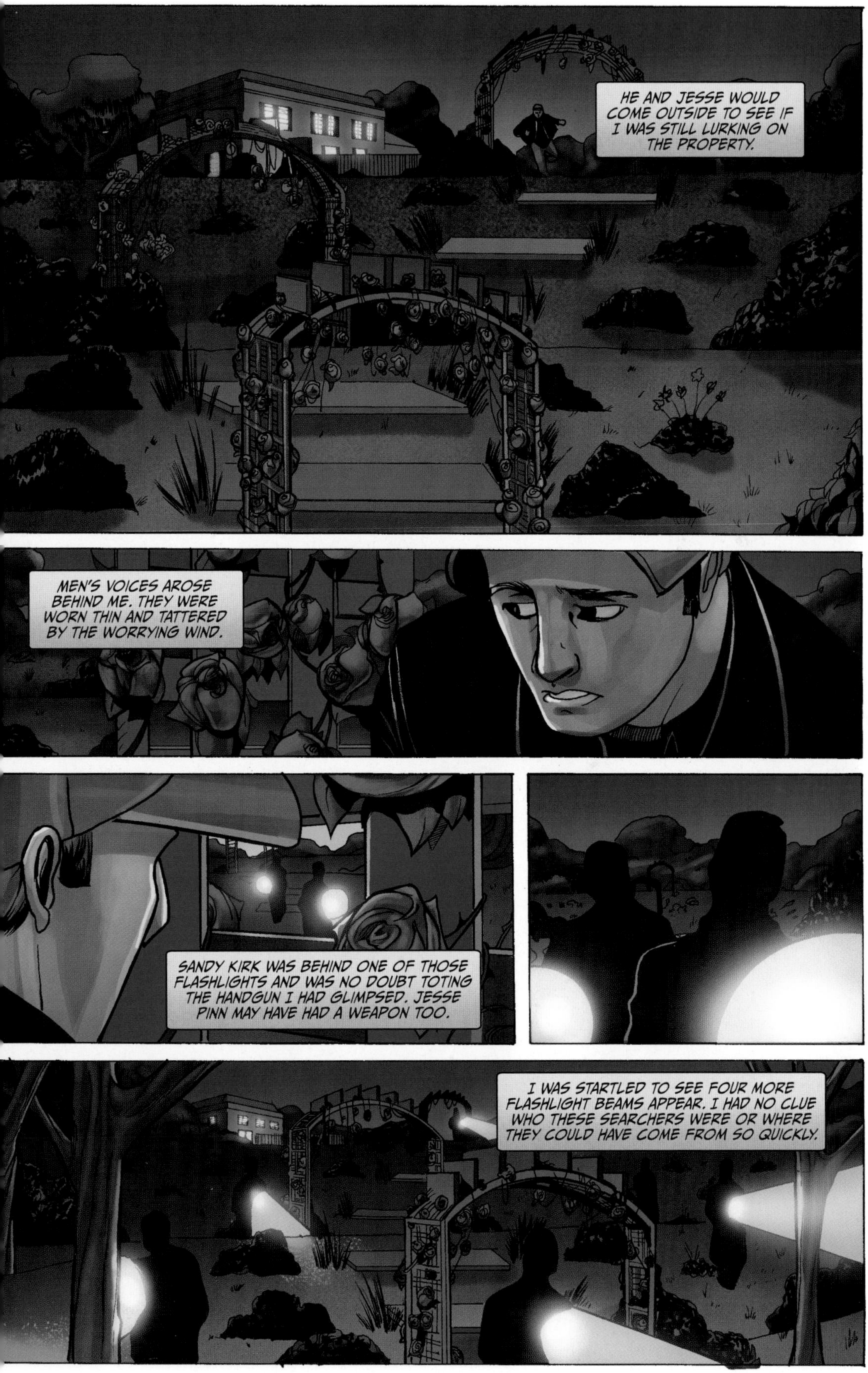
HE AND JESSE WOULD COME OUTSIDE TO SEE IF I WAS STILL LURKING ON THE PROPERTY.
MEN'S VOICES AROSE BEHIND ME. THEY WERE WORN THIN AND TATTERED BY THE WORRYING WIND.
SANDY KIRK WAS BEHIND ONE OF THOSE FLASHLIGHTS AND WAS NO DOUBT TOTING THE HANDGUN I HAD GLIMPSED. JESSE PINN MAY HAVE HAD A WEAPON TOO.
I WAS STARTLED TO SEE FOUR MORE FLASHLIGHT BEAMS APPEAR. I HAD NO CLUE WHO THESE SEARCHERS WERE OR WHERE THEY COULD HAVE COME FROM SO QUICKLY.

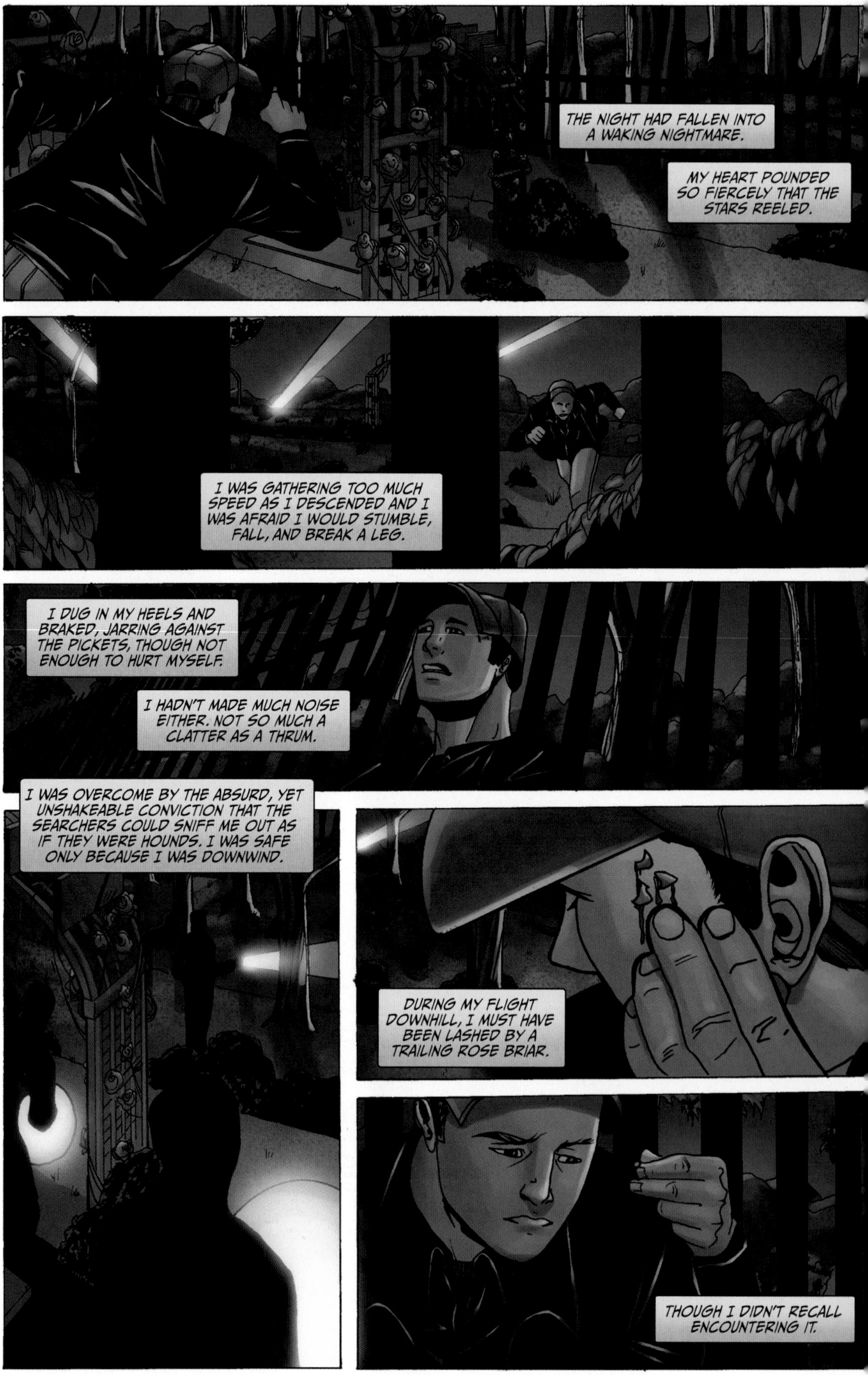
THE NIGHT HAD FALLEN INTO A WAKING NIGHTMARE.
MY HEART POUNDED SO FIERCELY THAT THE STARS REELED.
I WAS GATHERING TOO MUCH SPEED AS I DESCENDED AND I WAS AFRAID I WOULD STUMBLE, FALL, AND BREAK A LEG.
I DUG IN MY HEELS AND BRAKED, JARRING AGAINST THE PICKETS, THOUGH NOT ENOUGH TO HURT MYSELF.
I HADN'T MADE MUCH NOISE EITHER. NOT SO MUCH A CLATTER AS A THRUM.
I WAS OVERCOME BY THE ABSURD, YET UNSHAKEABLE CONVICTION THAT THE SEARCHERS COULD SNIFF ME OUT AS IF THEY WERE HOUNDS. I WAS SAFE ONLY BECAUSE I WAS DOWNWIND.
DURING MY FLIGHT DOWNHILL, I MUST HAVE BEEN LASHED BY A TRAILING ROSE BRIAR.
THOUGH I DIDN'T RECALL ENCOUNTERING IT.

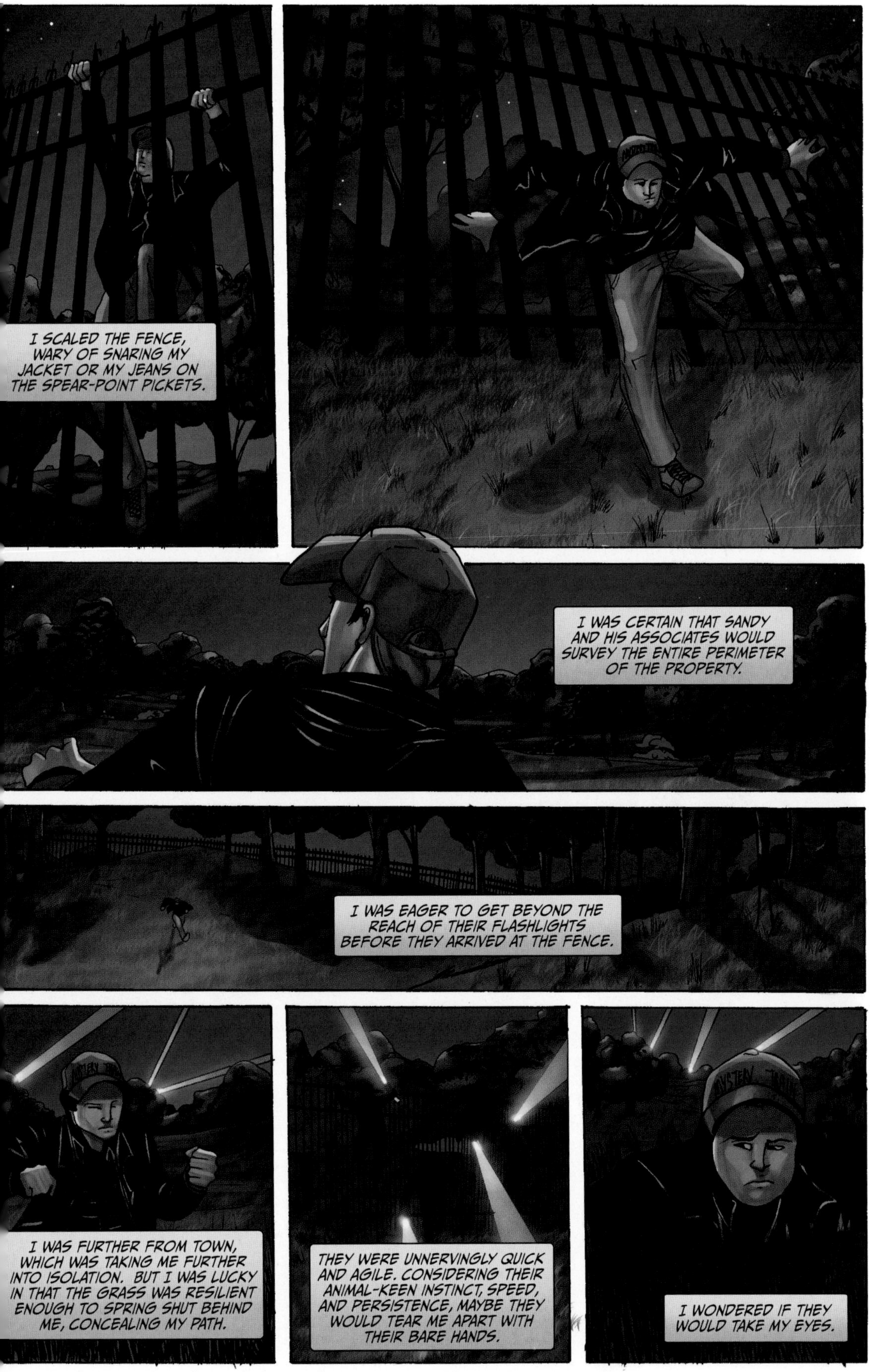
I SCALED THE FENCE, WARY OF SNARING MY JACKET OR MY JEANS ON THE SPEAR-POINT PICKETS.
I WAS CERTAIN THAT SANDY AND HIS ASSOCIATES WOULD SURVEY THE ENTIRE PERIMETER OF THE PROPERTY.
I WAS EAGER TO GET BEYOND THE REACH OF THEIR FLASHLIGHTS BEFORE THEY ARRIVED AT THE FENCE.
I WAS FURTHER FROM TOWN, WHICH WAS TAKING ME FURTHER INTO ISOLATION. BUT I WAS LUCKY IN THAT THE GRASS WAS RESILIENT ENOUGH TO SPRING SHUT BEHIND ME, CONCEALING MY PATH.
THEY WERE UNNERVINGLY QUICK AND AGILE. CONSIDERING THEIR ANIMAL-KEEN INSTINCT, SPEED, AND PERSISTENCE, MAYBE THEY WOULD TEAR ME APART WITH THEIR BARE HANDS.
I WONDERED IF THEY WOULD TAKE MY EYES.

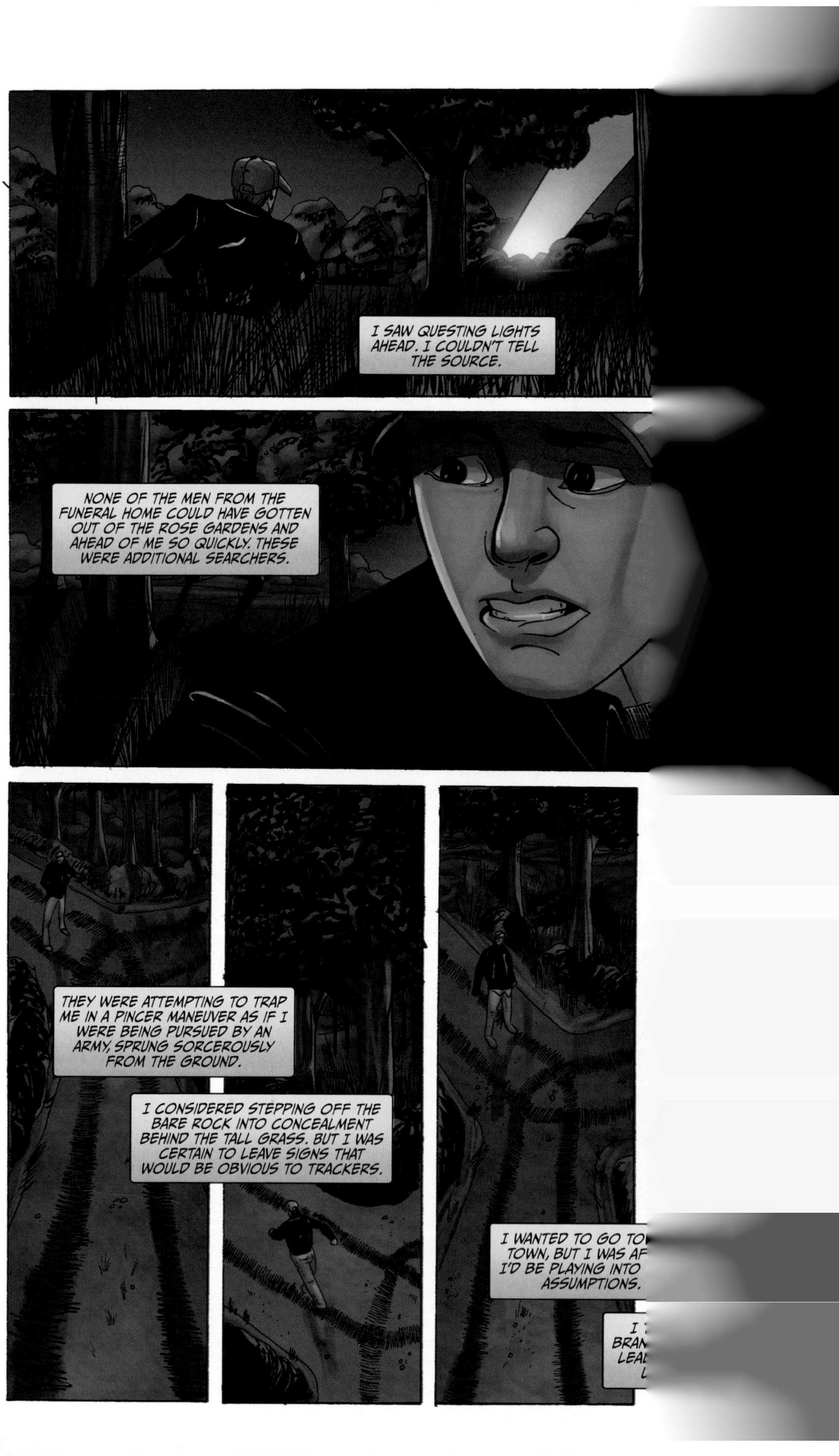
I SAW QUESTING LIGHTS AHEAD. I COULDN'T TELL THE SOURCE.
NONE OF THE MEN FROM THE FUNERAL HOME COULD HAVE GOTTEN OUT OF THE ROSE GARDENS AND AHEAD OF ME SO QUICKLY. THESE WERE ADDITIONAL SEARCHERS.
THEY WERE ATTEMPTING TO TRAP ME IN A PINCER MANEUVER AS IF I WERE BEING PURSUED BY AN ARMY, SPRUNG SORCEROUSLY FROM THE GROUND.
I CONSIDERED STEPPING OFF THE BARE ROCK INTO CONCEALMENT BEHIND THE TALL GRASS. BUT I WAS CERTAIN TO LEAVE SIGNS THAT WOULD BE OBVIOUS TO TRACKERS.
I WANTED TO GO TO TOWN, BUT I WAS I'D BE PLAYING INTO ASSUMPTIONS.

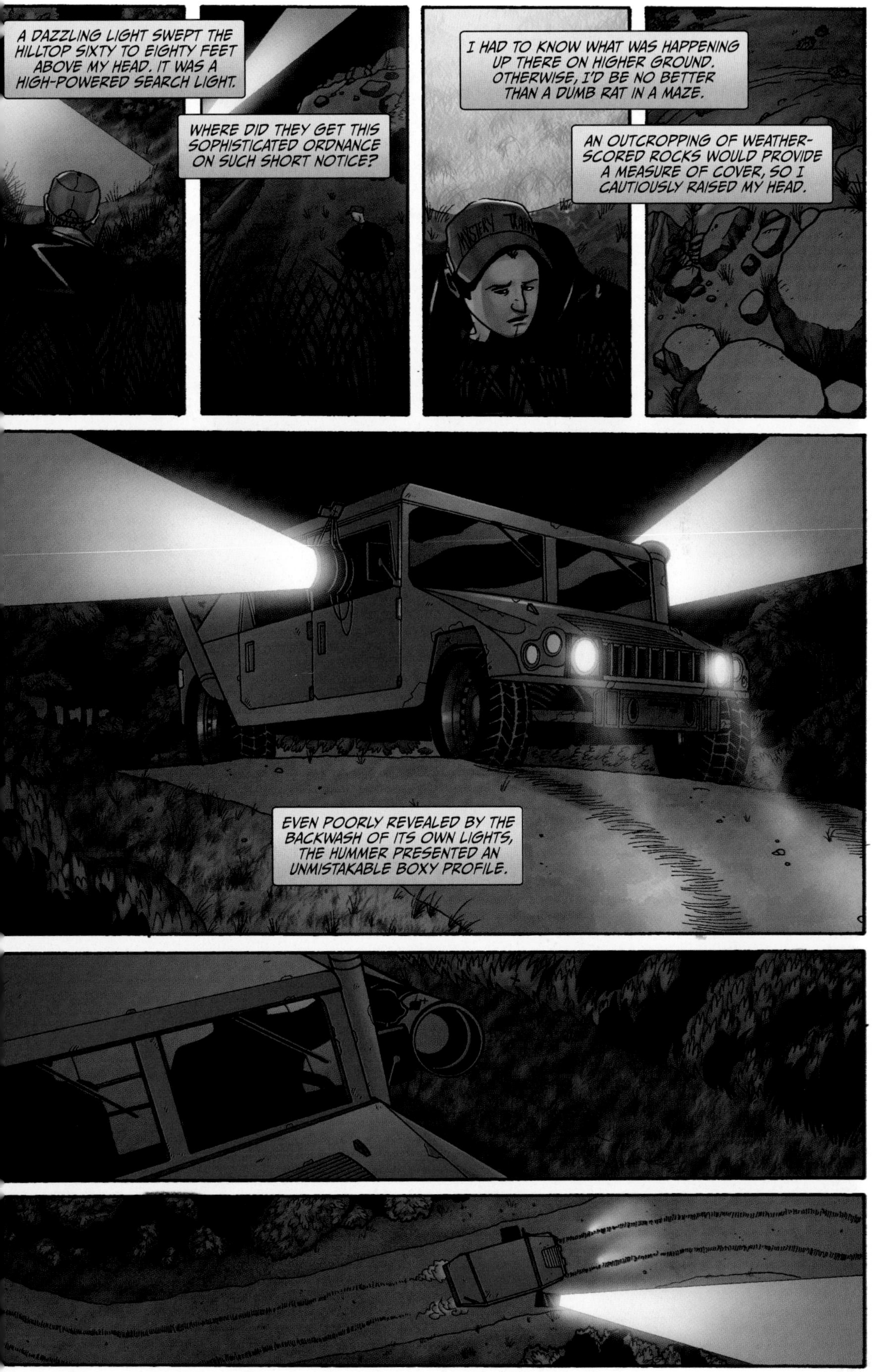
A DAZZLING LIGHT SWEPT THE HILLTOP SIXTY TO EIGHTY FEET ABOVE MY HEAD. IT WAS A HIGH-POWERED SEARCH LIGHT.
WHERE DID THEY GET THIS SOPHISTICATED ORDNANCE ON SUCH SHORT NOTICE?
I HAD TO KNOW WHAT WAS HAPPENING UP THERE ON HIGHER GROUND. OTHERWISE, I'D BE NO BETTER THAN A DUMB RAT IN A MAZE.
AN OUTCROPPING OF WEATHER-SCORED ROCKS WOULD PROVIDE A MEASURE OF COVER, SO I CAUTIOUSLY RAISED MY HEAD.
EVEN POORLY REVEALED BY THE BACKWASH OF ITS OWN LIGHTS, THE HUMMER PRESENTED AN UNMISTAKABLE BOXY PROFILE.

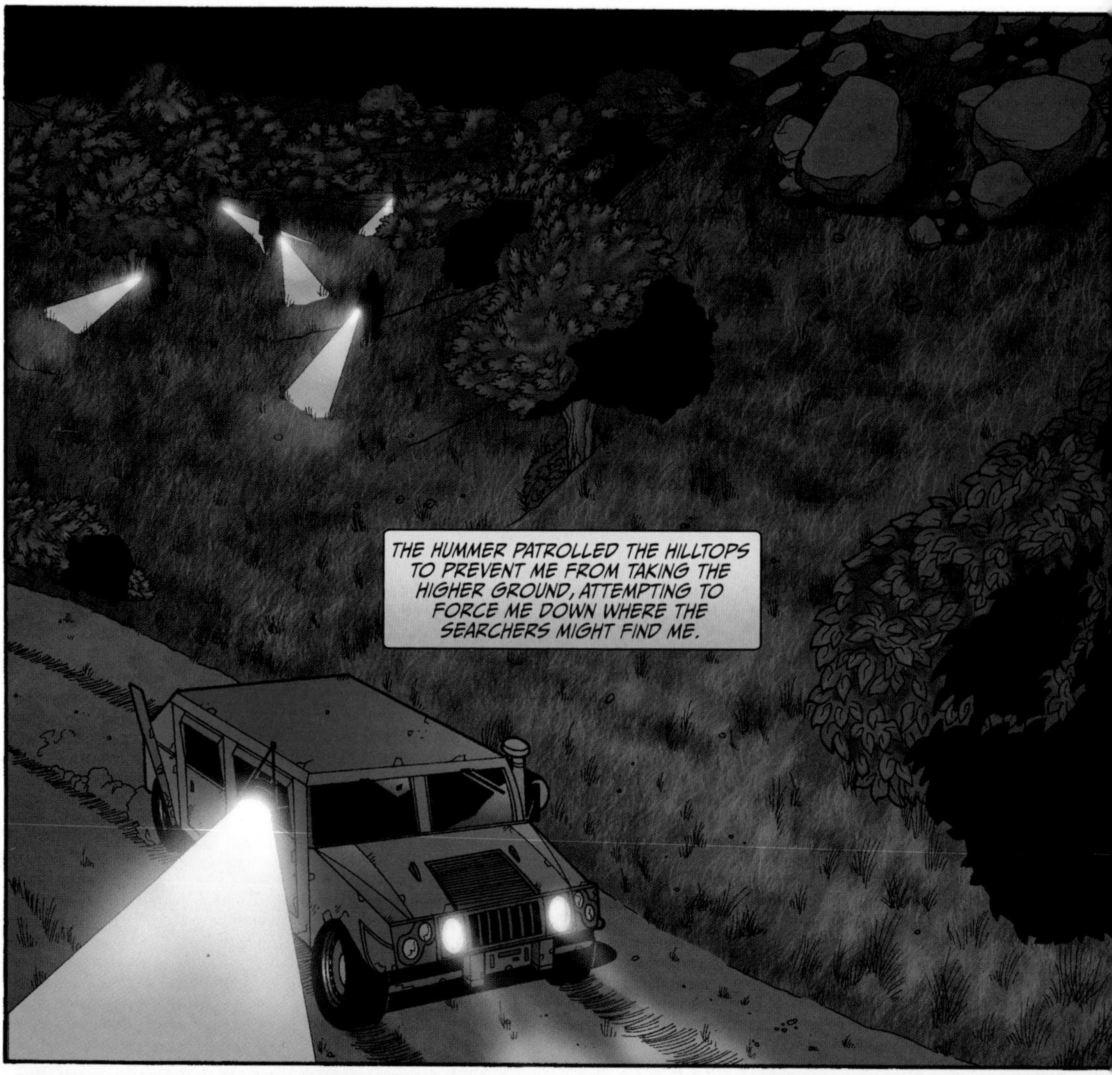
THE HUMMER PATROLLED THE HILLTOPS TO PREVENT ME FROM TAKING THE HIGHER GROUND, ATTEMPTING TO FORCE ME DOWN WHERE THE SEARCHERS MIGHT FIND ME.

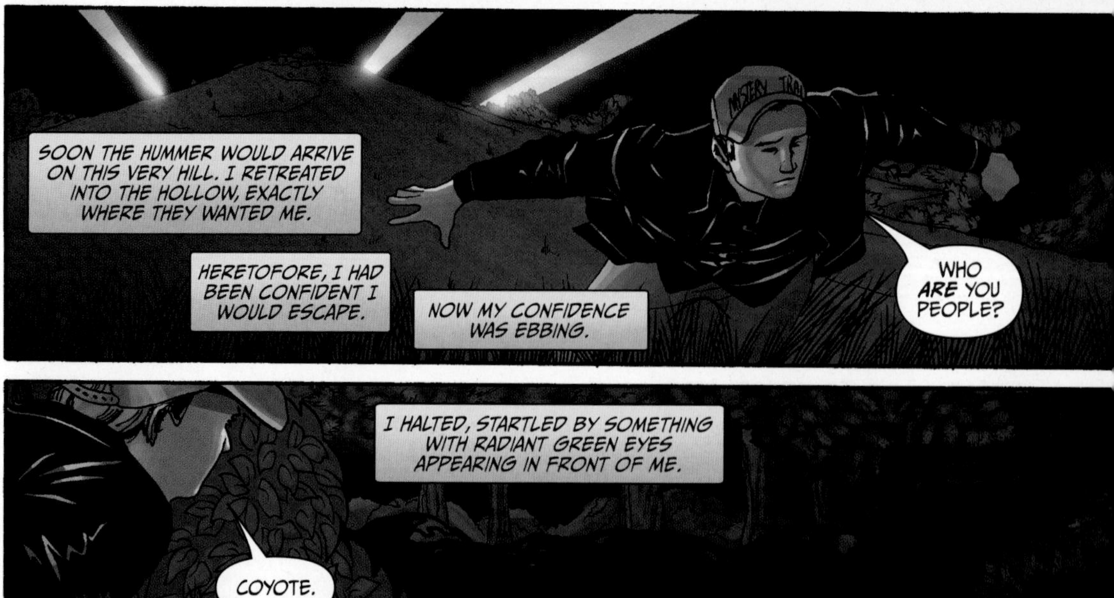
SOON THE HUMMER WOULD ARRIVE ON THIS VERY HILL. I RETREATED INTO THE HOLLOW, EXACTLY WHERE THEY WANTED ME.
HERETOFORE, I HAD BEEN CONFIDENT I WOULD ESCAPE.
NOW MY CONFIDENCE WAS EBBING.
WHO **ARE** YOU PEOPLE?

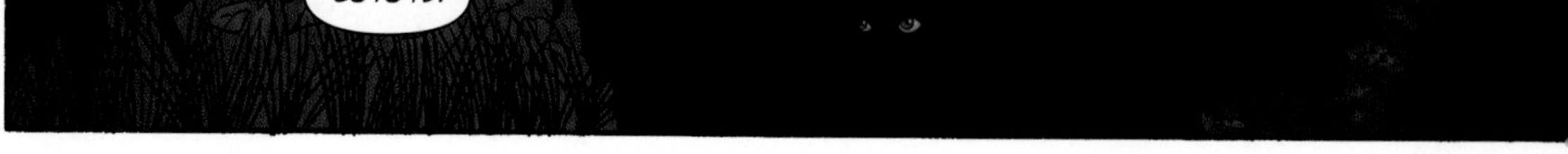
I HALTED, STARTLED BY SOMETHING WITH RADIANT GREEN EYES APPEARING IN FRONT OF ME.
COYOTE.

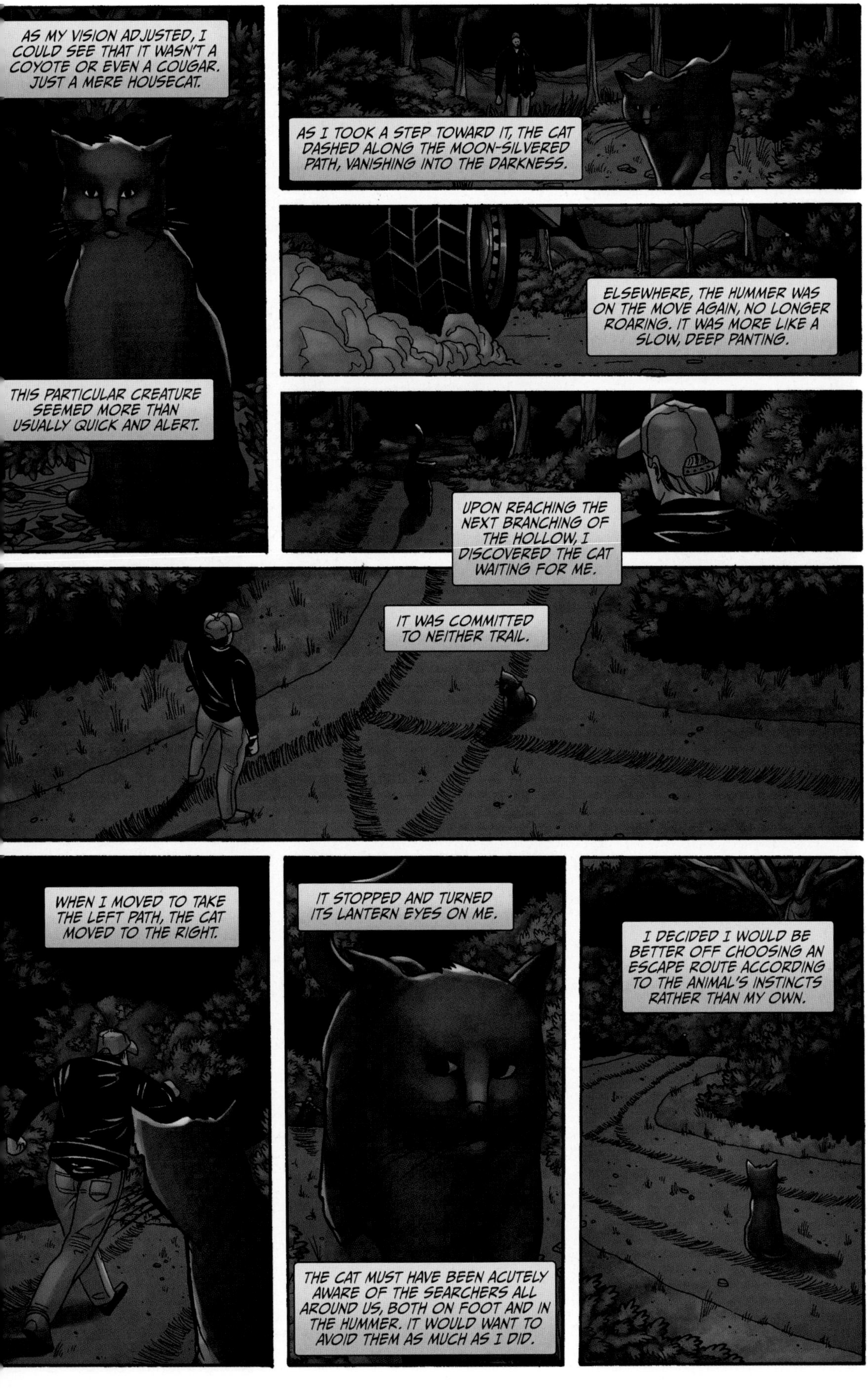
AS MY VISION ADJUSTED, I COULD SEE THAT IT WASN'T A COYOTE OR EVEN A COUGAR. JUST A MERE HOUSECAT.
THIS PARTICULAR CREATURE SEEMED MORE THAN USUALLY QUICK AND ALERT.
AS I TOOK A STEP TOWARD IT, THE CAT DASHED ALONG THE MOON-SILVERED PATH, VANISHING INTO THE DARKNESS.
ELSEWHERE, THE HUMMER WAS ON THE MOVE AGAIN, NO LONGER ROARING. IT WAS MORE LIKE A SLOW, DEEP PANTING.
UPON REACHING THE NEXT BRANCHING OF THE HOLLOW, I DISCOVERED THE CAT WAITING FOR ME.
IT WAS COMMITTED TO NEITHER TRAIL.
WHEN I MOVED TO TAKE THE LEFT PATH, THE CAT MOVED TO THE RIGHT.
IT STOPPED AND TURNED ITS LANTERN EYES ON ME.
THE CAT MUST HAVE BEEN ACUTELY AWARE OF THE SEARCHERS ALL AROUND US, BOTH ON FOOT AND IN THE HUMMER. IT WOULD WANT TO AVOID THEM AS MUCH AS I DID.
I DECIDED I WOULD BE BETTER OFF CHOOSING AN ESCAPE ROUTE ACCORDING TO THE ANIMAL'S INSTINCTS RATHER THAN MY OWN.

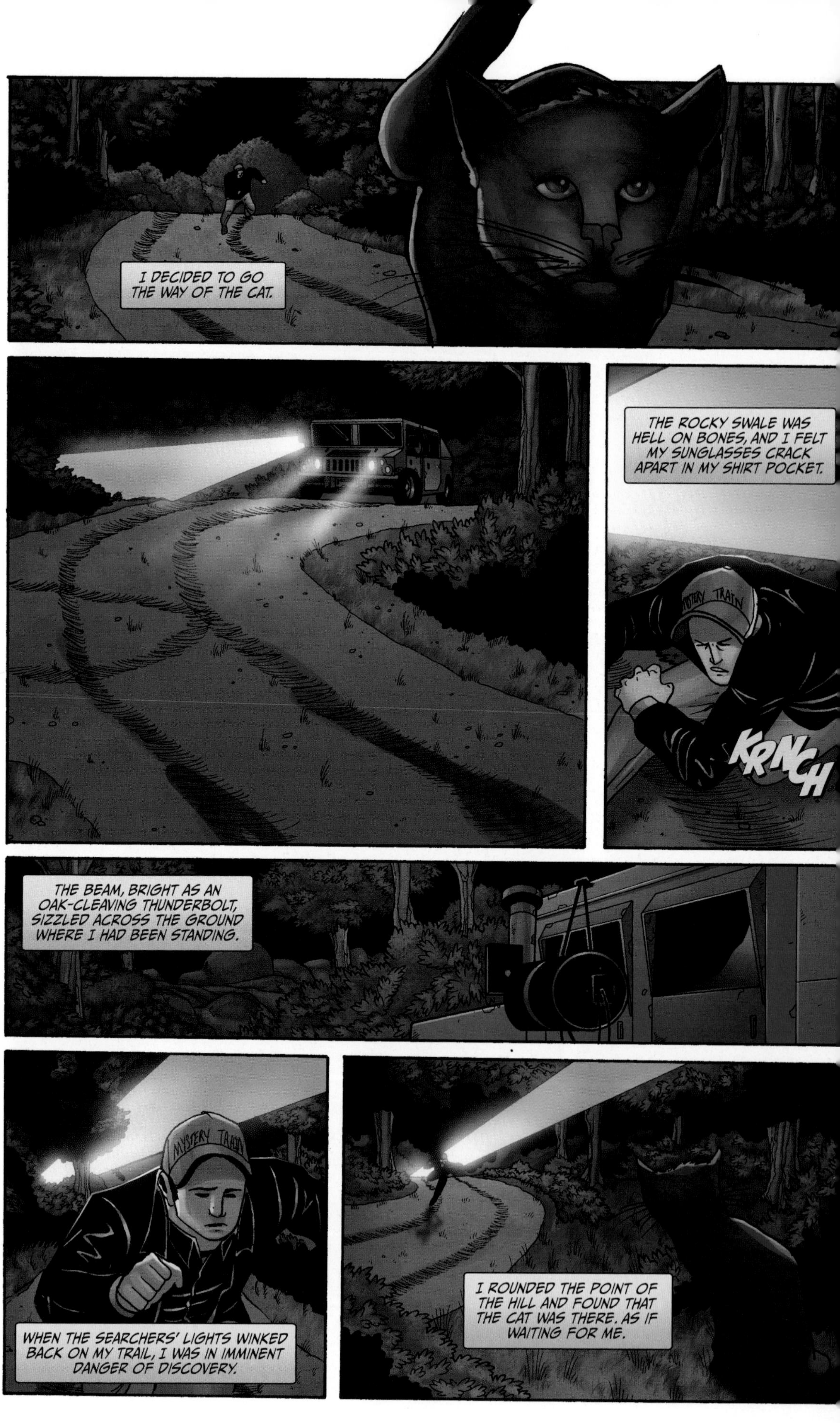
I DECIDED TO GO THE WAY OF THE CAT.
THE ROCKY SWALE WAS HELL ON BONES, AND I FELT MY SUNGLASSES CRACK APART IN MY SHIRT POCKET.
MYSTERY TRAIN
KRNCH
THE BEAM, BRIGHT AS AN OAK-CLEAVING THUNDERBOLT, SIZZLED ACROSS THE GROUND WHERE I HAD BEEN STANDING.
MYSTERY TRAIN
WHEN THE SEARCHERS' LIGHTS WINKED BACK ON MY TRAIL, I WAS IN IMMINENT DANGER OF DISCOVERY.
I ROUNDED THE POINT OF THE HILL AND FOUND THAT THE CAT WAS THERE. AS IF WAITING FOR ME.

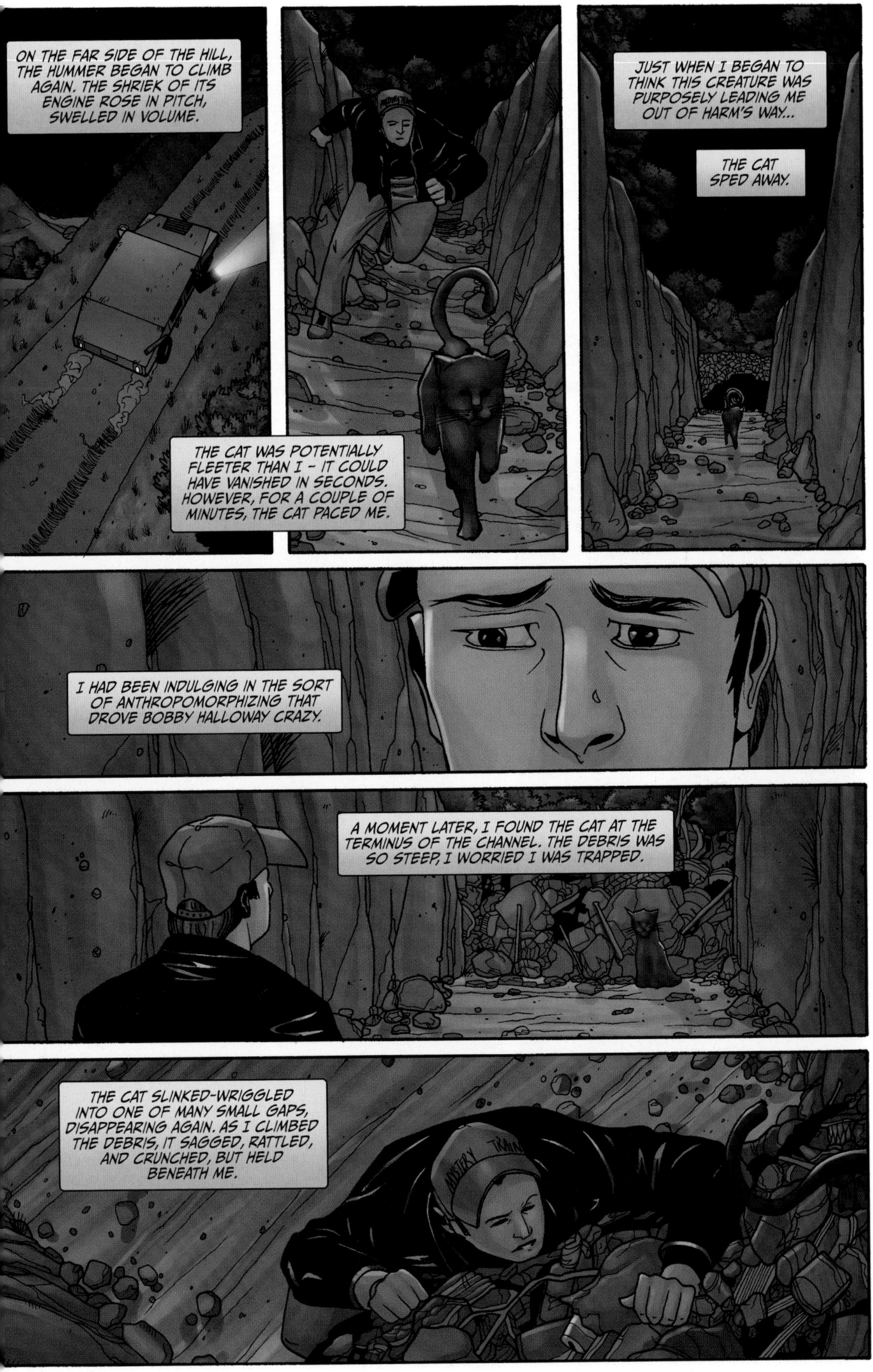
ON THE FAR SIDE OF THE HILL, THE HUMMER BEGAN TO CLIMB AGAIN. THE SHRIEK OF ITS ENGINE ROSE IN PITCH, SWELLED IN VOLUME.
THE CAT WAS POTENTIALLY FLEETER THAN I - IT COULD HAVE VANISHED IN SECONDS. HOWEVER, FOR A COUPLE OF MINUTES, THE CAT PACED ME.
JUST WHEN I BEGAN TO THINK THIS CREATURE WAS PURPOSELY LEADING ME OUT OF HARM'S WAY...
THE CAT SPED AWAY.
I HAD BEEN INDULGING IN THE SORT OF ANTHROPOMORPHIZING THAT DROVE BOBBY HALLOWAY CRAZY.
A MOMENT LATER, I FOUND THE CAT AT THE TERMINUS OF THE CHANNEL. THE DEBRIS WAS SO STEEP, I WORRIED I WAS TRAPPED.
THE CAT SLINKED-WRIGGLED INTO ONE OF MANY SMALL GAPS, DISAPPEARING AGAIN. AS I CLIMBED THE DEBRIS, IT SAGGED, RATTLED, AND CRUNCHED, BUT HELD BENEATH ME.

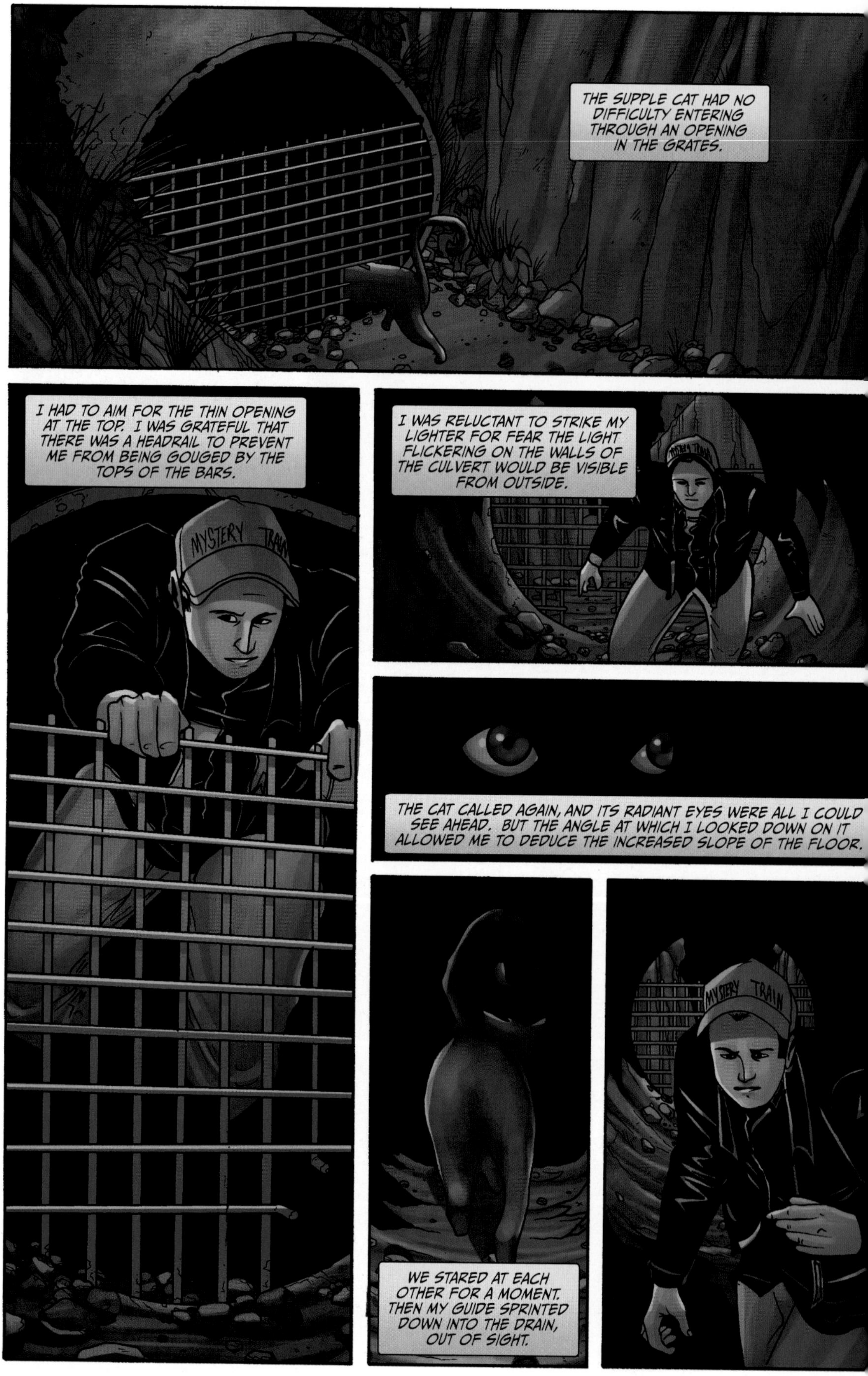
THE SUPPLE CAT HAD NO DIFFICULTY ENTERING THROUGH AN OPENING IN THE GRATES.
I HAD TO AIM FOR THE THIN OPENING AT THE TOP. I WAS GRATEFUL THAT THERE WAS A HEADRAIL TO PREVENT ME FROM BEING GOUGED BY THE TOPS OF THE BARS.
MYSTERY TRAIN
I WAS RELUCTANT TO STRIKE MY LIGHTER FOR FEAR THE LIGHT FLICKERING ON THE WALLS OF THE CULVERT WOULD BE VISIBLE FROM OUTSIDE.
THE CAT CALLED AGAIN, AND ITS RADIANT EYES WERE ALL I COULD SEE AHEAD. BUT THE ANGLE AT WHICH I LOOKED DOWN ON IT ALLOWED ME TO DEDUCE THE INCREASED SLOPE OF THE FLOOR.
WE STARED AT EACH OTHER FOR A MOMENT. THEN MY GUIDE SPRINTED DOWN INTO THE DRAIN, OUT OF SIGHT.
MYSTERY TRAIN

I USED THE LIGHTER TO FIND MY WAY, KEEPING THE FLAME LOW TO CONSERVE BUTANE.

THE SCUMMY STEPS WERE TREACHEROUS. BUT SAFETY CREWS HAD BOLTED A STEEL HANDRAIL TO THE WALL.

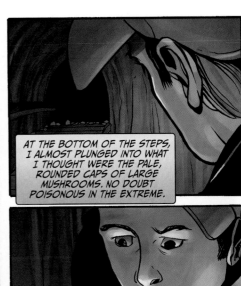

AT THE BOTTOM OF THE STEPS, I ALMOST PLUNGED INTO WHAT I THOUGHT WERE THE PALE, ROUNDED CAPS OF LARGE MUSHROOMS. NO DOUBT POISONOUS IN THE EXTREME.

WHEN I CRANKED UP THE FLAME, I DISCOVERED THAT BEFORE ME LAY NOT MUSHROOMS...

...BUT A COLLECTION OF SKULLS.

BIRDS, LIZARDS, CATS, DOGS, RACCOONS, ALL WITHOUT A SCRAP OF FLESH ADHERED TO THEM.

BUT IN THE MIDDLE OF THE ROW RESTED A MARKEDLY DIFFERENT SKULL. IT WAS SMALL, BUT HUMAN. LIKE THE SKULL OF AN INFANT

DEAR GOD!

ANXIOUS TO AVOID ENCOUNTERING WHOEVER HAD ACQUIRED THIS GRIM COLLECTION, I CONTINUED DOWN THE DRAIN.

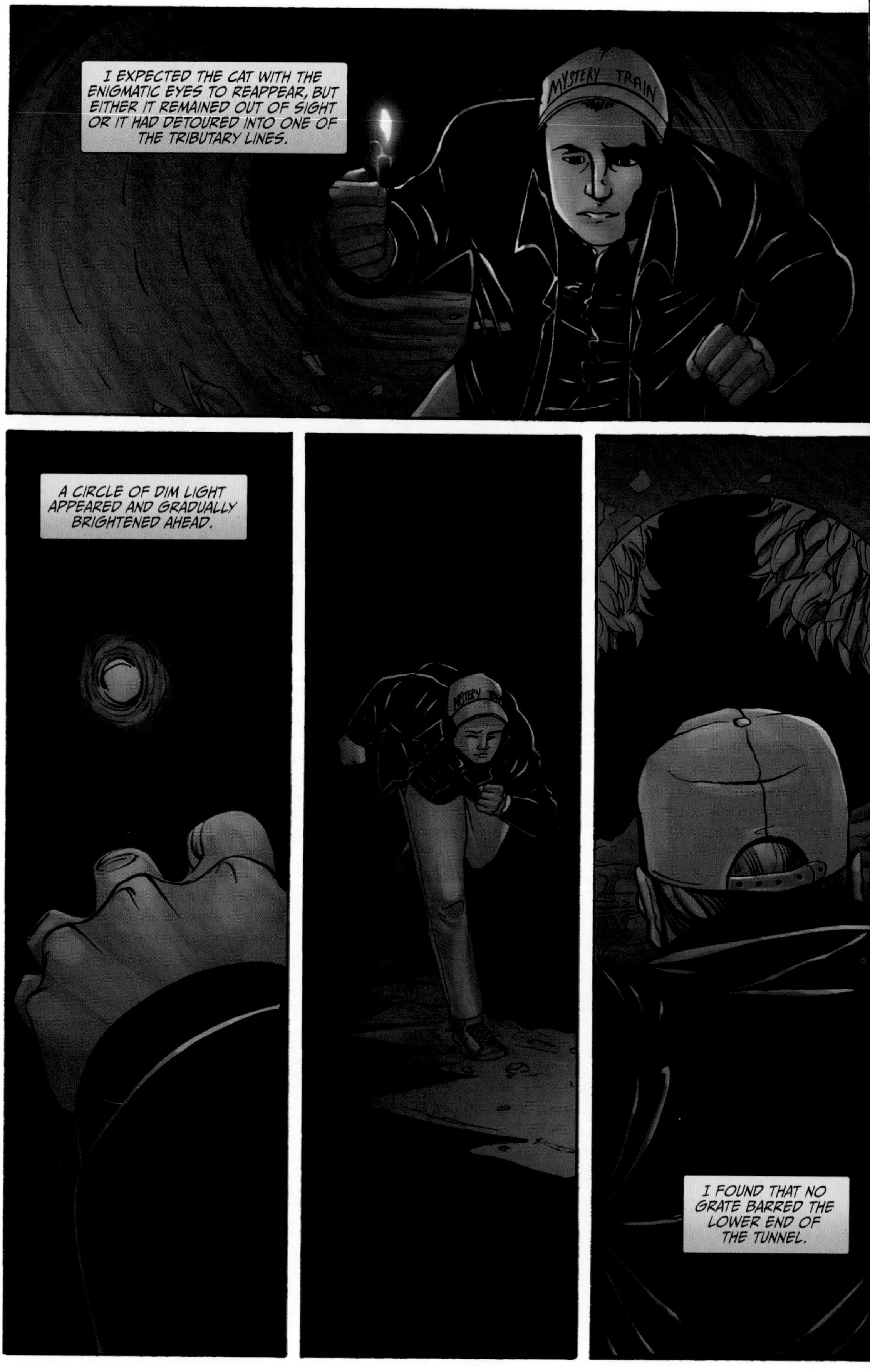
I EXPECTED THE CAT WITH THE ENIGMATIC EYES TO REAPPEAR, BUT EITHER IT REMAINED OUT OF SIGHT OR IT HAD DETOURED INTO ONE OF THE TRIBUTARY LINES.
MYSTERY TRAIN
A CIRCLE OF DIM LIGHT APPEARED AND GRADUALLY BRIGHTENED AHEAD.
I FOUND THAT NO GRATE BARRED THE LOWER END OF THE TUNNEL.

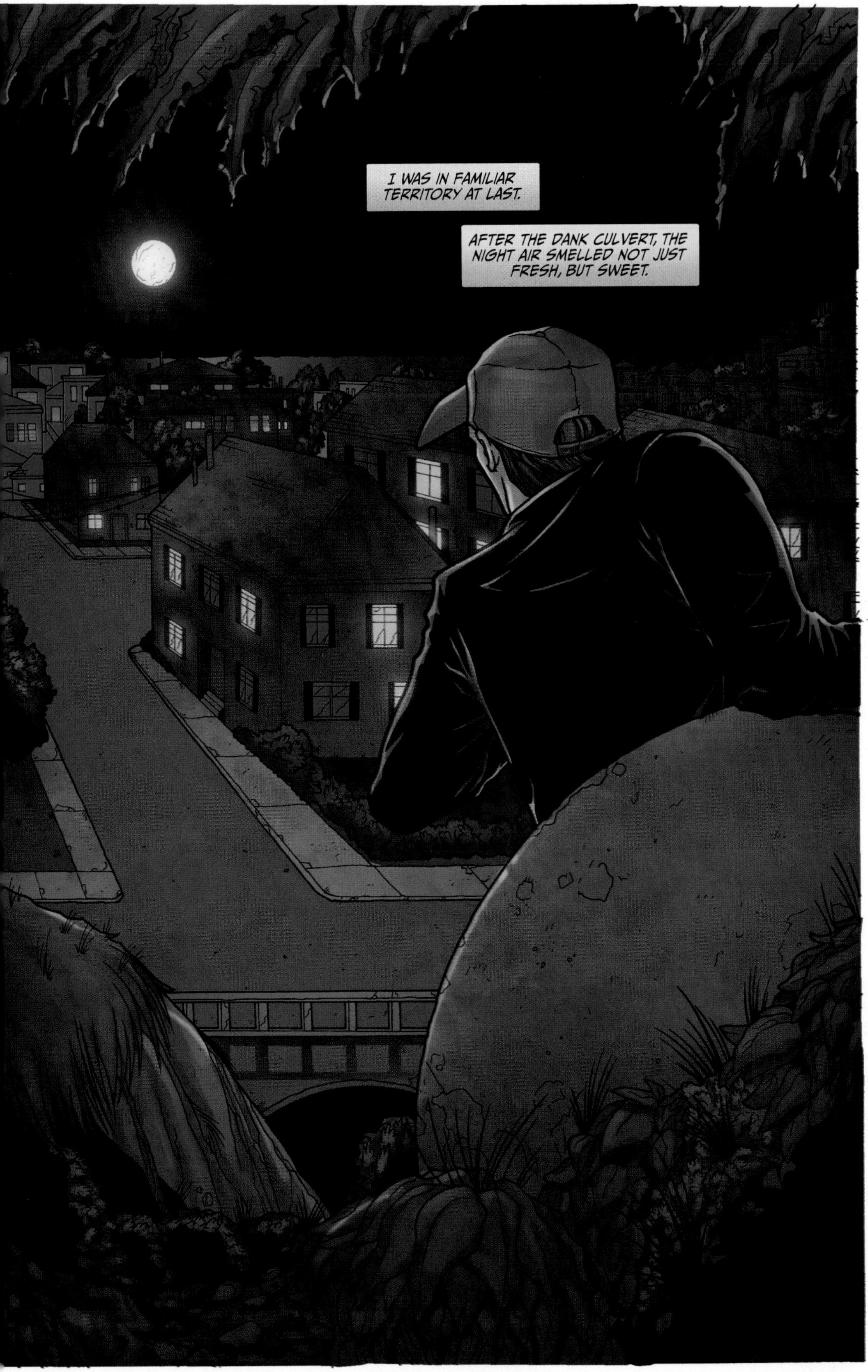
I WAS IN FAMILIAR TERRITORY AT LAST.
AFTER THE DANK CULVERT, THE NIGHT AIR SMELLED NOT JUST FRESH, BUT SWEET.

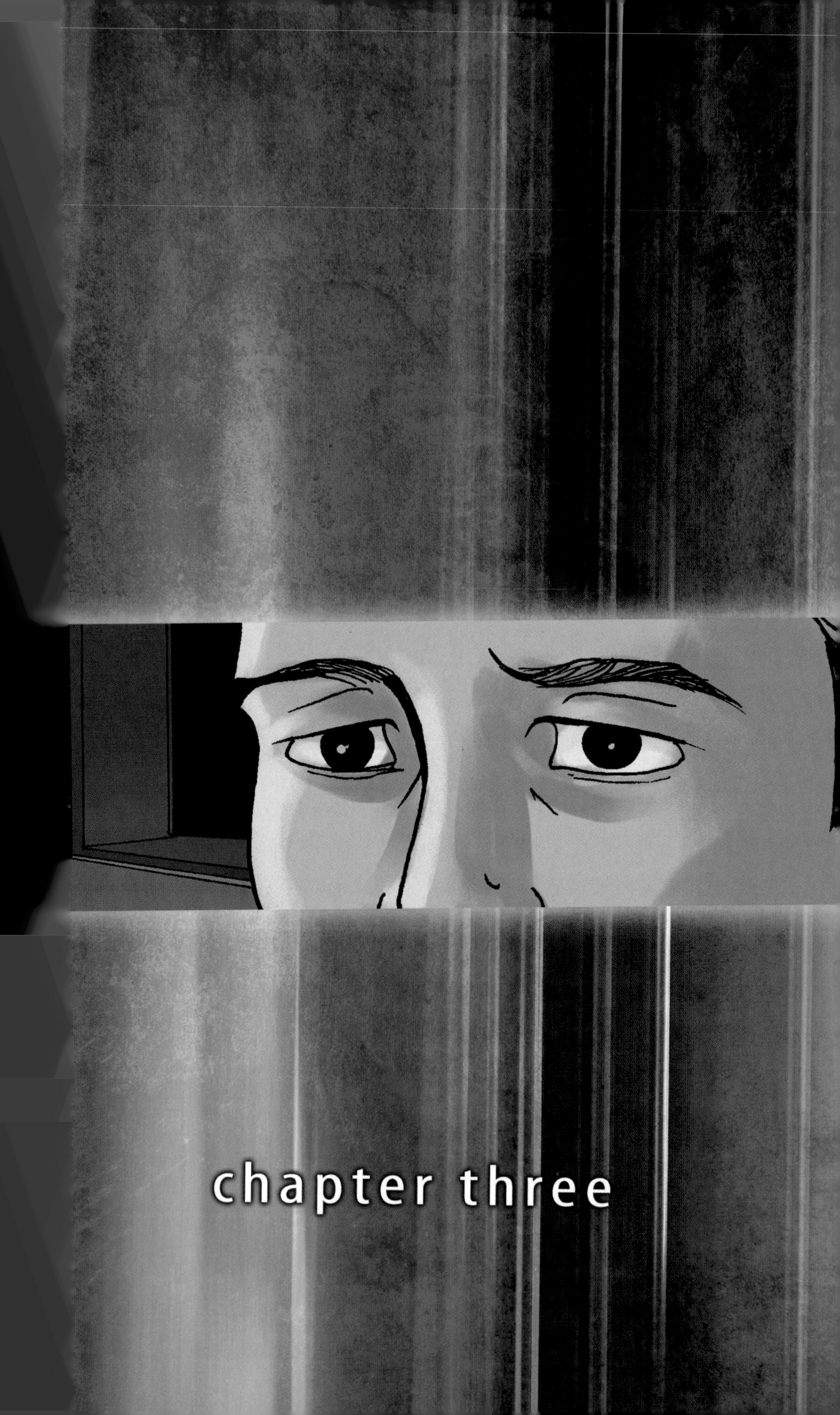
chapter three

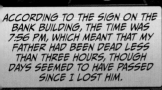

ACCORDING TO THE SIGN ON THE BANK BUILDING, THE TIME WAS 7:56 PM, WHICH MEANT THAT MY FATHER HAD BEEN DEAD LESS THAN THREE HOURS, THOUGH DAYS SEEMED TO HAVE PASSED SINCE I LOST HIM.

ABOVE THE PAYPHONE, I SPOTTED A POTENTIAL PROBLEM, A SECURITY LIGHT IN A CAGE.

I PUNCHED IN THE NUMBER OF THE MOONLIGHT BAY POLICE AND ASKED THE OPERATOR IF I COULD SPEAK TO OFFICER RAMIREZ.

CHRIS, I HEARD ABOUT YOUR DAD. I DON'T KNOW WHAT TO SAY.

NEITHER DO I, REALLY.

IN MY ESTIMATION, MANUEL IS THE BEST COP IN TOWN.

YOU GOING TO BE OKAY?

WE ARE FRIENDS.

YOU COME OVER WHEN I'M OFF DUTY. BEER, TAMALES, AND JACKIE CHAN MOVIES.

MANUEL, THERE'S SOMETHING MORE YOU CAN DO FOR ME. MORE THAN TAMALES.

YOU NAME IT, CHRIS.

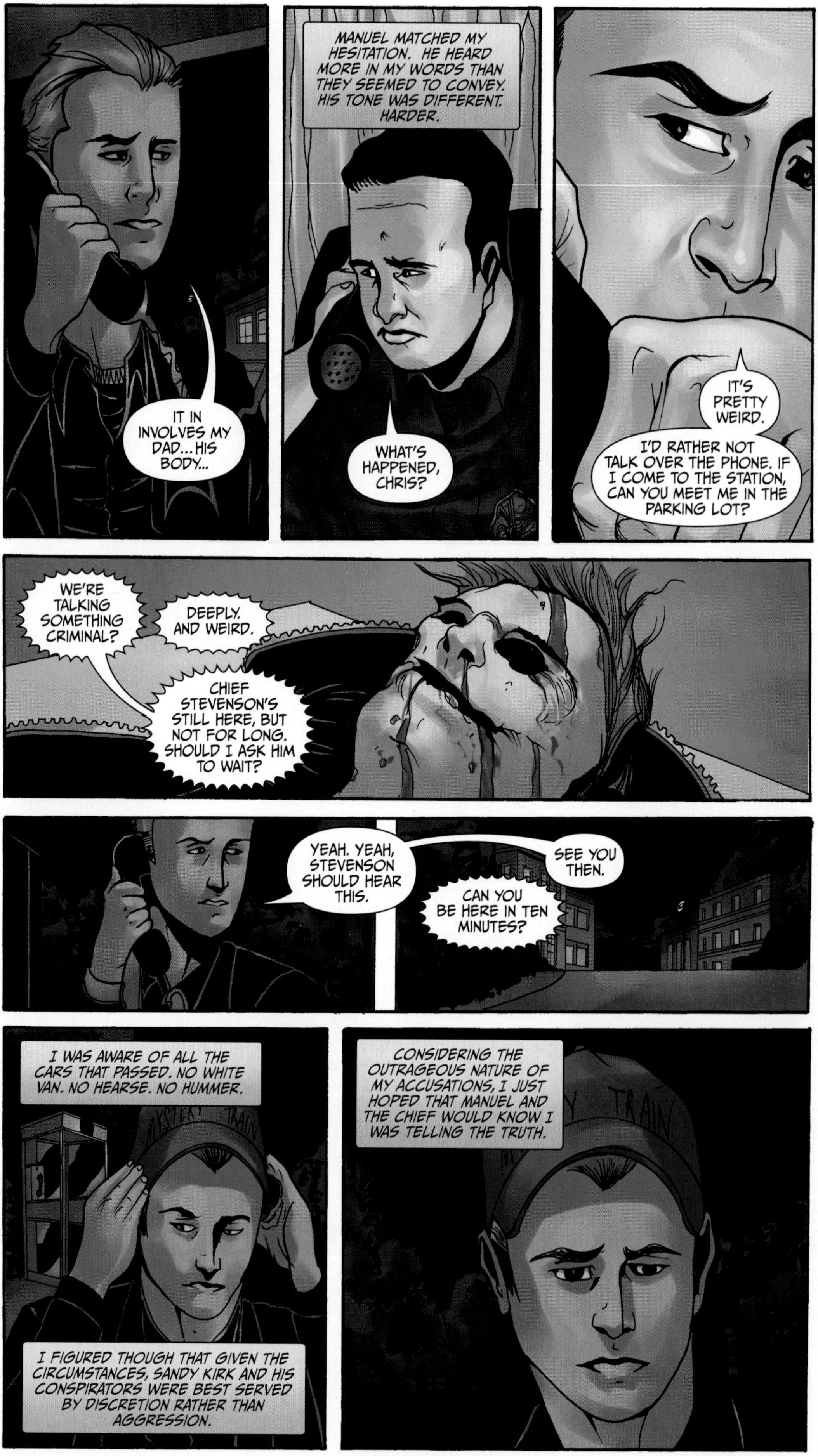
IT IN INVOLVES MY DAD... HIS BODY...
MANUEL MATCHED MY HESITATION. HE HEARD MORE IN MY WORDS THAN THEY SEEMED TO CONVEY. HIS TONE WAS DIFFERENT. HARDER.
WHAT'S HAPPENED, CHRIS?
IT'S PRETTY WEIRD.
I'D RATHER NOT TALK OVER THE PHONE. IF I COME TO THE STATION, CAN YOU MEET ME IN THE PARKING LOT?
WE'RE TALKING SOMETHING CRIMINAL?
DEEPLY. AND WEIRD.
CHIEF STEVENSON'S STILL HERE, BUT NOT FOR LONG. SHOULD I ASK HIM TO WAIT?
YEAH. YEAH, STEVENSON SHOULD HEAR THIS.
CAN YOU BE HERE IN TEN MINUTES?
SEE YOU THEN.
I WAS AWARE OF ALL THE CARS THAT PASSED. NO WHITE VAN. NO HEARSE. NO HUMMER.
I FIGURED THOUGH THAT GIVEN THE CIRCUMSTANCES, SANDY KIRK AND HIS CONSPIRATORS WERE BEST SERVED BY DISCRETION RATHER THAN AGGRESSION.
CONSIDERING THE OUTRAGEOUS NATURE OF MY ACCUSATIONS, I JUST HOPED THAT MANUEL AND THE CHIEF WOULD KNOW I WAS TELLING THE TRUTH.

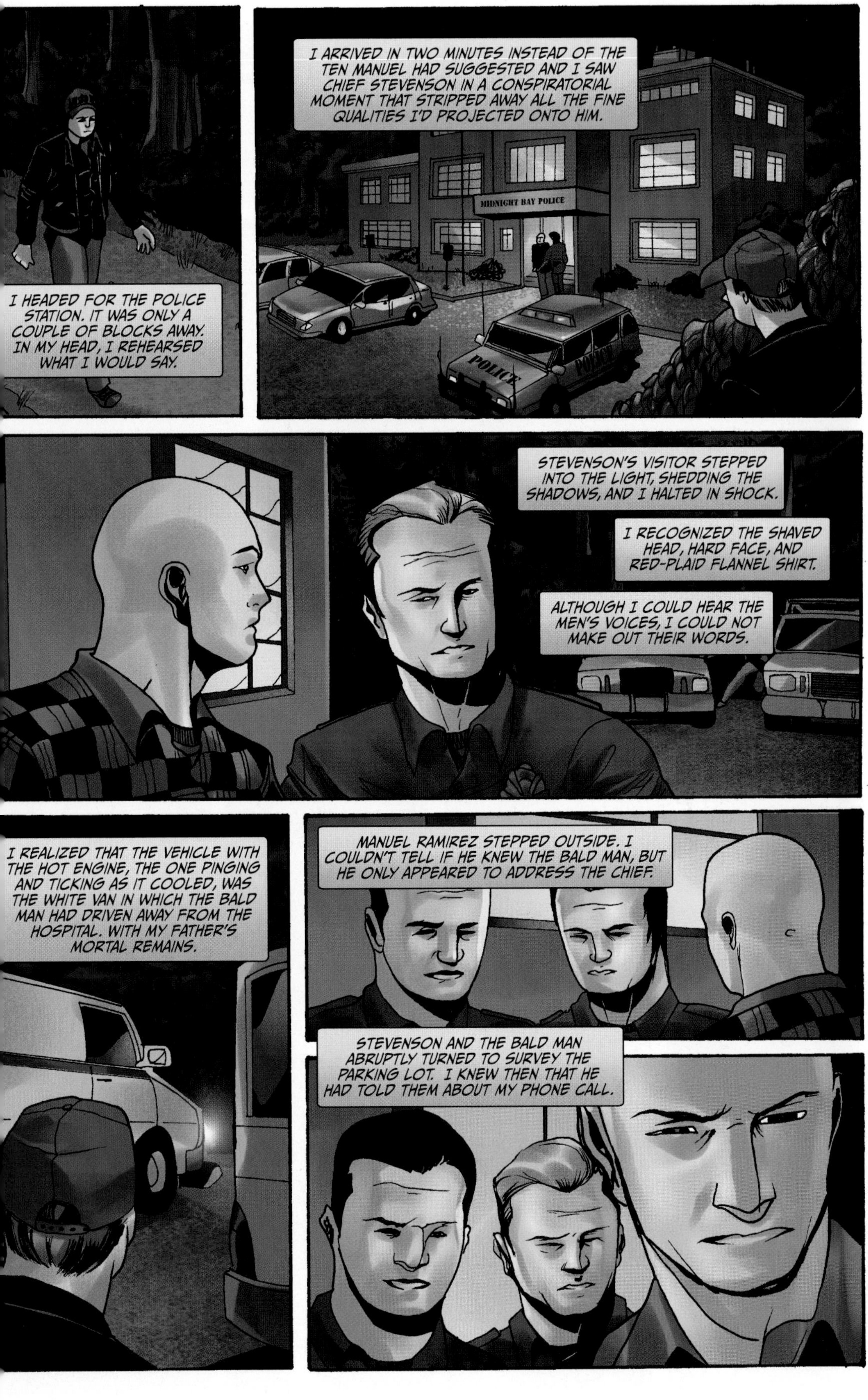
I HEADED FOR THE POLICE STATION. IT WAS ONLY A COUPLE OF BLOCKS AWAY. IN MY HEAD, I REHEARSED WHAT I WOULD SAY.
I ARRIVED IN TWO MINUTES INSTEAD OF THE TEN MANUEL HAD SUGGESTED AND I SAW CHIEF STEVENSON IN A CONSPIRATORIAL MOMENT THAT STRIPPED AWAY ALL THE FINE QUALITIES I'D PROJECTED ONTO HIM.
MIDNIGHT BAY POLICE
POLICE
POLICE
STEVENSON'S VISITOR STEPPED INTO THE LIGHT, SHEDDING THE SHADOWS, AND I HALTED IN SHOCK.
I RECOGNIZED THE SHAVED HEAD, HARD FACE, AND RED-PLAID FLANNEL SHIRT.
ALTHOUGH I COULD HEAR THE MEN'S VOICES, I COULD NOT MAKE OUT THEIR WORDS.
I REALIZED THAT THE VEHICLE WITH THE HOT ENGINE, THE ONE PINGING AND TICKING AS IT COOLED, WAS THE WHITE VAN IN WHICH THE BALD MAN HAD DRIVEN AWAY FROM THE HOSPITAL. WITH MY FATHER'S MORTAL REMAINS.
MANUEL RAMIREZ STEPPED OUTSIDE. I COULDN'T TELL IF HE KNEW THE BALD MAN, BUT HE ONLY APPEARED TO ADDRESS THE CHIEF.
STEVENSON AND THE BALD MAN ABRUPTLY TURNED TO SURVEY THE PARKING LOT. I KNEW THEN THAT HE HAD TOLD THEM ABOUT MY PHONE CALL.

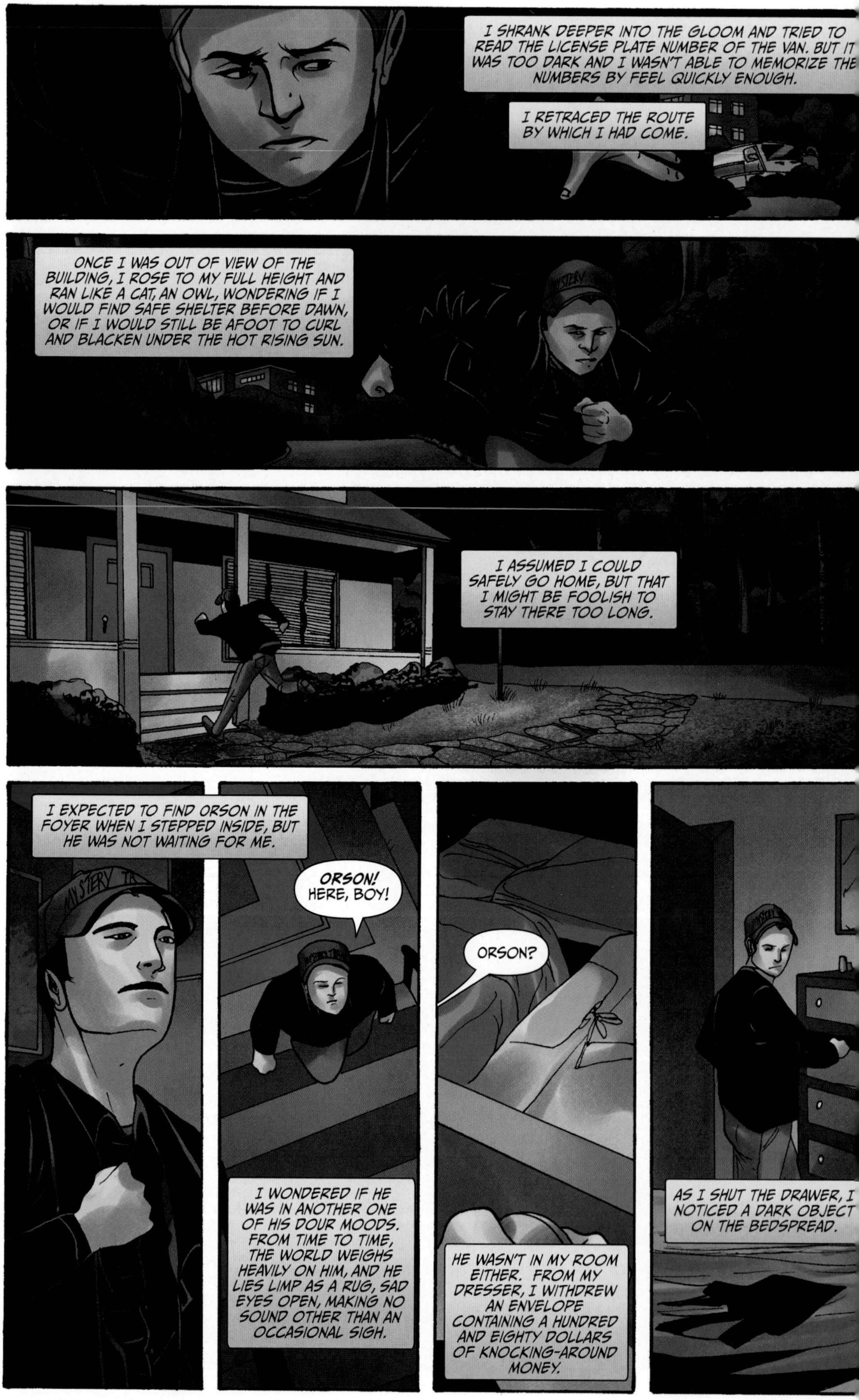

I SHRANK DEEPER INTO THE GLOOM AND TRIED TO READ THE LICENSE PLATE NUMBER OF THE VAN. BUT IT WAS TOO DARK AND I WASN'T ABLE TO MEMORIZE THE NUMBERS BY FEEL QUICKLY ENOUGH.
I RETRACED THE ROUTE BY WHICH I HAD COME.
ONCE I WAS OUT OF VIEW OF THE BUILDING, I ROSE TO MY FULL HEIGHT AND RAN LIKE A CAT, AN OWL, WONDERING IF I WOULD FIND SAFE SHELTER BEFORE DAWN, OR IF I WOULD STILL BE AFOOT TO CURL AND BLACKEN UNDER THE HOT RISING SUN.
I ASSUMED I COULD SAFELY GO HOME, BUT THAT I MIGHT BE FOOLISH TO STAY THERE TOO LONG.
I EXPECTED TO FIND ORSON IN THE FOYER WHEN I STEPPED INSIDE, BUT HE WAS NOT WAITING FOR ME.
ORSON! HERE, BOY!
I WONDERED IF HE WAS IN ANOTHER ONE OF HIS DOUR MOODS. FROM TIME TO TIME, THE WORLD WEIGHS HEAVILY ON HIM, AND HE LIES LIMP AS A RUG, SAD EYES OPEN, MAKING NO SOUND OTHER THAN AN OCCASIONAL SIGH.
ORSON?
HE WASN'T IN MY ROOM EITHER. FROM MY DRESSER, I WITHDREW AN ENVELOPE CONTAINING A HUNDRED AND EIGHTY DOLLARS OF KNOCKING-AROUND MONEY.
AS I SHUT THE DRAWER, I NOTICED A DARK OBJECT ON THE BEDSPREAD.

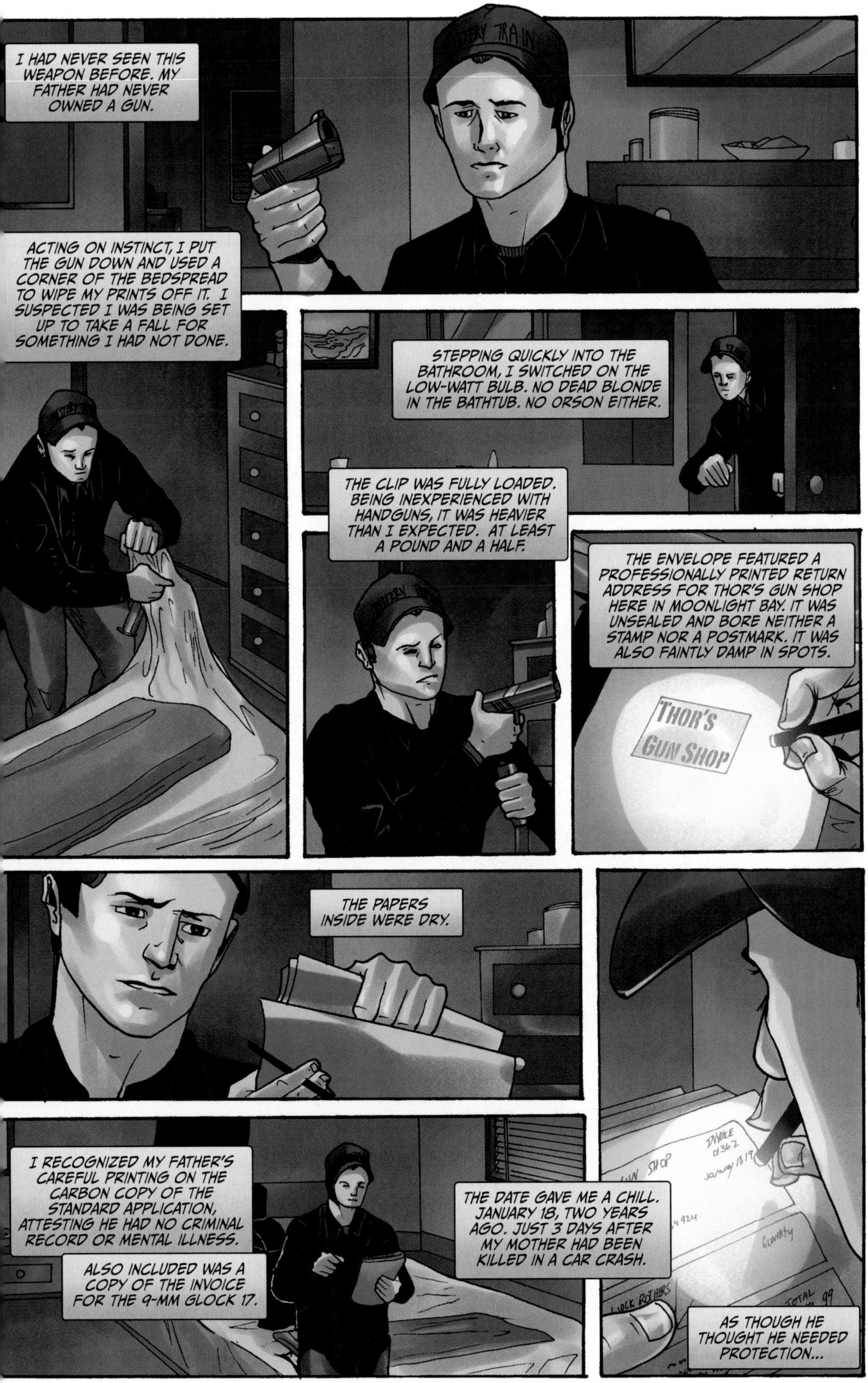
I HAD NEVER SEEN THIS WEAPON BEFORE. MY FATHER HAD NEVER OWNED A GUN.
ACTING ON INSTINCT, I PUT THE GUN DOWN AND USED A CORNER OF THE BEDSPREAD TO WIPE MY PRINTS OFF IT. I SUSPECTED I WAS BEING SET UP TO TAKE A FALL FOR SOMETHING I HAD NOT DONE.
STEPPING QUICKLY INTO THE BATHROOM, I SWITCHED ON THE LOW-WATT BULB. NO DEAD BLONDE IN THE BATHTUB. NO ORSON EITHER.
THE CLIP WAS FULLY LOADED. BEING INEXPERIENCED WITH HANDGUNS, IT WAS HEAVIER THAN I EXPECTED. AT LEAST A POUND AND A HALF.
THE ENVELOPE FEATURED A PROFESSIONALLY PRINTED RETURN ADDRESS FOR THOR'S GUN SHOP HERE IN MOONLIGHT BAY. IT WAS UNSEALED AND BORE NEITHER A STAMP NOR A POSTMARK. IT WAS ALSO FAINTLY DAMP IN SPOTS.
THOR'S GUN SHOP
THE PAPERS INSIDE WERE DRY.
I RECOGNIZED MY FATHER'S CAREFUL PRINTING ON THE CARBON COPY OF THE STANDARD APPLICATION, ATTESTING HE HAD NO CRIMINAL RECORD OR MENTAL ILLNESS.
ALSO INCLUDED WAS A COPY OF THE INVOICE FOR THE 9-MM GLOCK 17.
THE DATE GAVE ME A CHILL. JANUARY 18, TWO YEARS AGO. JUST 3 DAYS AFTER MY MOTHER HAD BEEN KILLED IN A CAR CRASH.
AS THOUGH HE THOUGHT HE NEEDED PROTECTION...

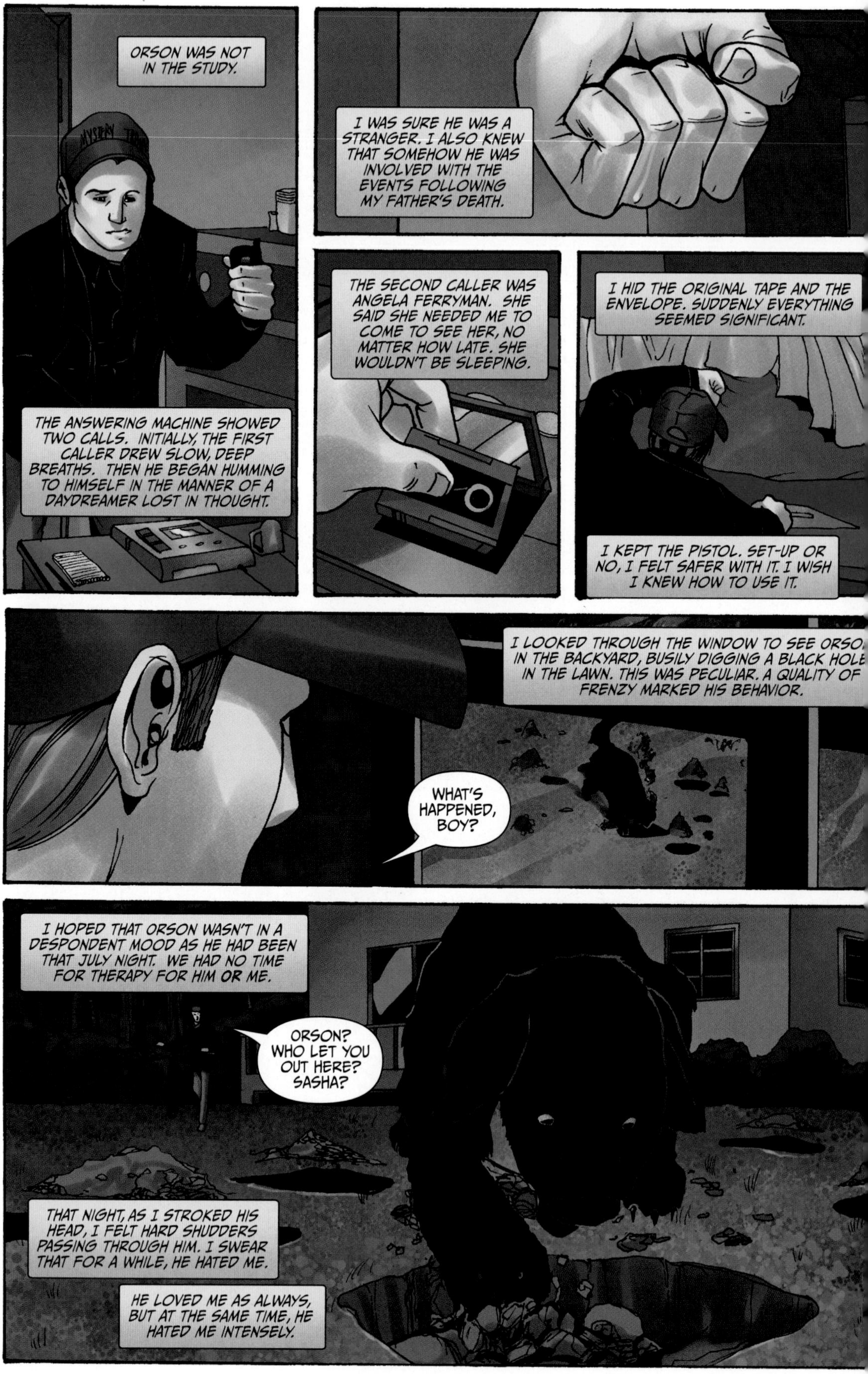
ORSON WAS NOT IN THE STUDY.
MYSTERY TRAIN
THE ANSWERING MACHINE SHOWED TWO CALLS. INITIALLY, THE FIRST CALLER DREW SLOW, DEEP BREATHS. THEN HE BEGAN HUMMING TO HIMSELF IN THE MANNER OF A DAYDREAMER LOST IN THOUGHT.
I WAS SURE HE WAS A STRANGER. I ALSO KNEW THAT SOMEHOW HE WAS INVOLVED WITH THE EVENTS FOLLOWING MY FATHER'S DEATH.
THE SECOND CALLER WAS ANGELA FERRYMAN. SHE SAID SHE NEEDED ME TO COME TO SEE HER, NO MATTER HOW LATE. SHE WOULDN'T BE SLEEPING.
I HID THE ORIGINAL TAPE AND THE ENVELOPE. SUDDENLY EVERYTHING SEEMED SIGNIFICANT.
I KEPT THE PISTOL. SET-UP OR NO, I FELT SAFER WITH IT. I WISH I KNEW HOW TO USE IT.
I LOOKED THROUGH THE WINDOW TO SEE ORSO IN THE BACKYARD, BUSILY DIGGING A BLACK HOLE IN THE LAWN. THIS WAS PECULIAR. A QUALITY OF FRENZY MARKED HIS BEHAVIOR.
WHAT'S HAPPENED, BOY?
I HOPED THAT ORSON WASN'T IN A DESPONDENT MOOD AS HE HAD BEEN THAT JULY NIGHT. WE HAD NO TIME FOR THERAPY FOR HIM OR ME.
ORSON? WHO LET YOU OUT HERE? SASHA?
THAT NIGHT, AS I STROKED HIS HEAD, I FELT HARD SHUDDERS PASSING THROUGH HIM. I SWEAR THAT FOR A WHILE, HE HATED ME.
HE LOVED ME AS ALWAYS, BUT AT THE SAME TIME, HE HATED ME INTENSELY.

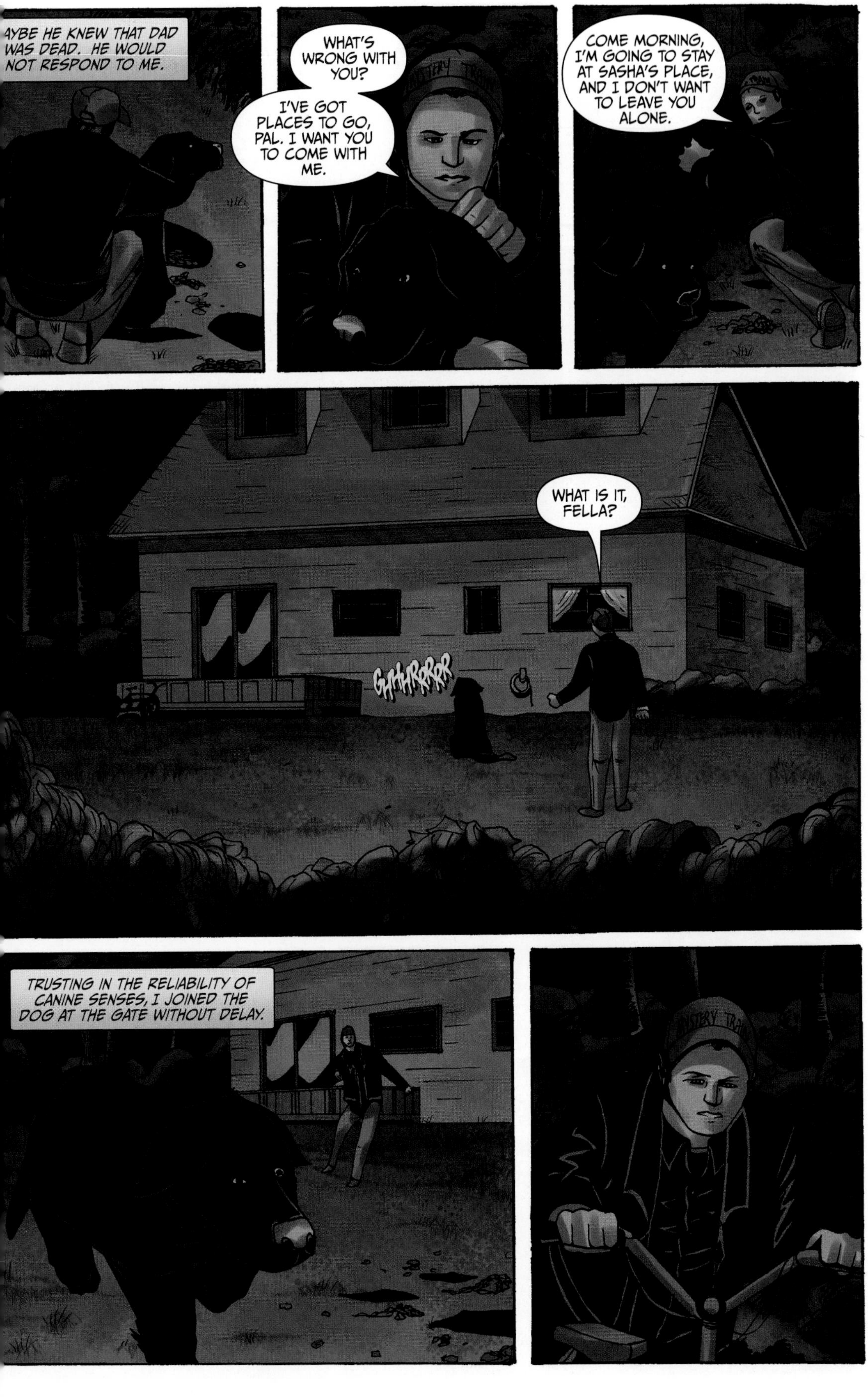
AYBE HE KNEW THAT DAD WAS DEAD. HE WOULD NOT RESPOND TO ME.
WHAT'S WRONG WITH YOU?
I'VE GOT PLACES TO GO, PAL. I WANT YOU TO COME WITH ME.
COME MORNING, I'M GOING TO STAY AT SASHA'S PLACE, AND I DON'T WANT TO LEAVE YOU ALONE.
WHAT IS IT, FELLA?
GHHHRRRR
TRUSTING IN THE RELIABILITY OF CANINE SENSES, I JOINED THE DOG AT THE GATE WITHOUT DELAY.

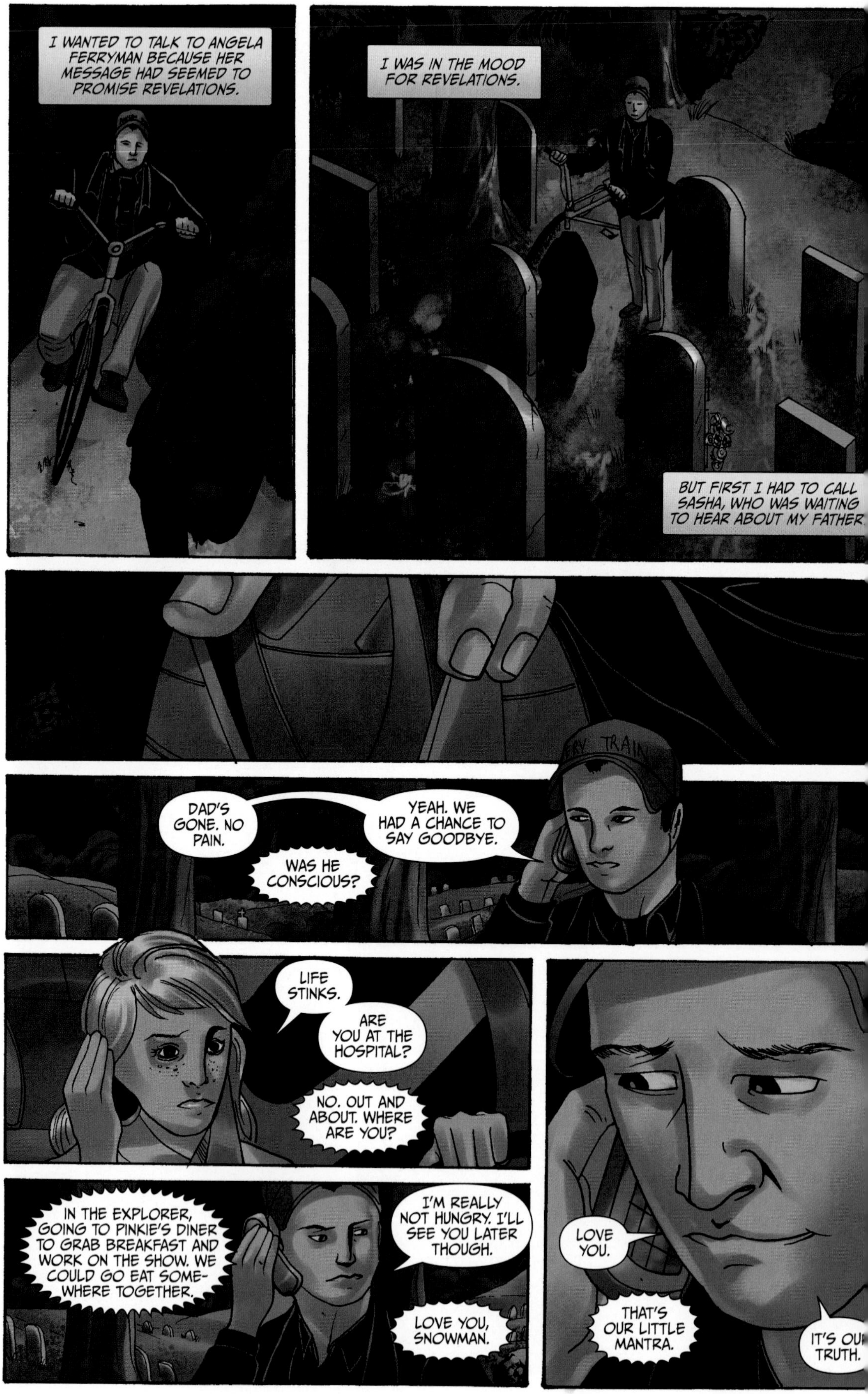
I WANTED TO TALK TO ANGELA FERRYMAN BECAUSE HER MESSAGE HAD SEEMED TO PROMISE REVELATIONS.
I WAS IN THE MOOD FOR REVELATIONS.
BUT FIRST I HAD TO CALL SASHA, WHO WAS WAITING TO HEAR ABOUT MY FATHER.
DAD'S GONE. NO PAIN.
YEAH. WE HAD A CHANCE TO SAY GOODBYE.
WAS HE CONSCIOUS?
LIFE STINKS.
ARE YOU AT THE HOSPITAL?
NO. OUT AND ABOUT. WHERE ARE YOU?
IN THE EXPLORER, GOING TO PINKIE'S DINER TO GRAB BREAKFAST AND WORK ON THE SHOW. WE COULD GO EAT SOME-WHERE TOGETHER.
I'M REALLY NOT HUNGRY. I'LL SEE YOU LATER THOUGH.
LOVE YOU, SNOWMAN.
LOVE YOU.
THAT'S OUR LITTLE MANTRA.
IT'S OU TRUTH.

I MADE MY WAY TO ANGELA FERRYMAN'S HOUSE AS FAR AS POSSIBLE BY ALLEYWAYS WHERE I WOULD NOT ENCOUNTER MUCH TRAFFIC AND ON STREETS WITH WIDELY SPACED LAMPPOSTS.

WHEN I HAD NO CHOICE BUT TO PASS UNDER CLUSTERS OF STREETLAMPS, I PEDALED HARD. ORSON SEEMED HAPPIER NOW THAT HE COULD TROT AT MY SIDE, BLACKER THAN ANY NIGHTSHADOW I COULD CAST.

ANGELA LIVED ON A HIGH STREET IN A CHARMING SPANISH BUNGALOW THAT SHELTERED UNDER MAGNOLIA TREES NOT YET IN BLOOM. NO LIGHTS WERE ON IN THE FRONT ROOMS.

BE VIGILANT. BE BIG. BE BAD.

TAP TAP

ANGELA'S QUICK, NERVOUS, HOPPING-HEN EYES PECKED AT ME AND THEN THE PATIO TO CONFIRM I HAD COME ALONE.

WITH A CONSPIRATORIAL DEMEANOR, SHE USHERED ME INSIDE, LOCKING THE DOOR BEHIND US. SHE ADJUSTED THE CURTAIN TO ENSURE THAT NO GAP EXISTED THROUGH WHICH ANYONE COULD PEER IN AT US.

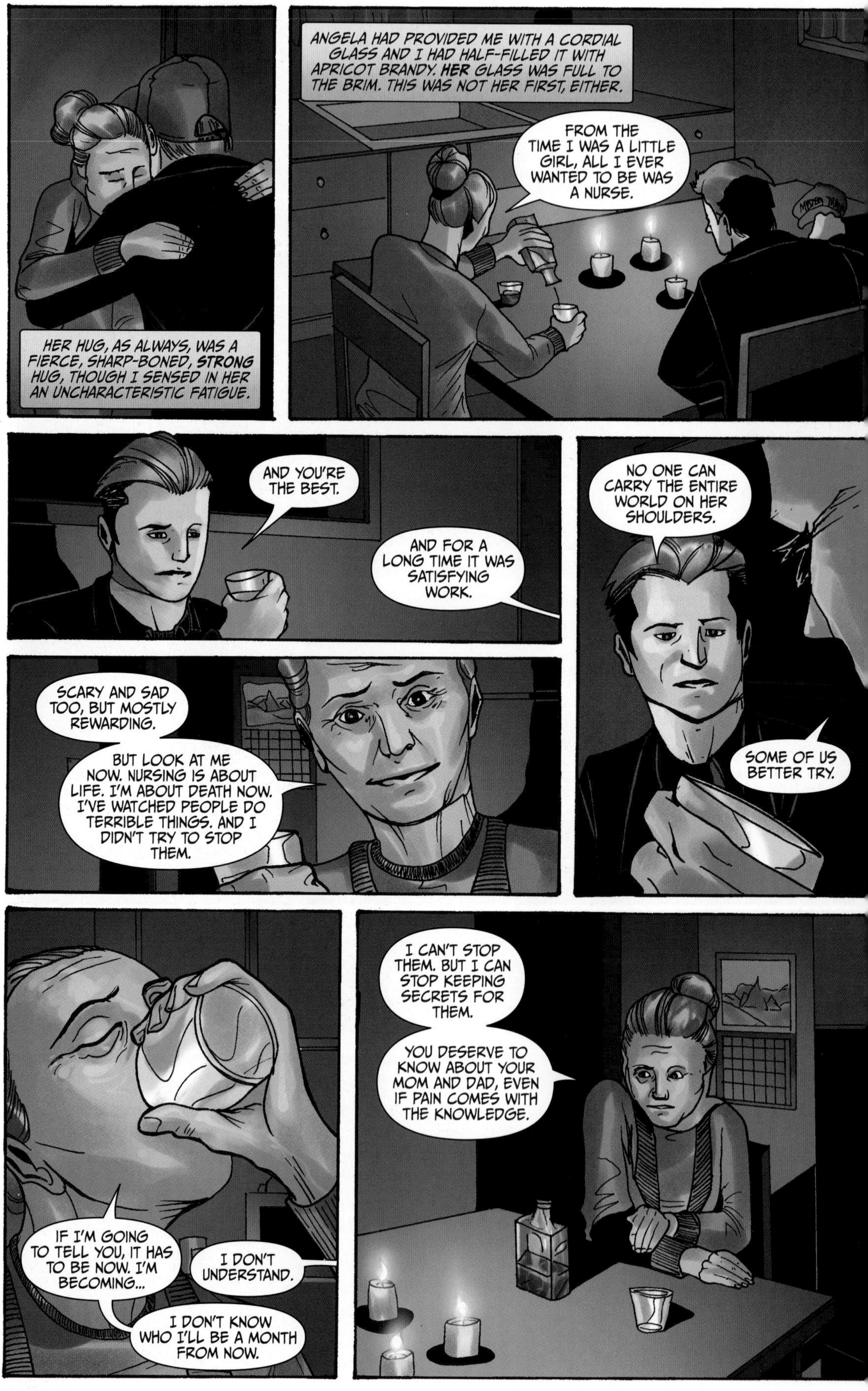
HER HUG, AS ALWAYS, WAS A FIERCE, SHARP-BONED, STRONG HUG, THOUGH I SENSED IN HER AN UNCHARACTERISTIC FATIGUE.
ANGELA HAD PROVIDED ME WITH A CORDIAL GLASS AND I HAD HALF-FILLED IT WITH APRICOT BRANDY. HER GLASS WAS FULL TO THE BRIM. THIS WAS NOT HER FIRST, EITHER.
FROM THE TIME I WAS A LITTLE GIRL, ALL I EVER WANTED TO BE WAS A NURSE.
AND YOU'RE THE BEST.
AND FOR A LONG TIME IT WAS SATISFYING WORK.
SCARY AND SAD TOO, BUT MOSTLY REWARDING.
BUT LOOK AT ME NOW. NURSING IS ABOUT LIFE. I'M ABOUT DEATH NOW. I'VE WATCHED PEOPLE DO TERRIBLE THINGS. AND I DIDN'T TRY TO STOP THEM.
NO ONE CAN CARRY THE ENTIRE WORLD ON HER SHOULDERS.
SOME OF US BETTER TRY.
IF I'M GOING TO TELL YOU, IT HAS TO BE NOW. I'M BECOMING...
I DON'T UNDERSTAND.
I DON'T KNOW WHO I'LL BE A MONTH FROM NOW.
I CAN'T STOP THEM. BUT I CAN STOP KEEPING SECRETS FOR THEM.
YOU DESERVE TO KNOW ABOUT YOUR MOM AND DAD, EVEN IF PAIN COMES WITH THE KNOWLEDGE.

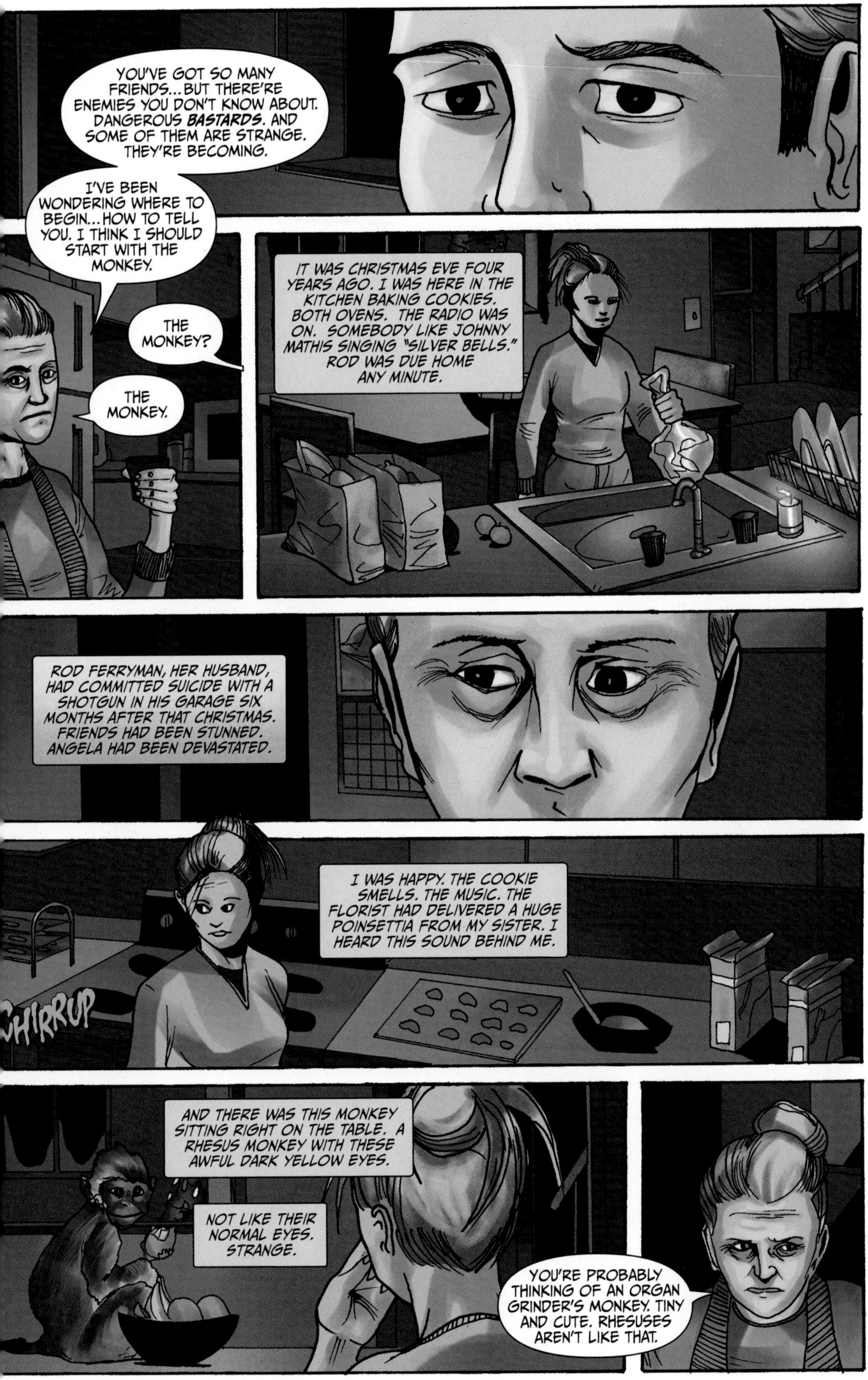
YOU'VE GOT SO MANY FRIENDS...BUT THERE'RE ENEMIES YOU DON'T KNOW ABOUT. DANGEROUS BASTARDS. AND SOME OF THEM ARE STRANGE. THEY'RE BECOMING.
I'VE BEEN WONDERING WHERE TO BEGIN...HOW TO TELL YOU. I THINK I SHOULD START WITH THE MONKEY.
THE MONKEY?
THE MONKEY.
IT WAS CHRISTMAS EVE FOUR YEARS AGO. I WAS HERE IN THE KITCHEN BAKING COOKIES. BOTH OVENS. THE RADIO WAS ON. SOMEBODY LIKE JOHNNY MATHIS SINGING "SILVER BELLS." ROD WAS DUE HOME ANY MINUTE.
ROD FERRYMAN, HER HUSBAND, HAD COMMITTED SUICIDE WITH A SHOTGUN IN HIS GARAGE SIX MONTHS AFTER THAT CHRISTMAS. FRIENDS HAD BEEN STUNNED. ANGELA HAD BEEN DEVASTATED.
I WAS HAPPY. THE COOKIE SMELLS. THE MUSIC. THE FLORIST HAD DELIVERED A HUGE POINSETTIA FROM MY SISTER. I HEARD THIS SOUND BEHIND ME.
CHIRRUP
AND THERE WAS THIS MONKEY SITTING RIGHT ON THE TABLE. A RHESUS MONKEY WITH THESE AWFUL DARK YELLOW EYES.
NOT LIKE THEIR NORMAL EYES. STRANGE.
YOU'RE PROBABLY THINKING OF AN ORGAN GRINDER'S MONKEY. TINY AND CUTE. RHESUSES AREN'T LIKE THAT.

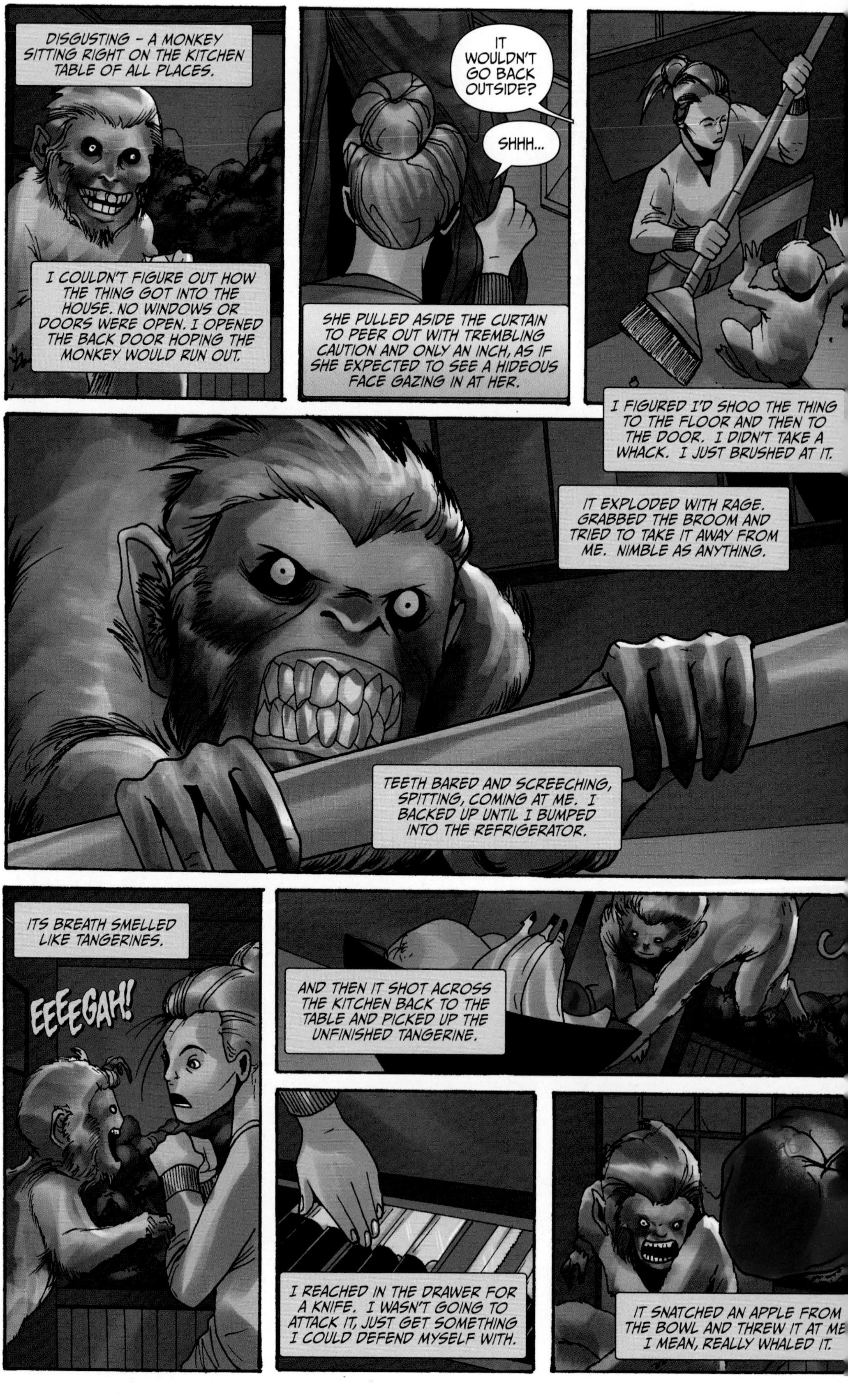
DISGUSTING – A MONKEY SITTING RIGHT ON THE KITCHEN TABLE OF ALL PLACES.
I COULDN'T FIGURE OUT HOW THE THING GOT INTO THE HOUSE. NO WINDOWS OR DOORS WERE OPEN. I OPENED THE BACK DOOR HOPING THE MONKEY WOULD RUN OUT.
IT WOULDN'T GO BACK OUTSIDE?
SHHH...
SHE PULLED ASIDE THE CURTAIN TO PEER OUT WITH TREMBLING CAUTION AND ONLY AN INCH, AS IF SHE EXPECTED TO SEE A HIDEOUS FACE GAZING IN AT HER.
I FIGURED I'D SHOO THE THING TO THE FLOOR AND THEN TO THE DOOR. I DIDN'T TAKE A WHACK. I JUST BRUSHED AT IT.
IT EXPLODED WITH RAGE. GRABBED THE BROOM AND TRIED TO TAKE IT AWAY FROM ME. NIMBLE AS ANYTHING.
TEETH BARED AND SCREECHING, SPITTING, COMING AT ME. I BACKED UP UNTIL I BUMPED INTO THE REFRIGERATOR.
ITS BREATH SMELLED LIKE TANGERINES.
EEEEGAH!
AND THEN IT SHOT ACROSS THE KITCHEN BACK TO THE TABLE AND PICKED UP THE UNFINISHED TANGERINE.
I REACHED IN THE DRAWER FOR A KNIFE. I WASN'T GOING TO ATTACK IT, JUST GET SOMETHING I COULD DEFEND MYSELF WITH.
IT SNATCHED AN APPLE FROM THE BOWL AND THREW IT AT ME. I MEAN, REALLY WHALED IT.

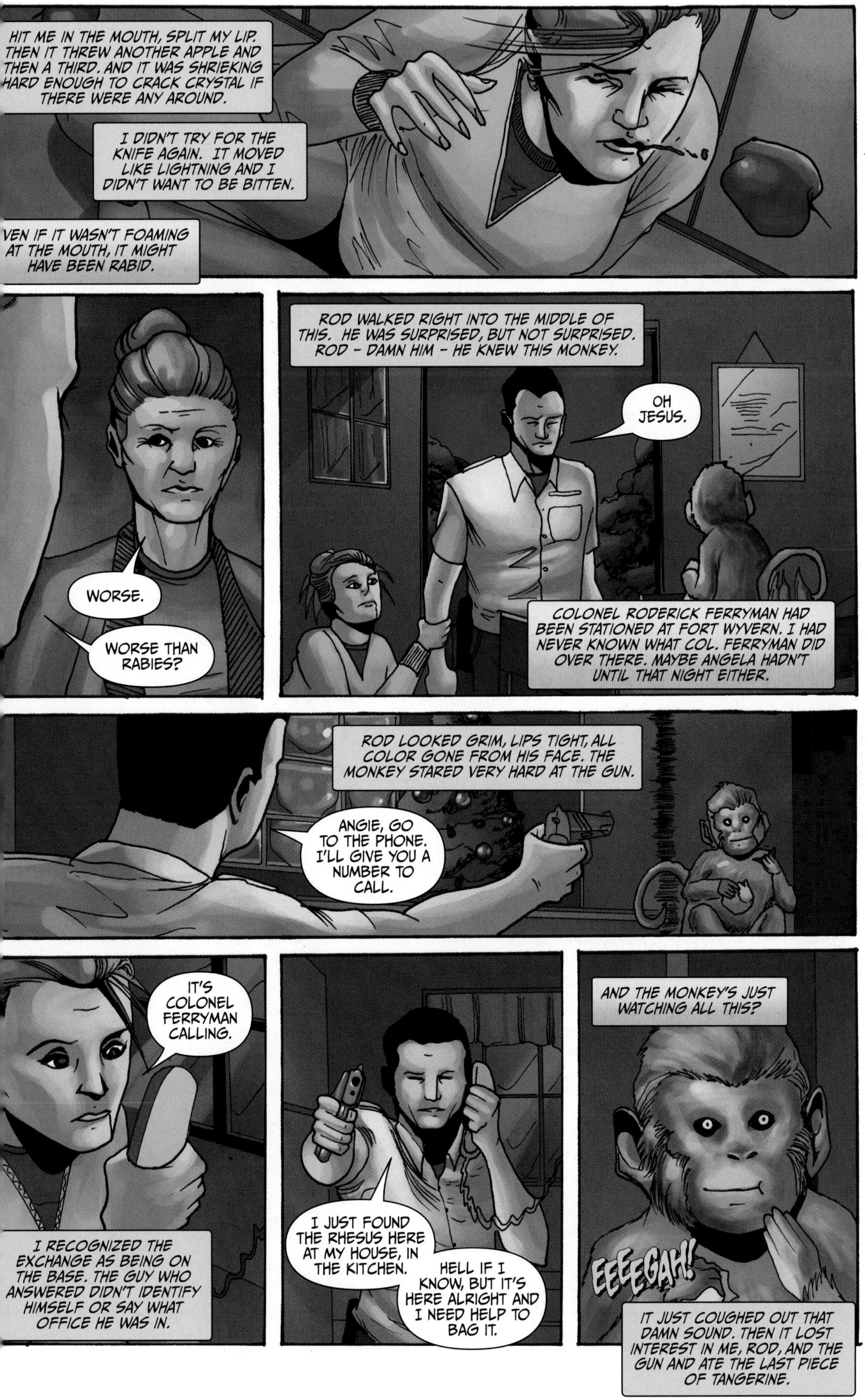
HIT ME IN THE MOUTH, SPLIT MY LIP. THEN IT THREW ANOTHER APPLE AND THEN A THIRD. AND IT WAS SHRIEKING HARD ENOUGH TO CRACK CRYSTAL IF THERE WERE ANY AROUND.
I DIDN'T TRY FOR THE KNIFE AGAIN. IT MOVED LIKE LIGHTNING AND I DIDN'T WANT TO BE BITTEN.
VEN IF IT WASN'T FOAMING AT THE MOUTH, IT MIGHT HAVE BEEN RABID.
WORSE.
WORSE THAN RABIES?
ROD WALKED RIGHT INTO THE MIDDLE OF THIS. HE WAS SURPRISED, BUT NOT SURPRISED. ROD - DAMN HIM - HE KNEW THIS MONKEY.
OH JESUS.
COLONEL RODERICK FERRYMAN HAD BEEN STATIONED AT FORT WYVERN. I HAD NEVER KNOWN WHAT COL. FERRYMAN DID OVER THERE. MAYBE ANGELA HADN'T UNTIL THAT NIGHT EITHER.
ROD LOOKED GRIM, LIPS TIGHT, ALL COLOR GONE FROM HIS FACE. THE MONKEY STARED VERY HARD AT THE GUN.
ANGIE, GO TO THE PHONE. I'LL GIVE YOU A NUMBER TO CALL.
IT'S COLONEL FERRYMAN CALLING.
I RECOGNIZED THE EXCHANGE AS BEING ON THE BASE. THE GUY WHO ANSWERED DIDN'T IDENTIFY HIMSELF OR SAY WHAT OFFICE HE WAS IN.
I JUST FOUND THE RHESUS HERE AT MY HOUSE, IN THE KITCHEN.
HELL IF I KNOW, BUT IT'S HERE ALRIGHT AND I NEED HELP TO BAG IT.
AND THE MONKEY'S JUST WATCHING ALL THIS?
EEEEGAH!
IT JUST COUGHED OUT THAT DAMN SOUND. THEN IT LOST INTEREST IN ME, ROD, AND THE GUN AND ATE THE LAST PIECE OF TANGERINE.

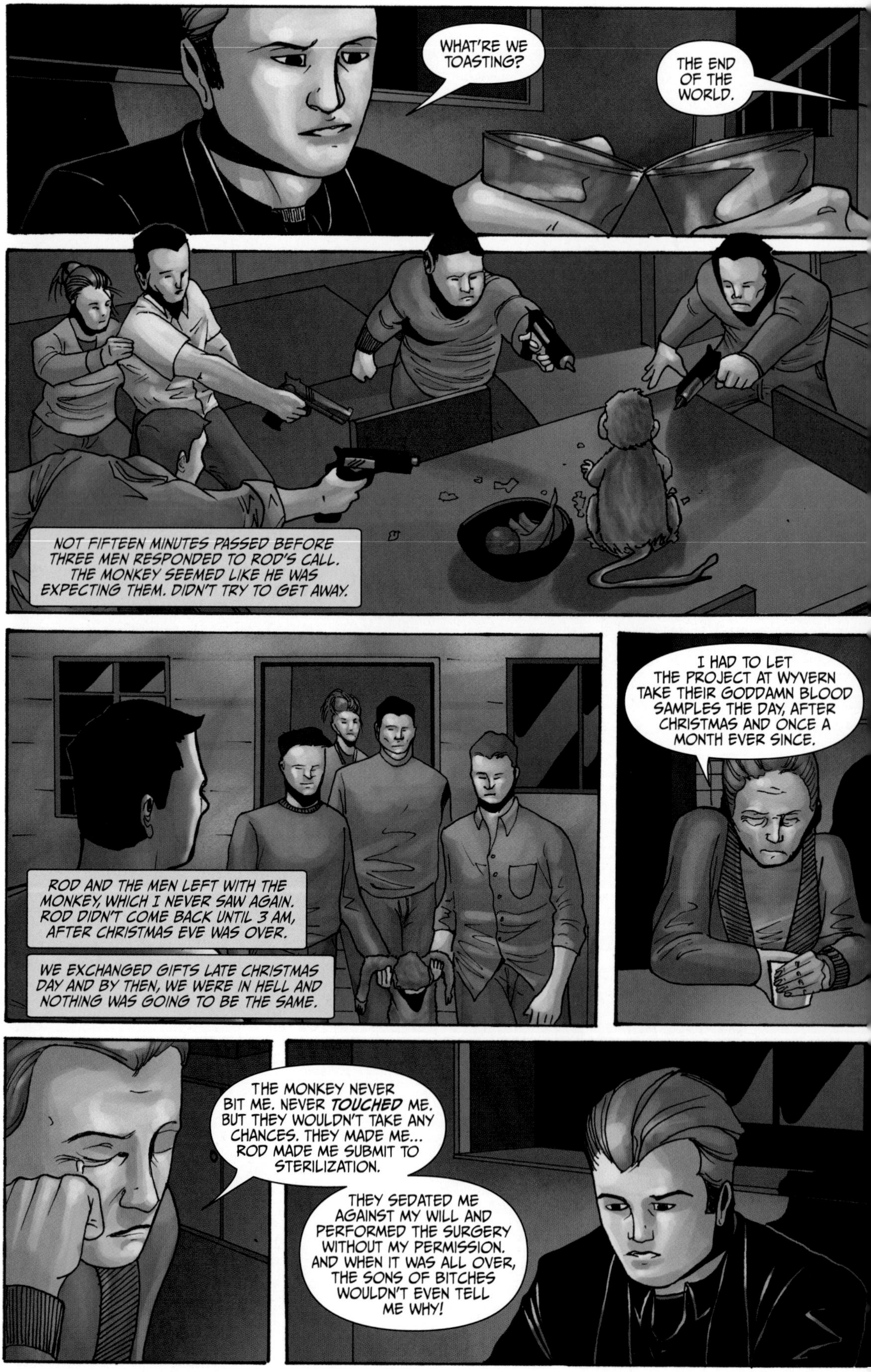
WHAT'RE WE TOASTING?
THE END OF THE WORLD.
NOT FIFTEEN MINUTES PASSED BEFORE THREE MEN RESPONDED TO ROD'S CALL. THE MONKEY SEEMED LIKE HE WAS EXPECTING THEM. DIDN'T TRY TO GET AWAY.
ROD AND THE MEN LEFT WITH THE MONKEY, WHICH I NEVER SAW AGAIN. ROD DIDN'T COME BACK UNTIL 3 AM, AFTER CHRISTMAS EVE WAS OVER.
WE EXCHANGED GIFTS LATE CHRISTMAS DAY AND BY THEN, WE WERE IN HELL AND NOTHING WAS GOING TO BE THE SAME.
I HAD TO LET THE PROJECT AT WYVERN TAKE THEIR GODDAMN BLOOD SAMPLES THE DAY, AFTER CHRISTMAS AND ONCE A MONTH EVER SINCE.
THE MONKEY NEVER BIT ME. NEVER ***TOUCHED*** ME. BUT THEY WOULDN'T TAKE ANY CHANCES. THEY MADE ME... ROD MADE ME SUBMIT TO STERILIZATION.
THEY SEDATED ME AGAINST MY WILL AND PERFORMED THE SURGERY WITHOUT MY PERMISSION. AND WHEN IT WAS ALL OVER, THE SONS OF BITCHES WOULDN'T EVEN TELL ME WHY!

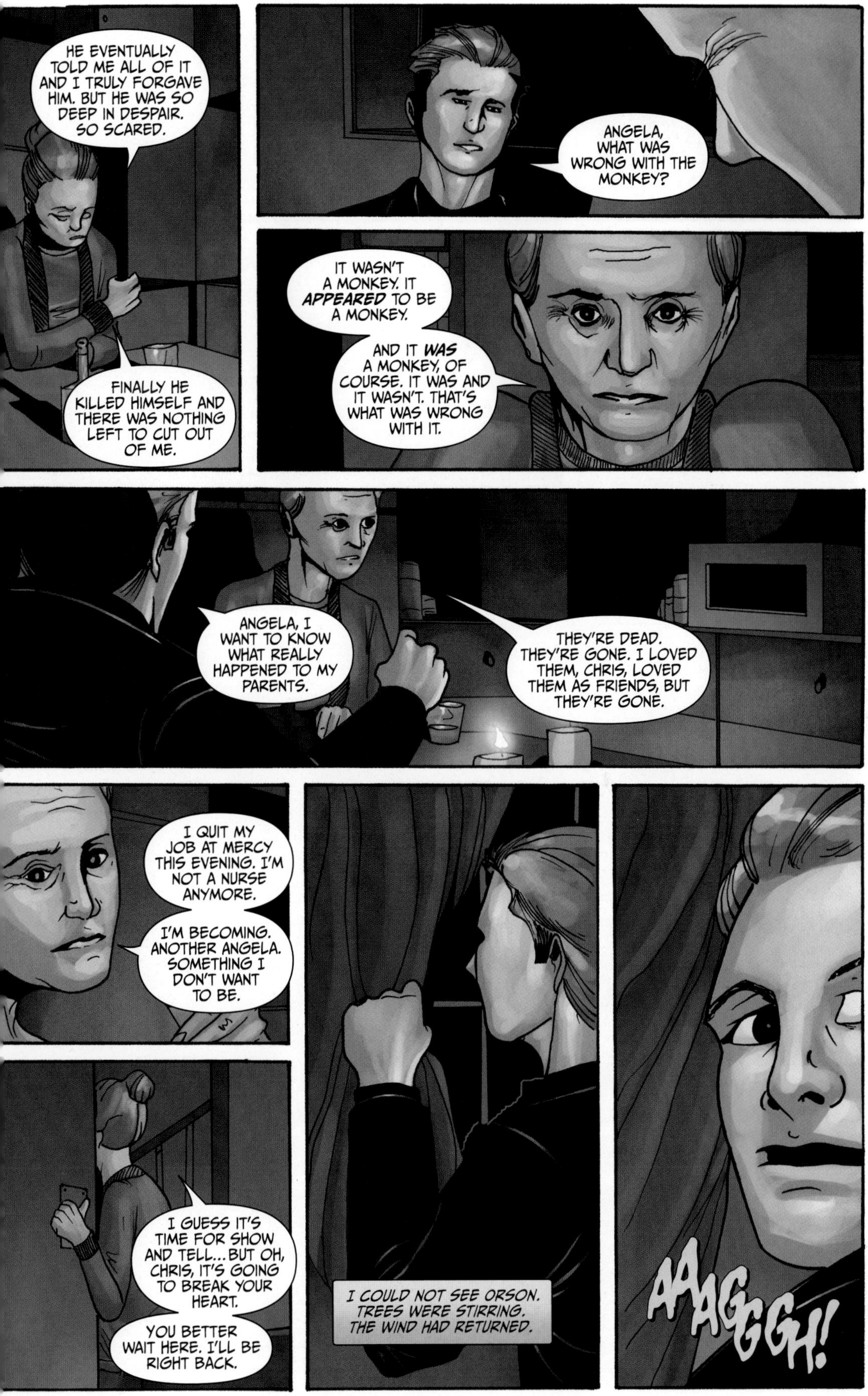

HE EVENTUALLY TOLD ME ALL OF IT AND I TRULY FORGAVE HIM. BUT HE WAS SO DEEP IN DESPAIR. SO SCARED.
FINALLY HE KILLED HIMSELF AND THERE WAS NOTHING LEFT TO CUT OUT OF ME.
ANGELA, WHAT WAS WRONG WITH THE MONKEY?
IT WASN'T A MONKEY. IT *APPEARED* TO BE A MONKEY.
AND IT *WAS* A MONKEY, OF COURSE. IT WAS AND IT WASN'T. THAT'S WHAT WAS WRONG WITH IT.
ANGELA, I WANT TO KNOW WHAT REALLY HAPPENED TO MY PARENTS.
THEY'RE DEAD. THEY'RE GONE. I LOVED THEM, CHRIS, LOVED THEM AS FRIENDS, BUT THEY'RE GONE.
I QUIT MY JOB AT MERCY THIS EVENING. I'M NOT A NURSE ANYMORE.
I'M BECOMING. ANOTHER ANGELA. SOMETHING I DON'T WANT TO BE.
I GUESS IT'S TIME FOR SHOW AND TELL... BUT OH, CHRIS, IT'S GOING TO BREAK YOUR HEART.
YOU BETTER WAIT HERE. I'LL BE RIGHT BACK.
I COULD NOT SEE ORSON. TREES WERE STIRRING. THE WIND HAD RETURNED.
AAAGGGH!

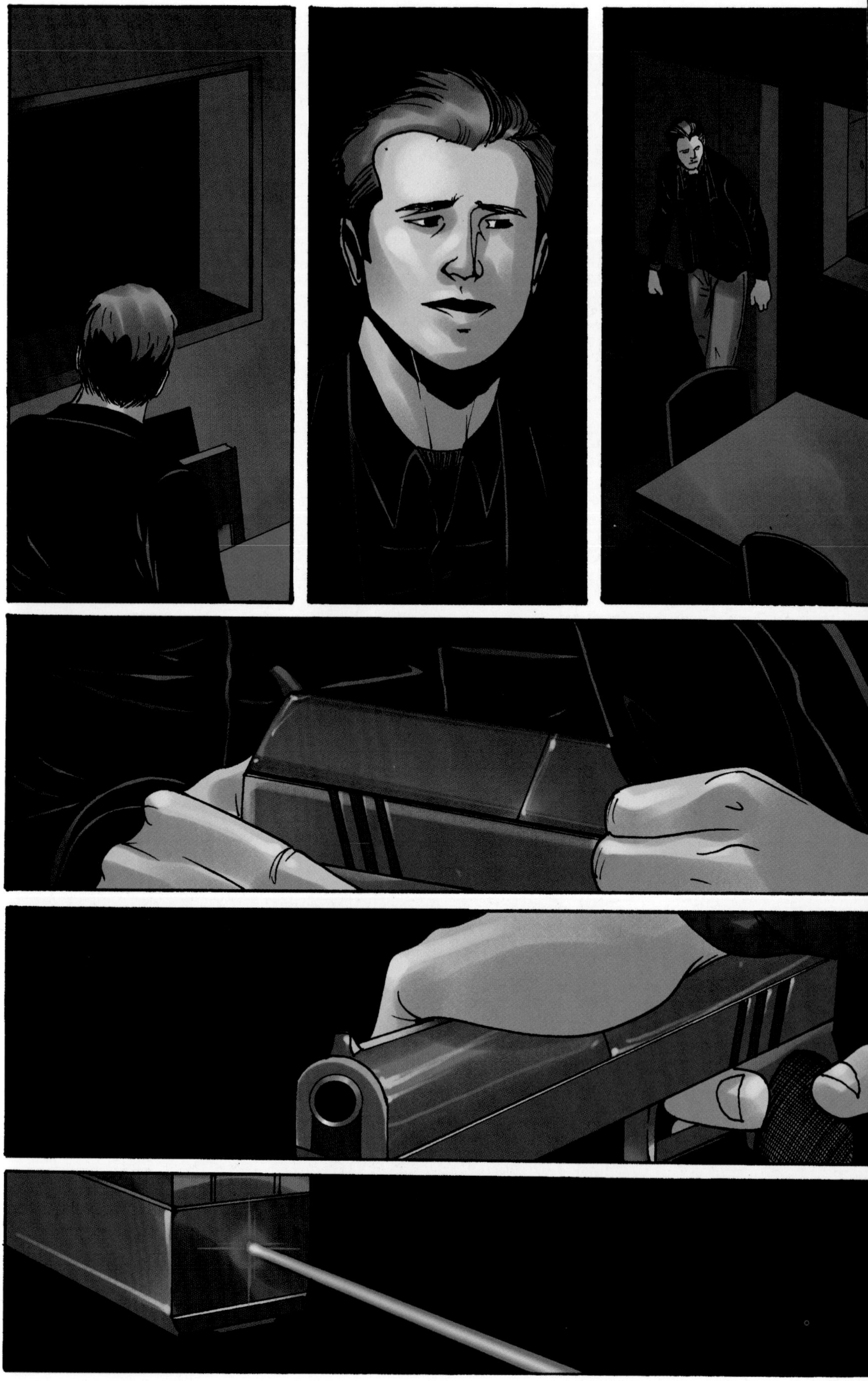

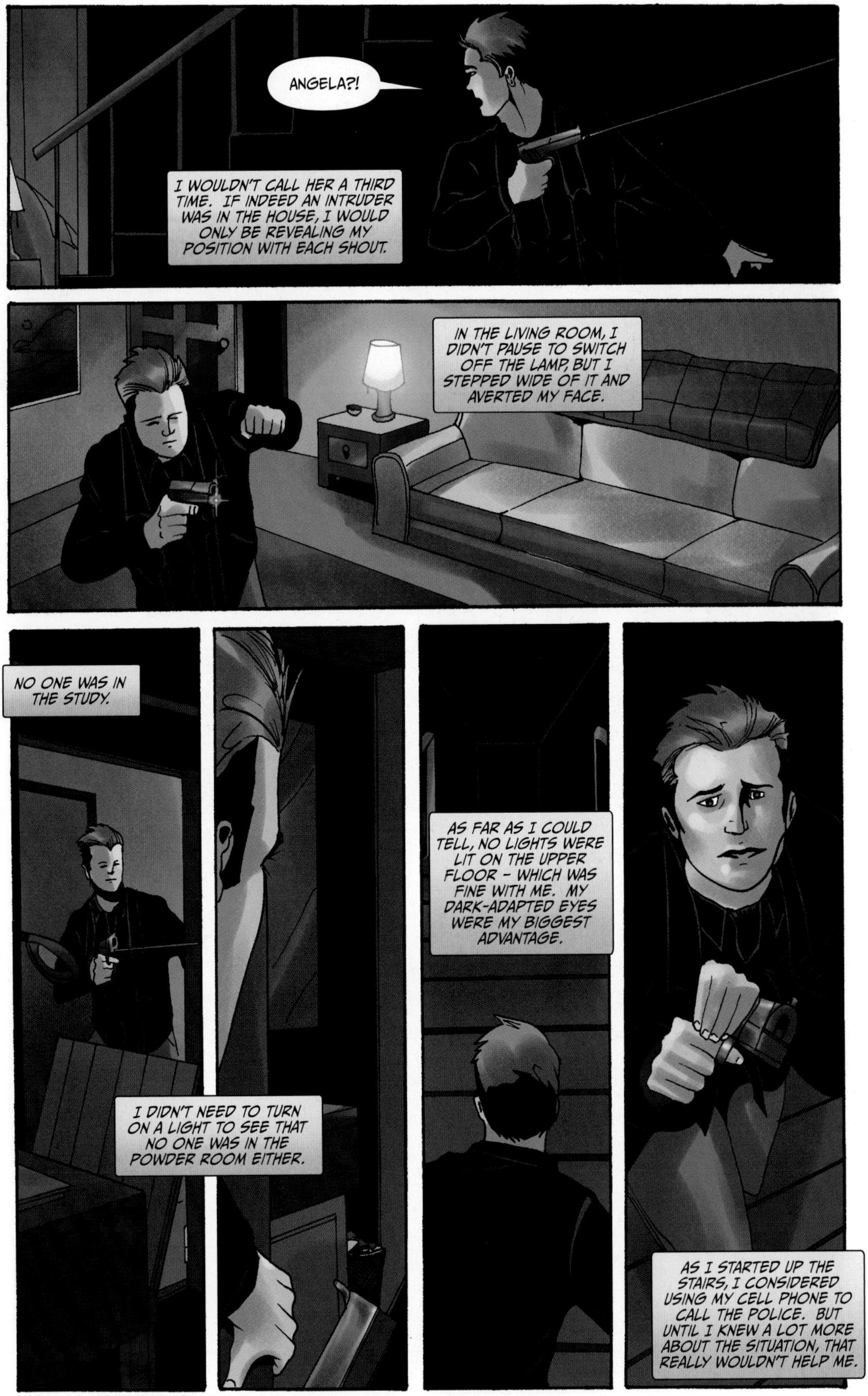
ANGELA?!
I WOULDN'T CALL HER A THIRD TIME. IF INDEED AN INTRUDER WAS IN THE HOUSE, I WOULD ONLY BE REVEALING MY POSITION WITH EACH SHOUT.
IN THE LIVING ROOM, I DIDN'T PAUSE TO SWITCH OFF THE LAMP, BUT I STEPPED WIDE OF IT AND AVERTED MY FACE.
NO ONE WAS IN THE STUDY.
I DIDN'T NEED TO TURN ON A LIGHT TO SEE THAT NO ONE WAS IN THE POWDER ROOM EITHER.
AS FAR AS I COULD TELL, NO LIGHTS WERE LIT ON THE UPPER FLOOR – WHICH WAS FINE WITH ME. MY DARK-ADAPTED EYES WERE MY BIGGEST ADVANTAGE.
AS I STARTED UP THE STAIRS, I CONSIDERED USING MY CELL PHONE TO CALL THE POLICE. BUT UNTIL I KNEW A LOT MORE ABOUT THE SITUATION, THAT REALLY WOULDN'T HELP ME.

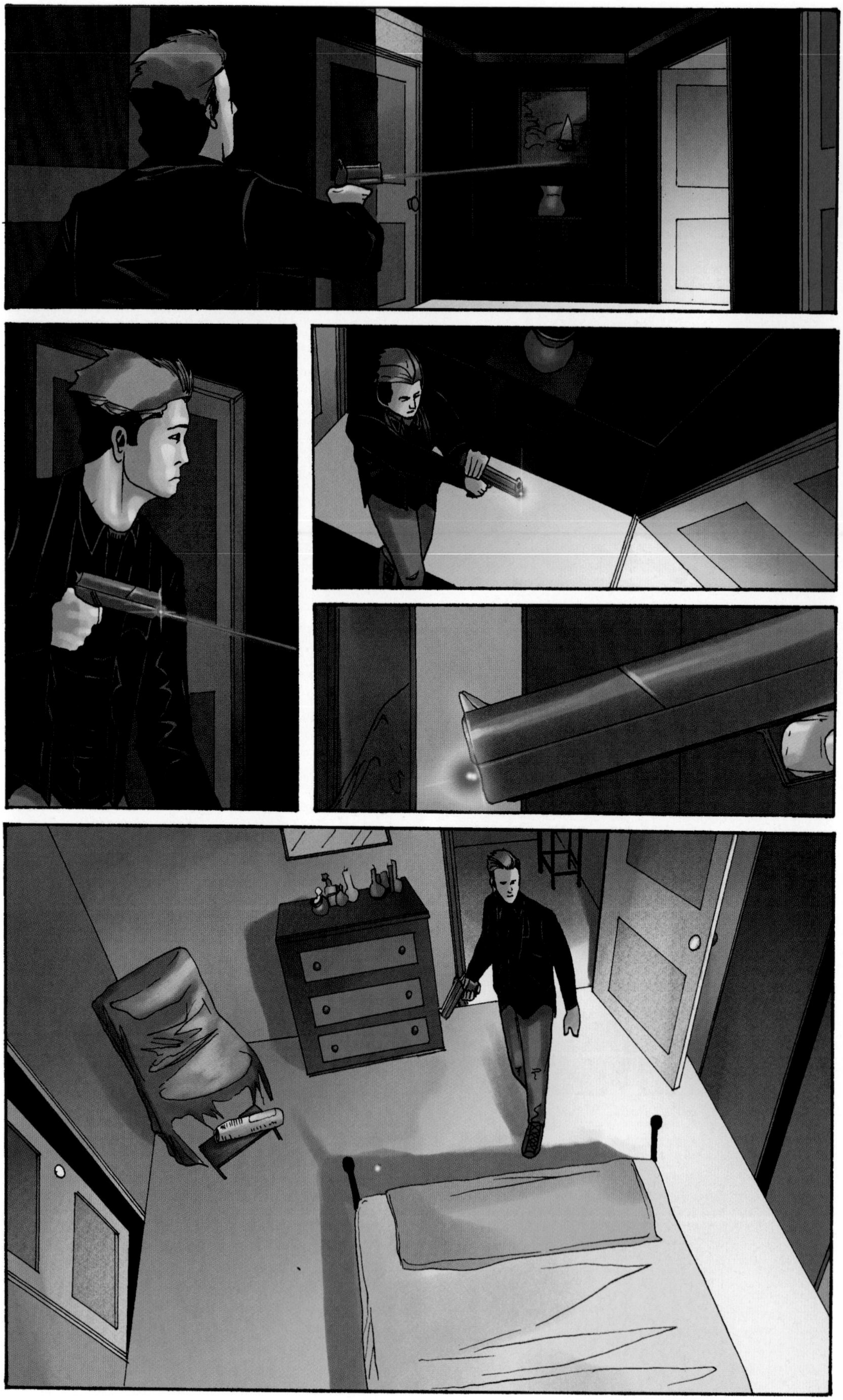

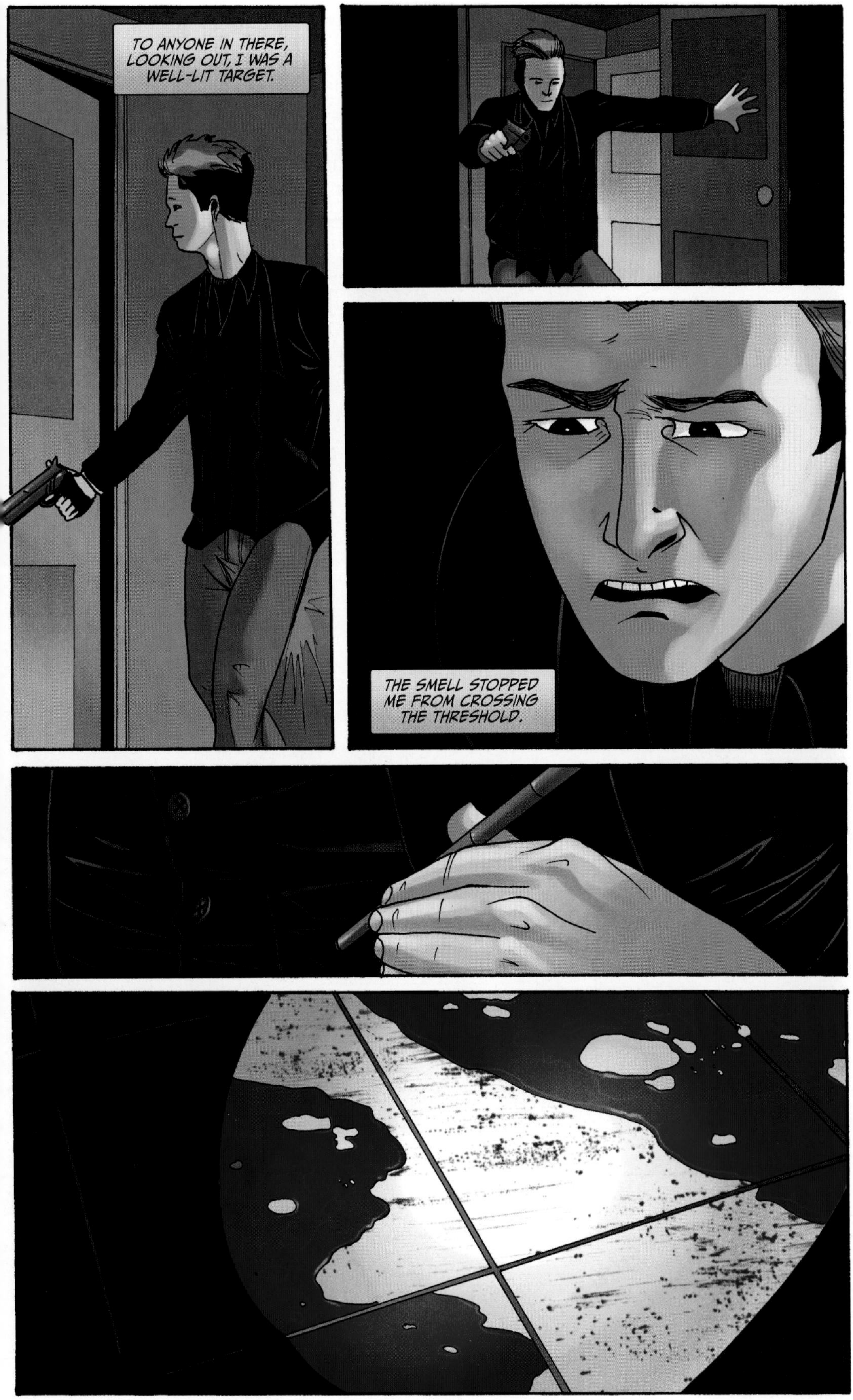
TO ANYONE IN THERE, LOOKING OUT, I WAS A WELL-LIT TARGET.
THE SMELL STOPPED ME FROM CROSSING THE THRESHOLD.

AT FIRST GLANCE, I THOUGHT HER THROAT APPEARED TO HAVE BEEN SLASHED REPEATEDLY WITH A HALF-SHARP KNIFE. I COULDN'T BEAR TO LOOK AT IT FOR TOO LONG.

THE SMELL WAS NOT MERELY BLOOD. DYING, SHE HAD FOULED HERSELF.

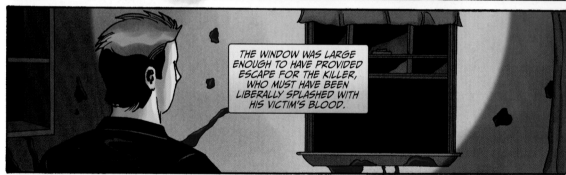

THE WINDOW WAS LARGE ENOUGH TO HAVE PROVIDED ESCAPE FOR THE KILLER, WHO MUST HAVE BEEN LIBERALLY SPLASHED WITH HIS VICTIM'S BLOOD.

ANGUISHED, SHAKING UNCONTROLLABLY, I TURNED AWAY FROM THE BATHROOM.

I HADN'T APPROACHED ANGELA WITH QUESTIONS. I HADN'T BROUGHT HER TO THIS HIDEOUS END.

SHE WAS A WOMAN WITH NOTHING TO LOSE, BEYOND THEIR CONTROL. THEY WOULD HAVE KILLED HER EVEN IF I HAD NOT RESPONDED TO HER CALL.

NEVERTHELESS, I WAS AWASH IN GUILT, ROBBED OF BREATH AND I STOOD GASPING.

BRRIINNG

WHEN THE PHONE RANG, I KEPT MY DISTANCE FROM IT. I HAD THE QUEER FEELING THAT THE CALLER WAS THE DEEP-BREATHER WHO HAD LEFT THE MESSAGE ON MY MACHINE.

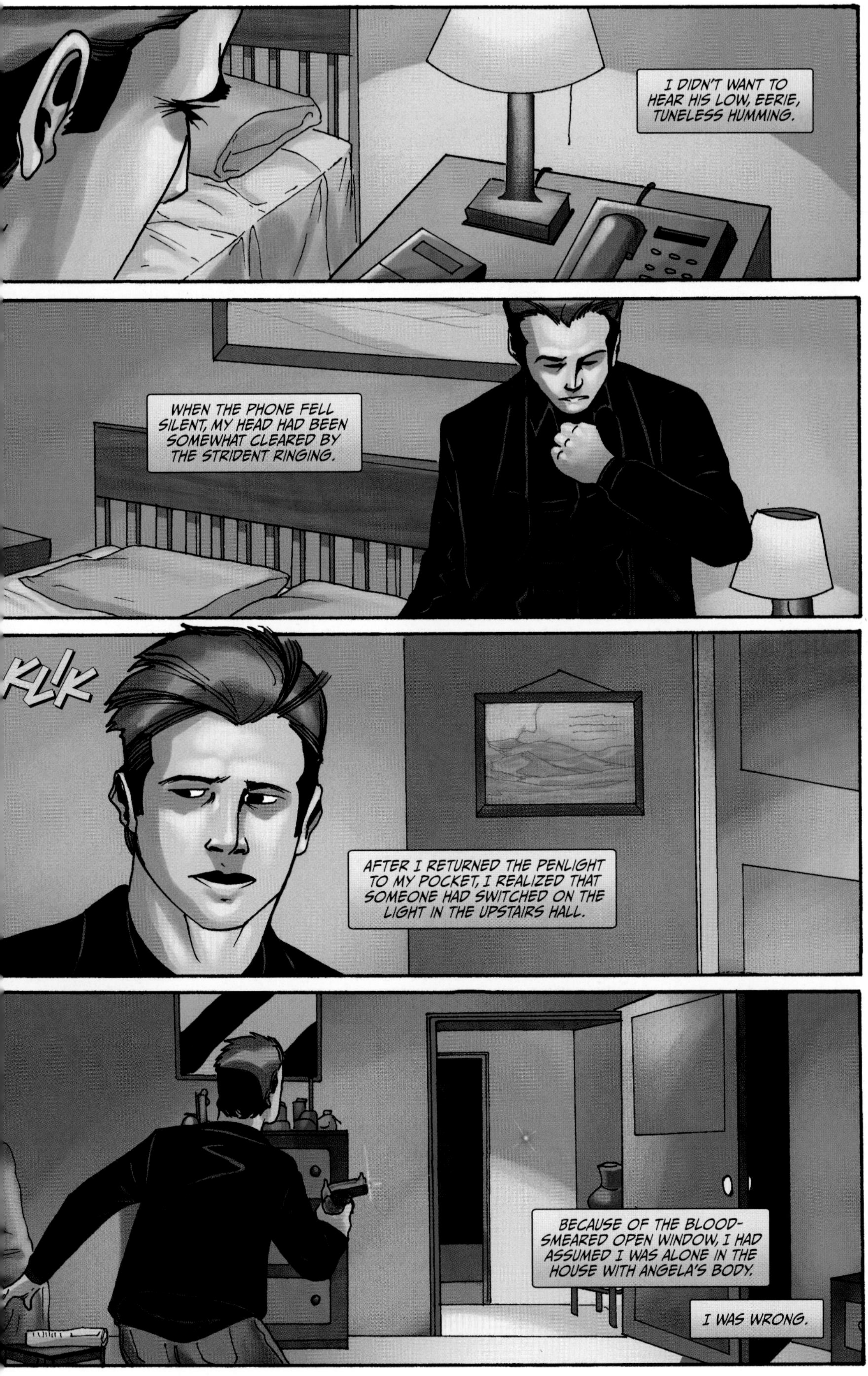
I DIDN'T WANT TO HEAR HIS LOW, EERIE, TUNELESS HUMMING.
WHEN THE PHONE FELL SILENT, MY HEAD HAD BEEN SOMEWHAT CLEARED BY THE STRIDENT RINGING.
KLIK
AFTER I RETURNED THE PENLIGHT TO MY POCKET, I REALIZED THAT SOMEONE HAD SWITCHED ON THE LIGHT IN THE UPSTAIRS HALL.
BECAUSE OF THE BLOOD-SMEARED OPEN WINDOW, I HAD ASSUMED I WAS ALONE IN THE HOUSE WITH ANGELA'S BODY.
I WAS WRONG.

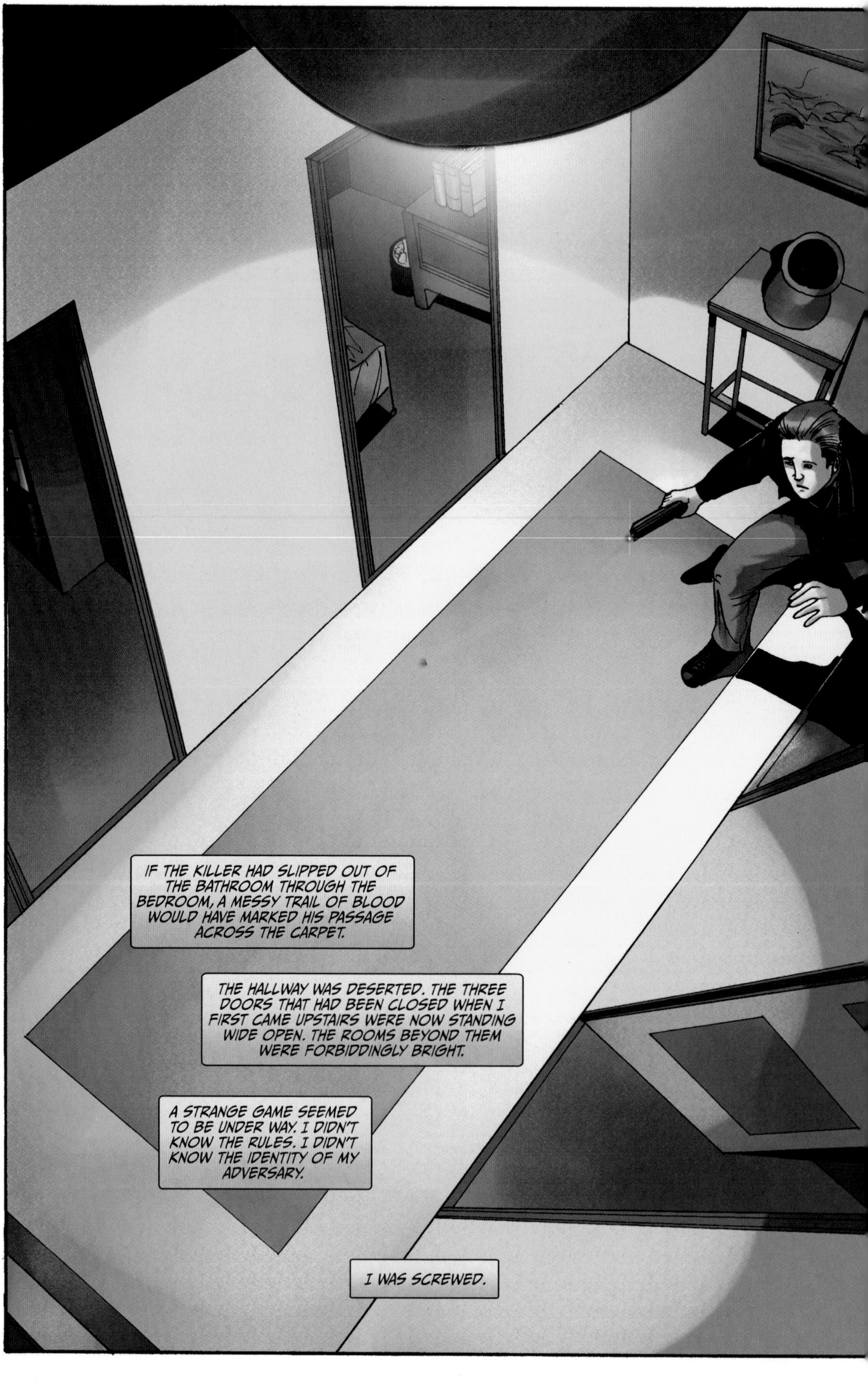
IF THE KILLER HAD SLIPPED OUT OF THE BATHROOM THROUGH THE BEDROOM, A MESSY TRAIL OF BLOOD WOULD HAVE MARKED HIS PASSAGE ACROSS THE CARPET.
THE HALLWAY WAS DESERTED. THE THREE DOORS THAT HAD BEEN CLOSED WHEN I FIRST CAME UPSTAIRS WERE NOW STANDING WIDE OPEN. THE ROOMS BEYOND THEM WERE FORBIDDINGLY BRIGHT.
A STRANGE GAME SEEMED TO BE UNDER WAY. I DIDN'T KNOW THE RULES. I DIDN'T KNOW THE IDENTITY OF MY ADVERSARY.
I WAS SCREWED.

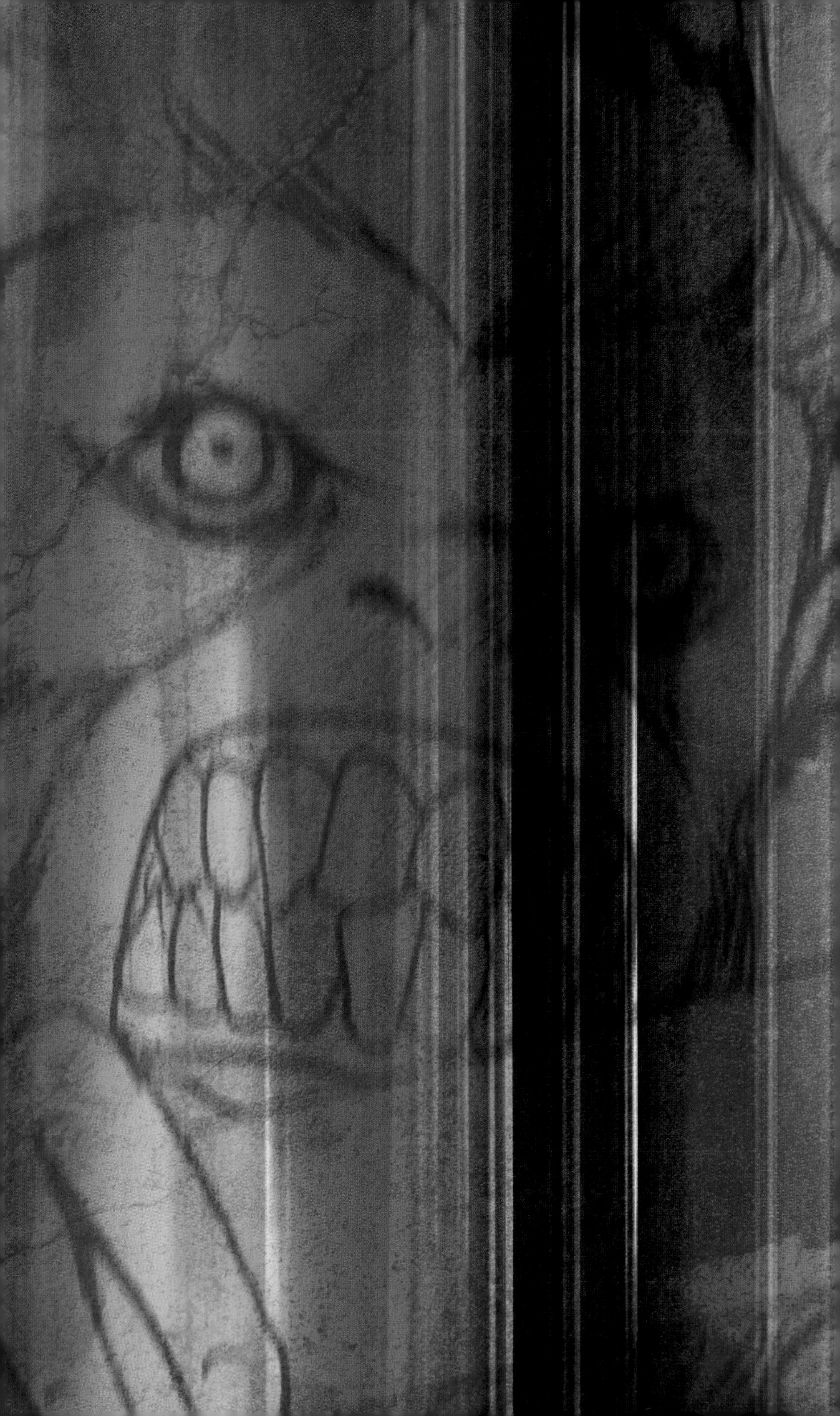

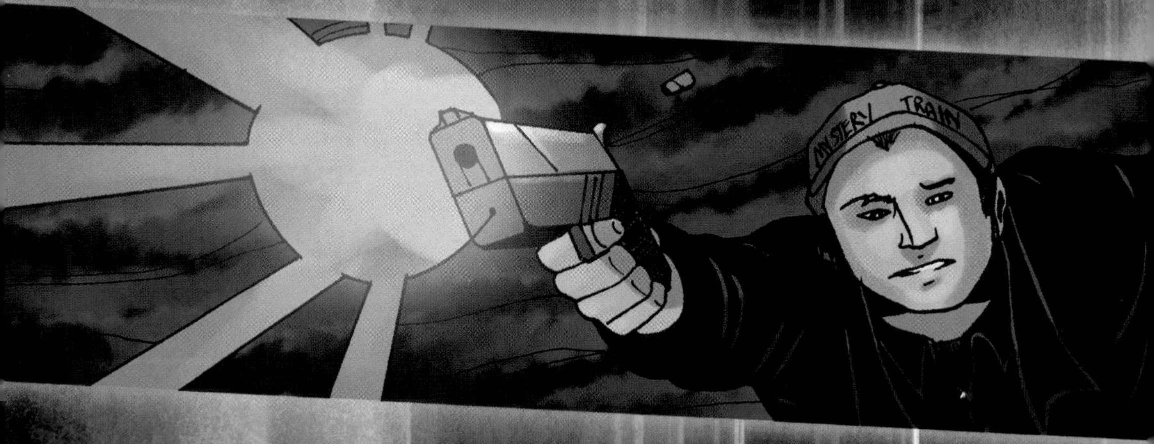
MYSTERY TRAIN

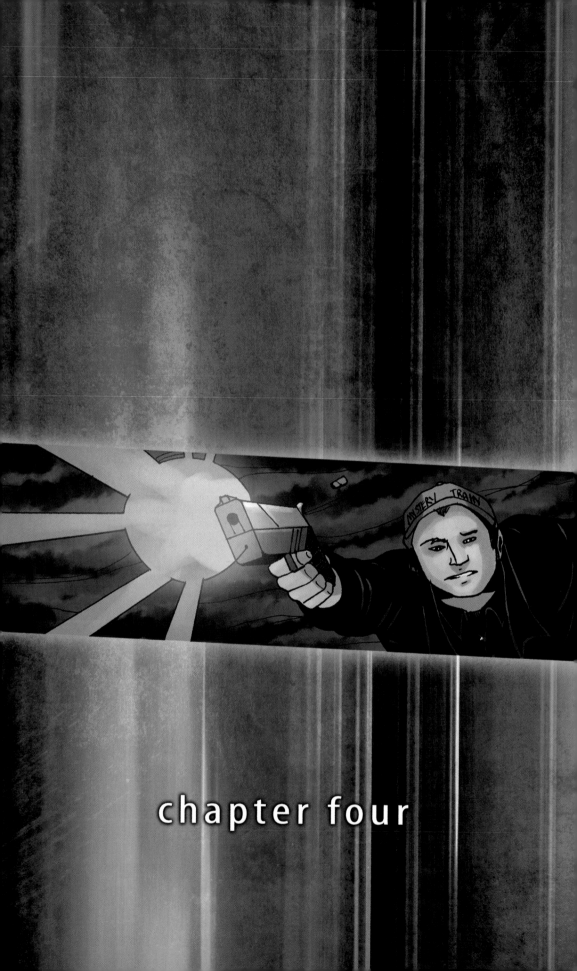

chapter four

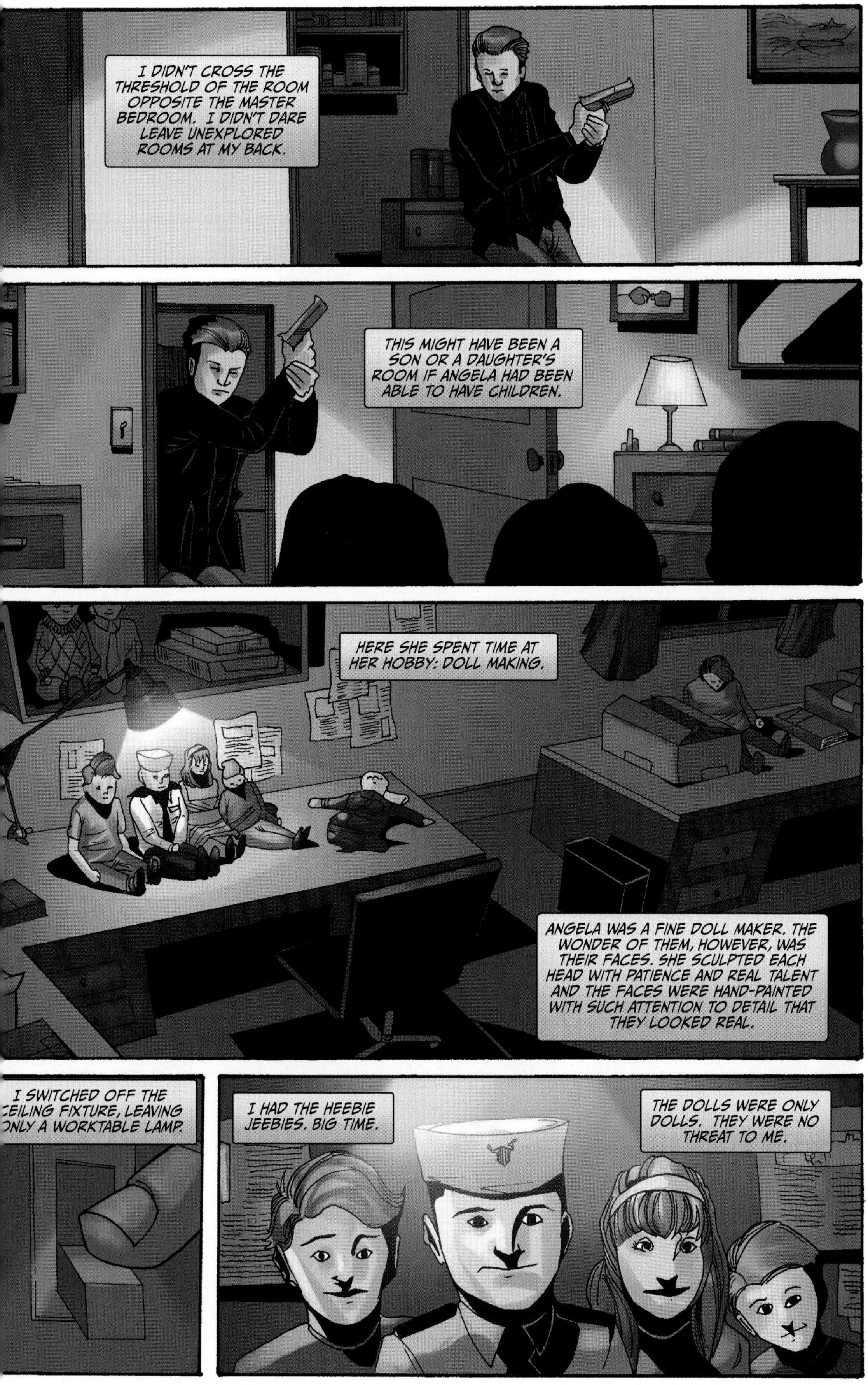
I DIDN'T CROSS THE THRESHOLD OF THE ROOM OPPOSITE THE MASTER BEDROOM. I DIDN'T DARE LEAVE UNEXPLORED ROOMS AT MY BACK.
THIS MIGHT HAVE BEEN A SON OR A DAUGHTER'S ROOM IF ANGELA HAD BEEN ABLE TO HAVE CHILDREN.
HERE SHE SPENT TIME AT HER HOBBY: DOLL MAKING.
ANGELA WAS A FINE DOLL MAKER. THE WONDER OF THEM, HOWEVER, WAS THEIR FACES. SHE SCULPTED EACH HEAD WITH PATIENCE AND REAL TALENT AND THE FACES WERE HAND-PAINTED WITH SUCH ATTENTION TO DETAIL THAT THEY LOOKED REAL.
I SWITCHED OFF THE CEILING FIXTURE, LEAVING ONLY A WORKTABLE LAMP.
I HAD THE HEEBIE JEEBIES. BIG TIME.
THE DOLLS WERE ONLY DOLLS. THEY WERE NO THREAT TO ME.

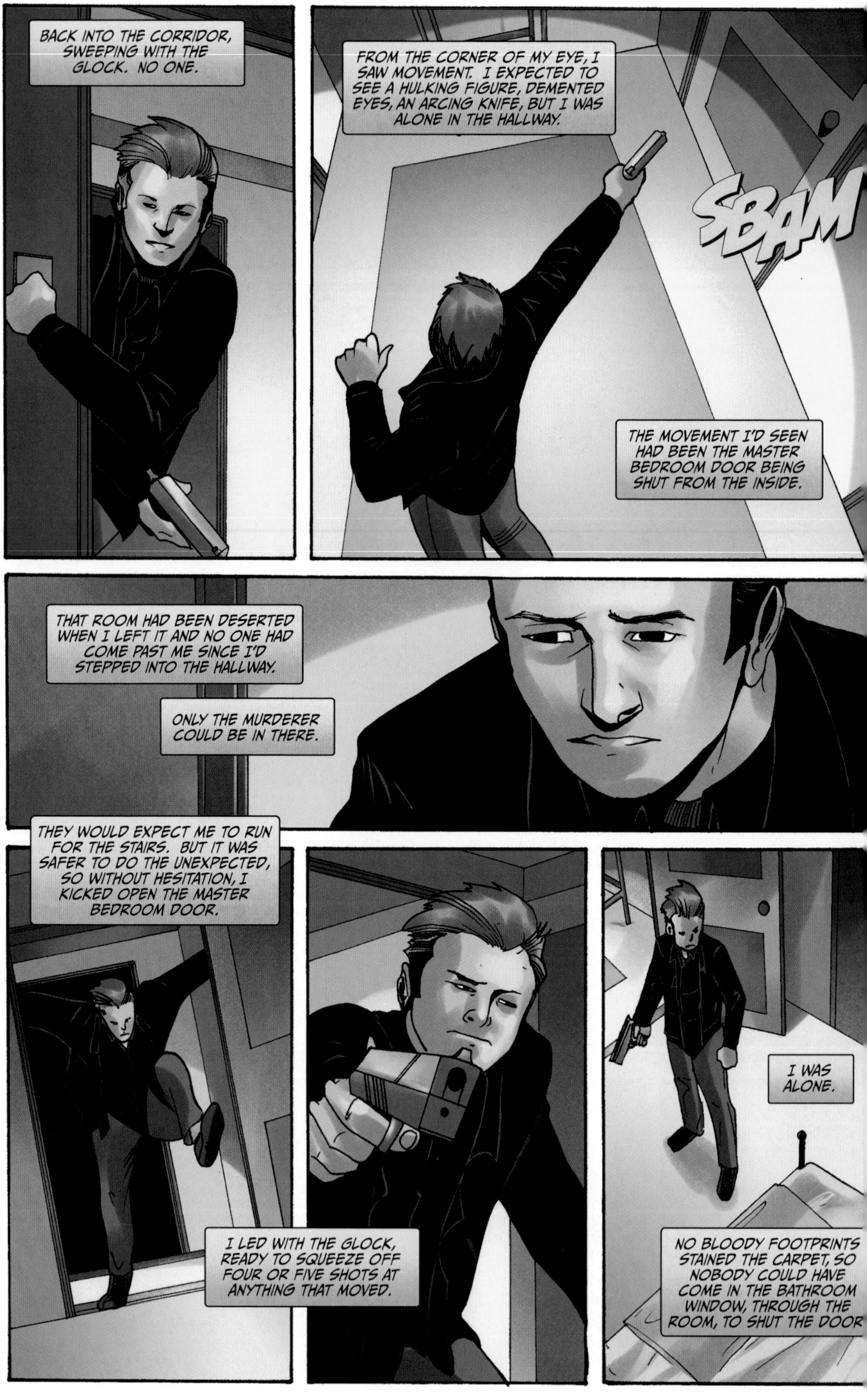
BACK INTO THE CORRIDOR, SWEEPING WITH THE GLOCK. NO ONE.
FROM THE CORNER OF MY EYE, I SAW MOVEMENT. I EXPECTED TO SEE A HULKING FIGURE, DEMENTED EYES, AN ARCING KNIFE, BUT I WAS ALONE IN THE HALLWAY.
SBAM
THE MOVEMENT I'D SEEN HAD BEEN THE MASTER BEDROOM DOOR BEING SHUT FROM THE INSIDE.
THAT ROOM HAD BEEN DESERTED WHEN I LEFT IT AND NO ONE HAD COME PAST ME SINCE I'D STEPPED INTO THE HALLWAY.
ONLY THE MURDERER COULD BE IN THERE.
THEY WOULD EXPECT ME TO RUN FOR THE STAIRS. BUT IT WAS SAFER TO DO THE UNEXPECTED, SO WITHOUT HESITATION, I KICKED OPEN THE MASTER BEDROOM DOOR.
I LED WITH THE GLOCK, READY TO SQUEEZE OFF FOUR OR FIVE SHOTS AT ANYTHING THAT MOVED.
I WAS ALONE.
NO BLOODY FOOTPRINTS STAINED THE CARPET, SO NOBODY COULD HAVE COME IN THE BATHROOM WINDOW, THROUGH THE ROOM, TO SHUT THE DOOR

I CHECKED THE BATHROOM ANYWAY. I LEFT THE PENLIGHT IN MY POCKET. I DIDN'T WANT TO SEE ALL THE VIVID DETAILS AGAIN.

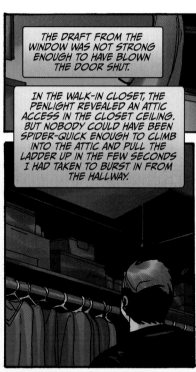

THE DRAFT FROM THE WINDOW WAS NOT STRONG ENOUGH TO HAVE BLOWN THE DOOR SHUT.

IN THE WALK-IN CLOSET, THE PENLIGHT REVEALED AN ATTIC ACCESS IN THE CLOSET CEILING. BUT NOBODY COULD HAVE BEEN SPIDER-QUICK ENOUGH TO CLIMB INTO THE ATTIC AND PULL THE LADDER UP IN THE FEW SECONDS I HAD TAKEN TO BURST IN FROM THE HALLWAY.

MY BACK TO THE BATHROOM, SUDDENLY I FELT AS THOUGH SPIDERS WERE TWITCHING THROUGH THE HOLLOWS OF MY SPINE. SOMETIMES THERE IS NO DARKER PLACE THAN OUR OWN THOUGHTS: THE MOONLESS MIDNIGHT OF THE MIND.

I STOPPED CHASING GHOSTS AND RELUCTANTLY RETURNED TO THE UPSTAIRS HALLWAY. A DOLL WAS WAITING FOR ME.

THIS WAS NOT GOOD. FULLY, TOTALLY, RADICALLY NOT GOOD. IN THE MOVIES, THIS WAS FOLLOWED BY THE ENTRANCE OF A REALLY BIG GUY WITH A BAD ATTITUDE CARRYING A CHAINSAW, A COMPRESSED AIR NAIL GUN, OR IN AN UNPLUGGED MOOD, AN AXE BIG ENOUGH TO DECAPITATE A T-REX.

FOR A MOMENT, I THOUGHT THE DOLL HELD A CAP LIKE MINE. THEN I SAW THAT IT WAS MY OWN, WHICH I'D LEFT DOWNSTAIRS ON THE KITCHEN TABLE.

THE DOLL HAD MY FACE. IT HAD BEEN MODELED AFTER ME.

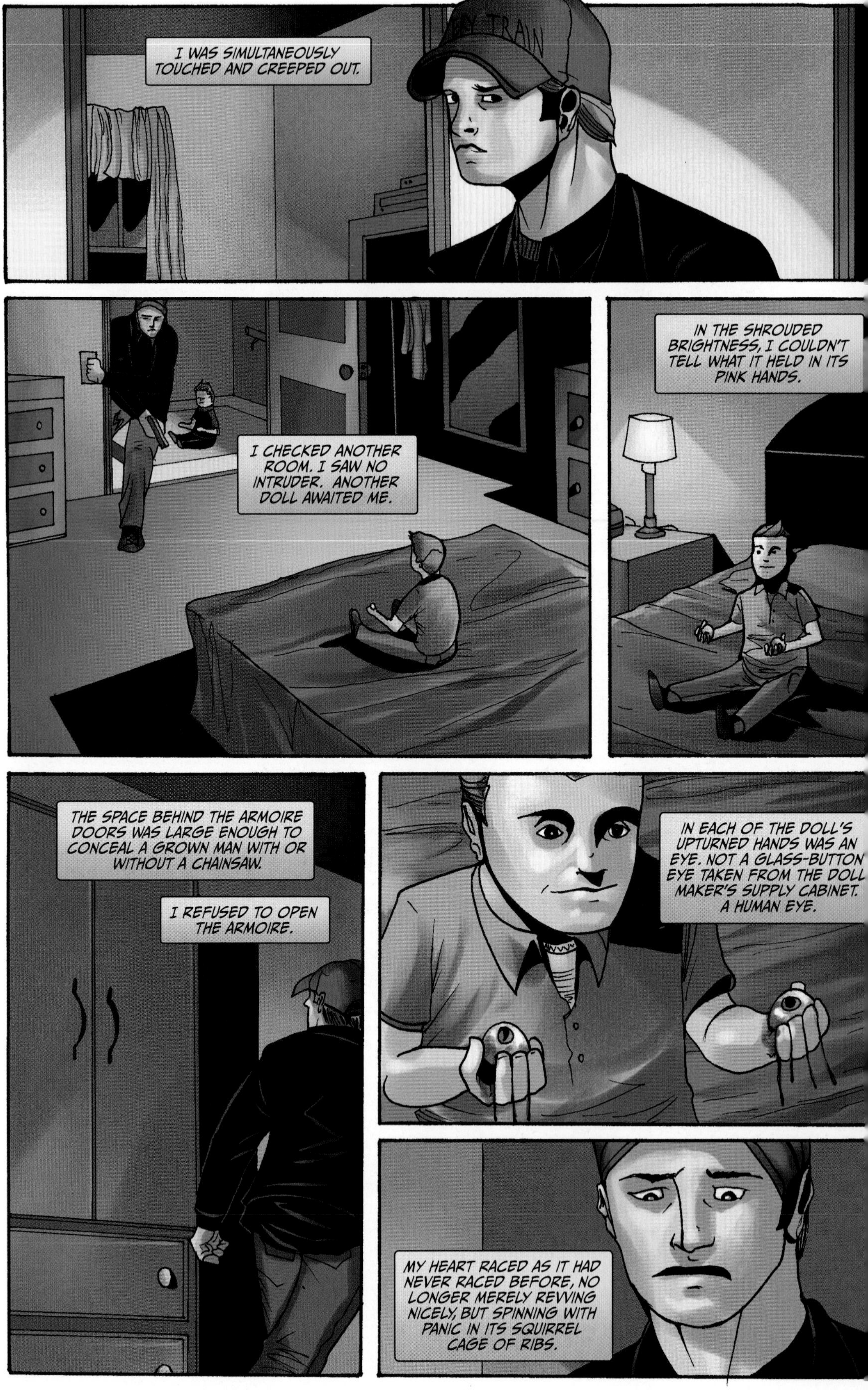

I WAS SIMULTANEOUSLY TOUCHED AND CREEPED OUT.
I CHECKED ANOTHER ROOM. I SAW NO INTRUDER. ANOTHER DOLL AWAITED ME.
IN THE SHROUDED BRIGHTNESS, I COULDN'T TELL WHAT IT HELD IN ITS PINK HANDS.
THE SPACE BEHIND THE ARMOIRE DOORS WAS LARGE ENOUGH TO CONCEAL A GROWN MAN WITH OR WITHOUT A CHAINSAW.
I REFUSED TO OPEN THE ARMOIRE.
IN EACH OF THE DOLL'S UPTURNED HANDS WAS AN EYE. NOT A GLASS-BUTTON EYE TAKEN FROM THE DOLL MAKER'S SUPPLY CABINET. A HUMAN EYE.
MY HEART RACED AS IT HAD NEVER RACED BEFORE, NO LONGER MERELY REVVING NICELY, BUT SPINNING WITH PANIC IN ITS SQUIRREL CAGE OF RIBS.

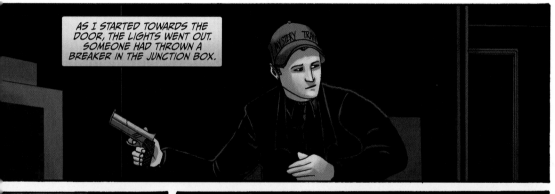

AS I STARTED TOWARDS THE DOOR, THE LIGHTS WENT OUT. SOMEONE HAD THROWN A BREAKER IN THE JUNCTION BOX.

THIS DARKNESS WAS SO BOTTOMLESS THAT IT DIDN'T WELCOME EVEN *ME*. ALL WAS BLACKNESS ON BLACKNESS.

BLINDLY, I RUSHED TOWARD THE DOOR.

I ANGLED TO ONE SIDE OF IT WHEN I WAS OVERCOME BY THE CONVICTION THAT SOMEONE WAS IN THE HALL AND THAT I WOULD ENCOUNTER THE THRUST OF A SHARP BLADE AT THE THRESHOLD.

KREEEE

EEEEEEEKK

OVER THE THUNDERING STAMPEDE OF MY HEART, I HEARD THE CREAK OF THE ARMOIRE HINGES – THE DOORS WERE OPENING.

JESUS.

IT WAS A PRAYER, NOT A CURSE. OR MAYBE BOTH.

I COULDN'T RISK PUMPING OUT ROUNDS INDISCRIMINATELY. THERE WAS A CHANCE THAT I WOULD ONLY WOUND HIM AND A SMALLER BUT VERY REAL CHANCE I WOULD MERELY PISS HIM OFF.

I PUT THE DOOR BETWEEN MYSELF AND WHOEVER HAD COME OUT OF THE ARMOIRE.

INSTEAD OF WAITING TO SEE WHO OR WHAT WOULD BURST OUT OF THE GUEST ROOM, I RAN TO THE STAIRS. EVIDENTLY, THE LIGHTS ON THE LOWER FLOOR WERE ON THEIR OWN CIRCUIT. THEY WERE STILL ON.

SPASH

I WAS ALMOST TO THE LANDING WHEN MY HEAD IN MINIATURE SAILED PAST ME AND SHATTERED AGAINST THE WALL IN FRONT OF ME. CHINA SHRAPNEL TATTOOED MY FACE AND CHEST.

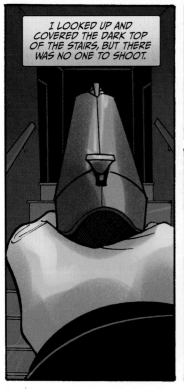

I LOOKED UP AND COVERED THE DARK TOP OF THE STAIRS, BUT THERE WAS NO ONE TO SHOOT.

THE DOWNSTAIRS LIGHTS WENT OUT.

THROUGH THE FORBIDDING BLACKNESS CAME THE SMELL OF SOMETHING BURNING.

A GREAT PULSING MASS OF FOUL-SMELLING SMOKE POURED INTO THE STAIRWELL FROM BELOW.

I SAW A THROBBING LIGHT ABOVE. FIRE.

TWO FIRES HAD BE SET, ONE ABOVE AN ONE BELOW.

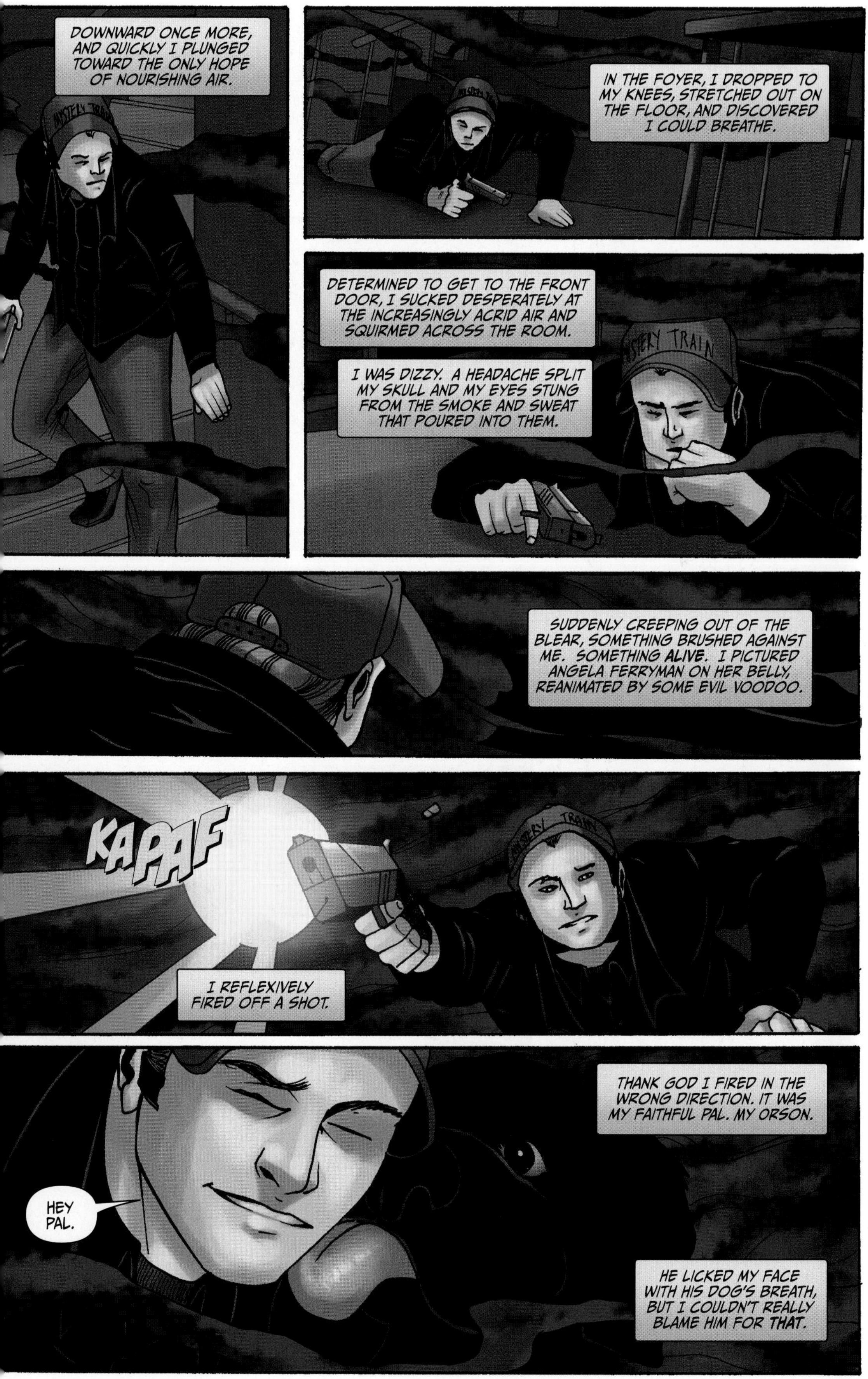
DOWNWARD ONCE MORE, AND QUICKLY I PLUNGED TOWARD THE ONLY HOPE OF NOURISHING AIR.
MYSTERY TRAIN
IN THE FOYER, I DROPPED TO MY KNEES, STRETCHED OUT ON THE FLOOR, AND DISCOVERED I COULD BREATHE.
DETERMINED TO GET TO THE FRONT DOOR, I SUCKED DESPERATELY AT THE INCREASINGLY ACRID AIR AND SQUIRMED ACROSS THE ROOM.
I WAS DIZZY. A HEADACHE SPLIT MY SKULL AND MY EYES STUNG FROM THE SMOKE AND SWEAT THAT POURED INTO THEM.
SUDDENLY CREEPING OUT OF THE BLEAR, SOMETHING BRUSHED AGAINST ME. SOMETHING **ALIVE**. I PICTURED ANGELA FERRYMAN ON HER BELLY, REANIMATED BY SOME EVIL VOODOO.
KAPAF
I REFLEXIVELY FIRED OFF A SHOT.
THANK GOD I FIRED IN THE WRONG DIRECTION. IT WAS MY FAITHFUL PAL. MY ORSON.
HEY PAL.
HE LICKED MY FACE WITH HIS DOG'S BREATH, BUT I COULDN'T REALLY BLAME HIM FOR **THAT**.

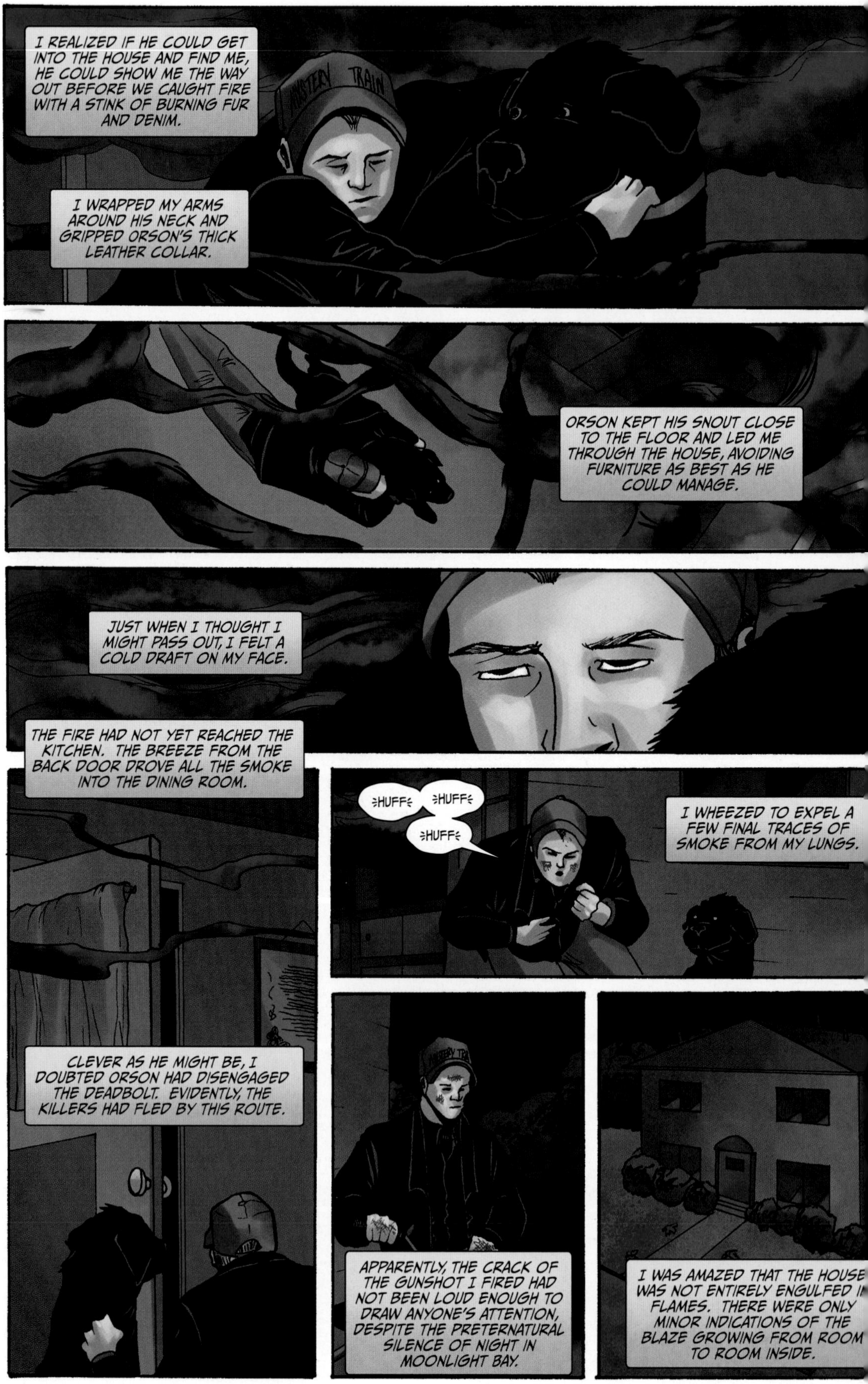
I REALIZED IF HE COULD GET INTO THE HOUSE AND FIND ME, HE COULD SHOW ME THE WAY OUT BEFORE WE CAUGHT FIRE WITH A STINK OF BURNING FUR AND DENIM.
MYSTERY TRAIN
I WRAPPED MY ARMS AROUND HIS NECK AND GRIPPED ORSON'S THICK LEATHER COLLAR.
ORSON KEPT HIS SNOUT CLOSE TO THE FLOOR AND LED ME THROUGH THE HOUSE, AVOIDING FURNITURE AS BEST AS HE COULD MANAGE.
JUST WHEN I THOUGHT I MIGHT PASS OUT, I FELT A COLD DRAFT ON MY FACE.
THE FIRE HAD NOT YET REACHED THE KITCHEN. THE BREEZE FROM THE BACK DOOR DROVE ALL THE SMOKE INTO THE DINING ROOM.
CLEVER AS HE MIGHT BE, I DOUBTED ORSON HAD DISENGAGED THE DEADBOLT. EVIDENTLY, THE KILLERS HAD FLED BY THIS ROUTE.
HUFF
HUFF
HUFF
I WHEEZED TO EXPEL A FEW FINAL TRACES OF SMOKE FROM MY LUNGS.
APPARENTLY, THE CRACK OF THE GUNSHOT I FIRED HAD NOT BEEN LOUD ENOUGH TO DRAW ANYONE'S ATTENTION, DESPITE THE PRETERNATURAL SILENCE OF NIGHT IN MOONLIGHT BAY.
I WAS AMAZED THAT THE HOUSE WAS NOT ENTIRELY ENGULFED IN FLAMES. THERE WERE ONLY MINOR INDICATIONS OF THE BLAZE GROWING FROM ROOM TO ROOM INSIDE.

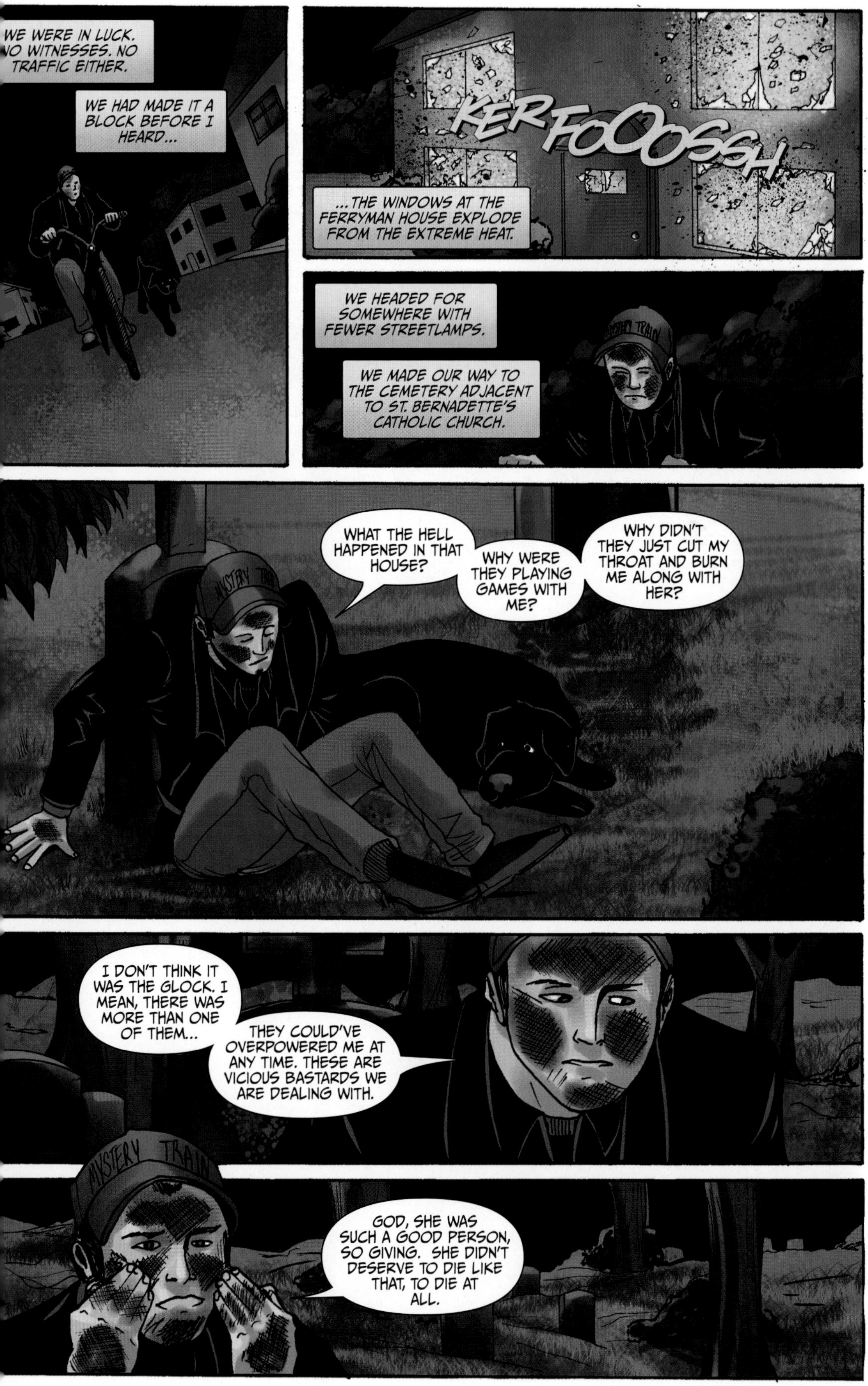
WE WERE IN LUCK. NO WITNESSES. NO TRAFFIC EITHER.
WE HAD MADE IT A BLOCK BEFORE I HEARD...
KERFOOOOSSH
...THE WINDOWS AT THE FERRYMAN HOUSE EXPLODE FROM THE EXTREME HEAT.
WE HEADED FOR SOMEWHERE WITH FEWER STREETLAMPS.
WE MADE OUR WAY TO THE CEMETERY ADJACENT TO ST. BERNADETTE'S CATHOLIC CHURCH.
MYSTERY TRAIN
WHAT THE HELL HAPPENED IN THAT HOUSE?
WHY WERE THEY PLAYING GAMES WITH ME?
WHY DIDN'T THEY JUST CUT MY THROAT AND BURN ME ALONG WITH HER?
I DON'T THINK IT WAS THE GLOCK. I MEAN, THERE WAS MORE THAN ONE OF THEM...
THEY COULD'VE OVERPOWERED ME AT ANY TIME. THESE ARE VICIOUS BASTARDS WE ARE DEALING WITH.
MYSTERY TRAIN
GOD, SHE WAS SUCH A GOOD PERSON, SO GIVING. SHE DIDN'T DESERVE TO DIE LIKE THAT, TO DIE AT ALL.

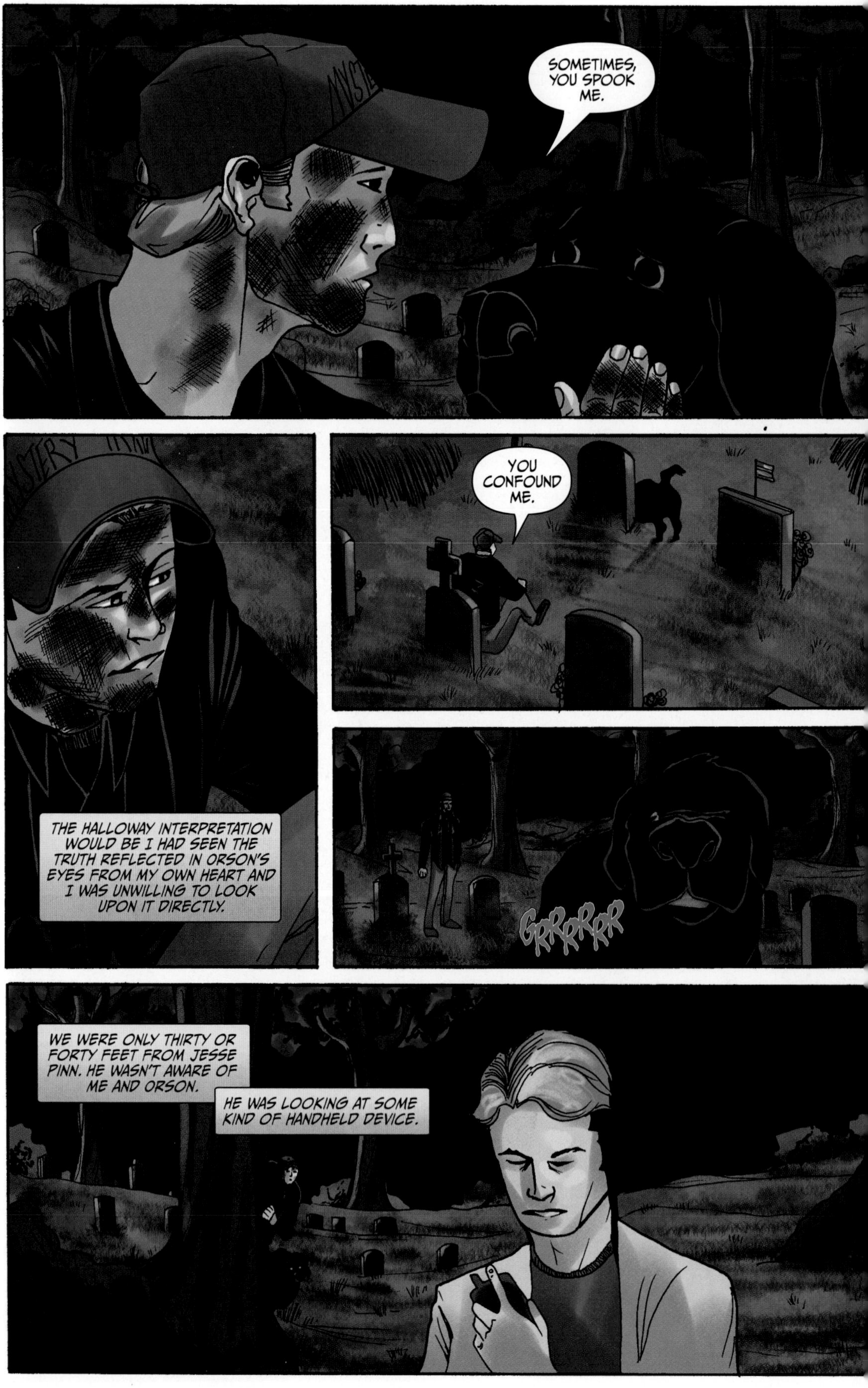
SOMETIMES, YOU SPOOK ME.
YOU CONFOUND ME.
THE HALLOWAY INTERPRETATION WOULD BE I HAD SEEN THE TRUTH REFLECTED IN ORSON'S EYES FROM MY OWN HEART AND I WAS UNWILLING TO LOOK UPON IT DIRECTLY.
GRRRRRR
WE WERE ONLY THIRTY OR FORTY FEET FROM JESSE PINN. HE WASN'T AWARE OF ME AND ORSON.
HE WAS LOOKING AT SOME KIND OF HANDHELD DEVICE.

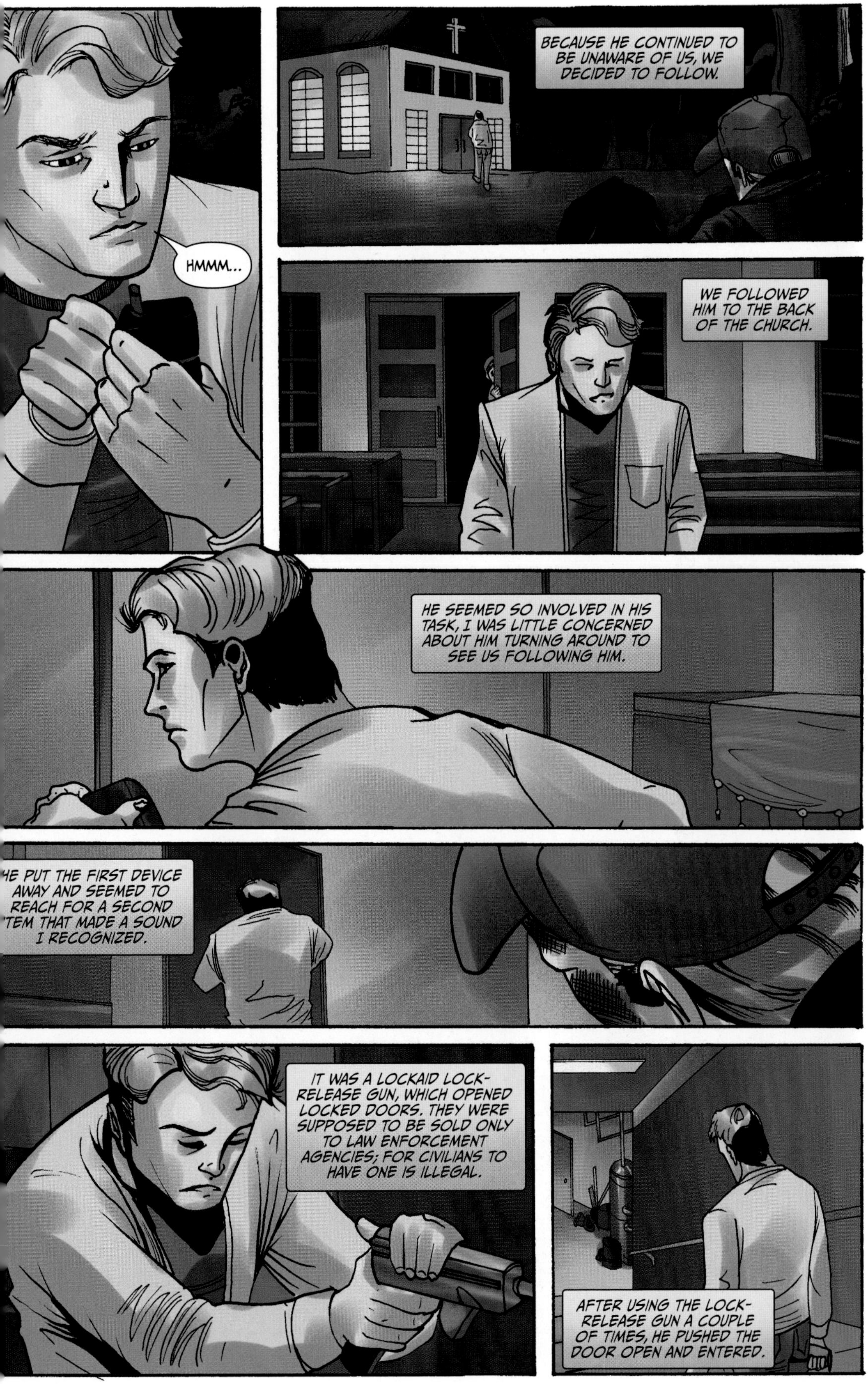
HMMM...
BECAUSE HE CONTINUED TO BE UNAWARE OF US, WE DECIDED TO FOLLOW.
WE FOLLOWED HIM TO THE BACK OF THE CHURCH.
HE SEEMED SO INVOLVED IN HIS TASK, I WAS LITTLE CONCERNED ABOUT HIM TURNING AROUND TO SEE US FOLLOWING HIM.
HE PUT THE FIRST DEVICE AWAY AND SEEMED TO REACH FOR A SECOND ITEM THAT MADE A SOUND I RECOGNIZED.
IT WAS A LOCKAID LOCK-RELEASE GUN, WHICH OPENED LOCKED DOORS. THEY WERE SUPPOSED TO BE SOLD ONLY TO LAW ENFORCEMENT AGENCIES; FOR CIVILIANS TO HAVE ONE IS ILLEGAL.
AFTER USING THE LOCK-RELEASE GUN A COUPLE OF TIMES, HE PUSHED THE DOOR OPEN AND ENTERED.

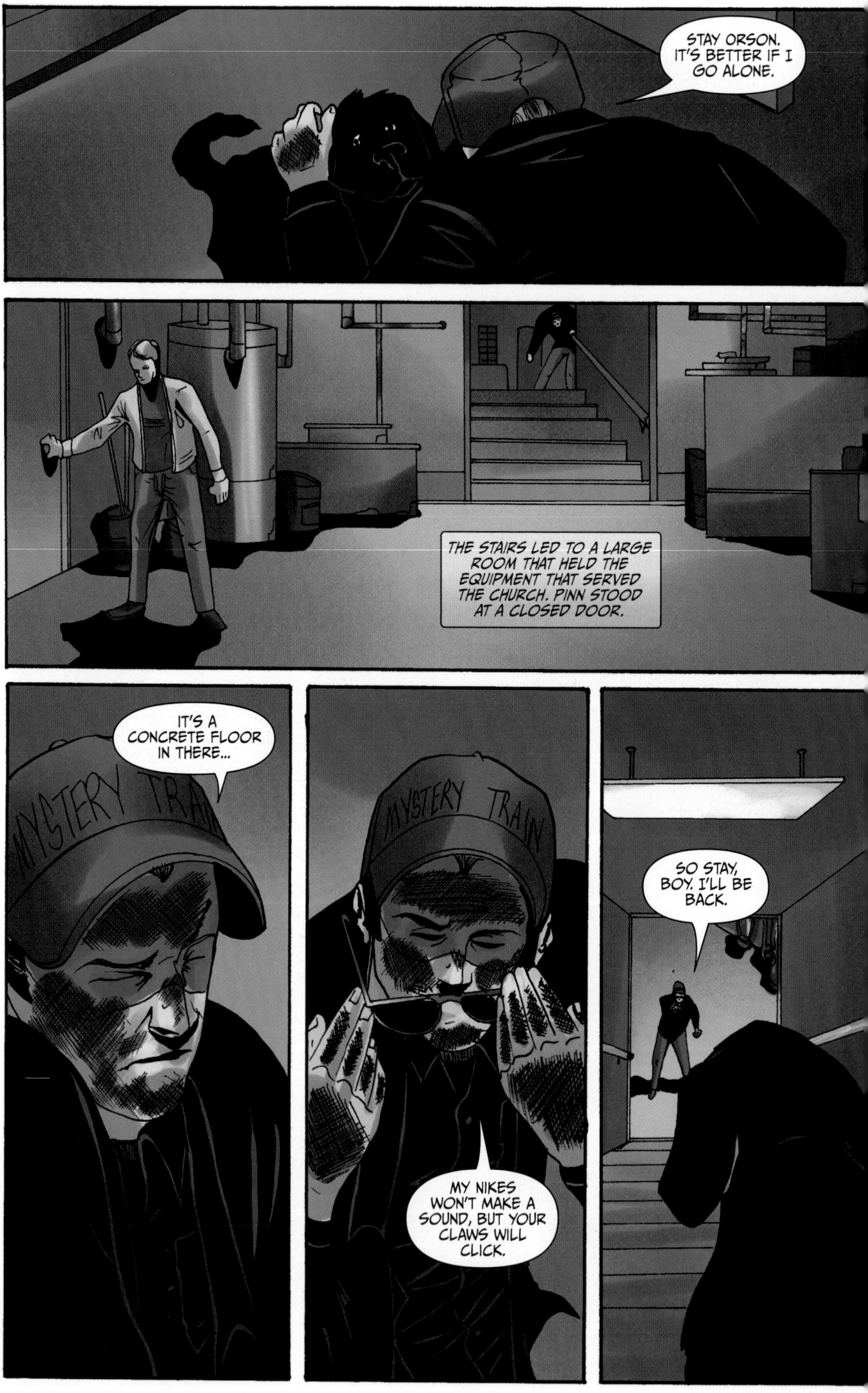
STAY ORSON. IT'S BETTER IF I GO ALONE.
THE STAIRS LED TO A LARGE ROOM THAT HELD THE EQUIPMENT THAT SERVED THE CHURCH. PINN STOOD AT A CLOSED DOOR.
IT'S A CONCRETE FLOOR IN THERE...
MYSTERY TRAIN
MYSTERY TRAIN
MY NIKES WON'T MAKE A SOUND, BUT YOUR CLAWS WILL CLICK.
SO STAY, BOY. I'LL BE BACK.

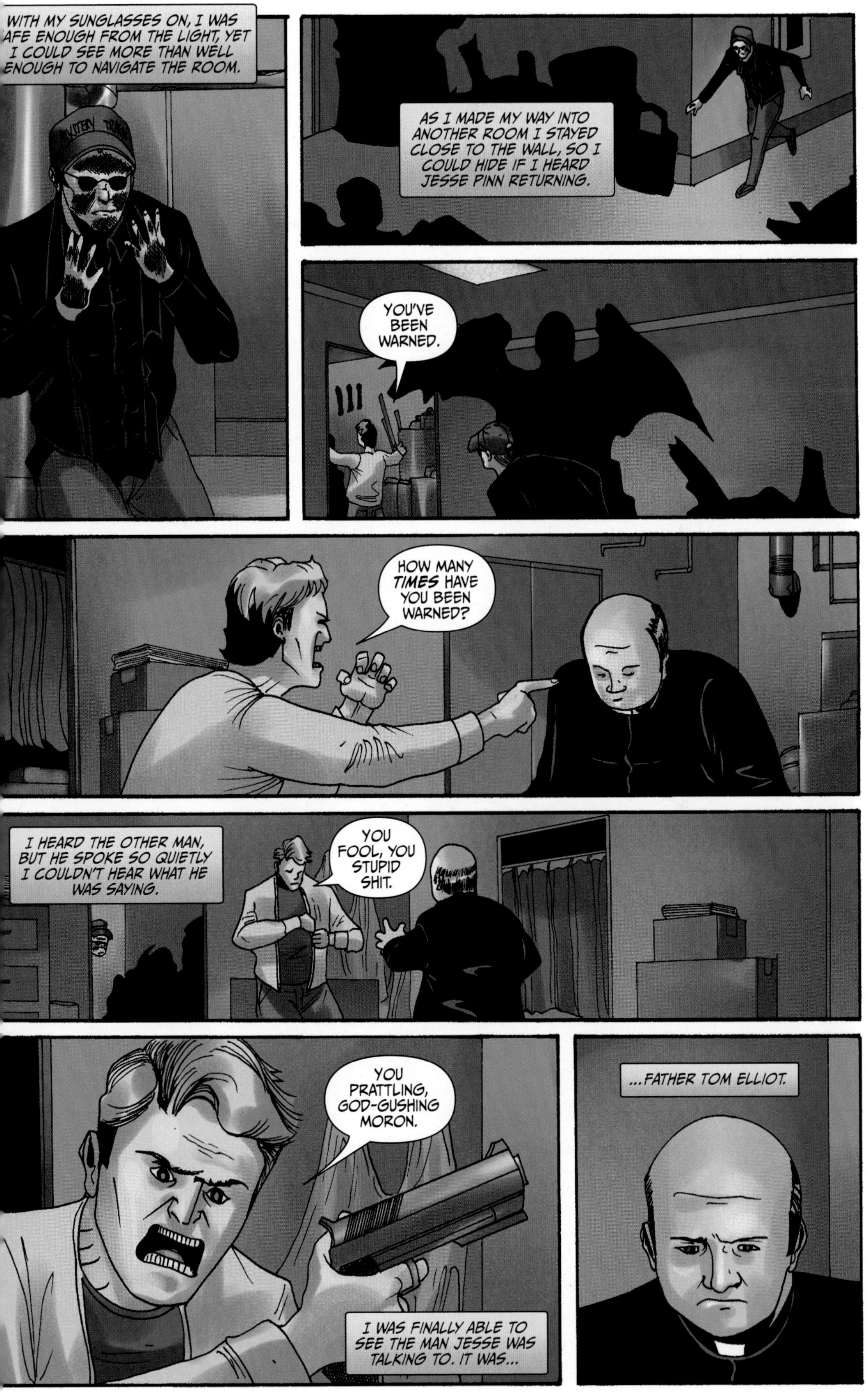
WITH MY SUNGLASSES ON, I WAS AFE ENOUGH FROM THE LIGHT, YET I COULD SEE MORE THAN WELL ENOUGH TO NAVIGATE THE ROOM.
AS I MADE MY WAY INTO ANOTHER ROOM I STAYED CLOSE TO THE WALL, SO I COULD HIDE IF I HEARD JESSE PINN RETURNING.
YOU'VE BEEN WARNED.
HOW MANY *TIMES* HAVE YOU BEEN WARNED?
I HEARD THE OTHER MAN, BUT HE SPOKE SO QUIETLY I COULDN'T HEAR WHAT HE WAS SAYING.
YOU FOOL, YOU STUPID SHIT.
YOU PRATTLING, GOD-GUSHING MORON.
I WAS FINALLY ABLE TO SEE THE MAN JESSE WAS TALKING TO. IT WAS...
...FATHER TOM ELLIOT.

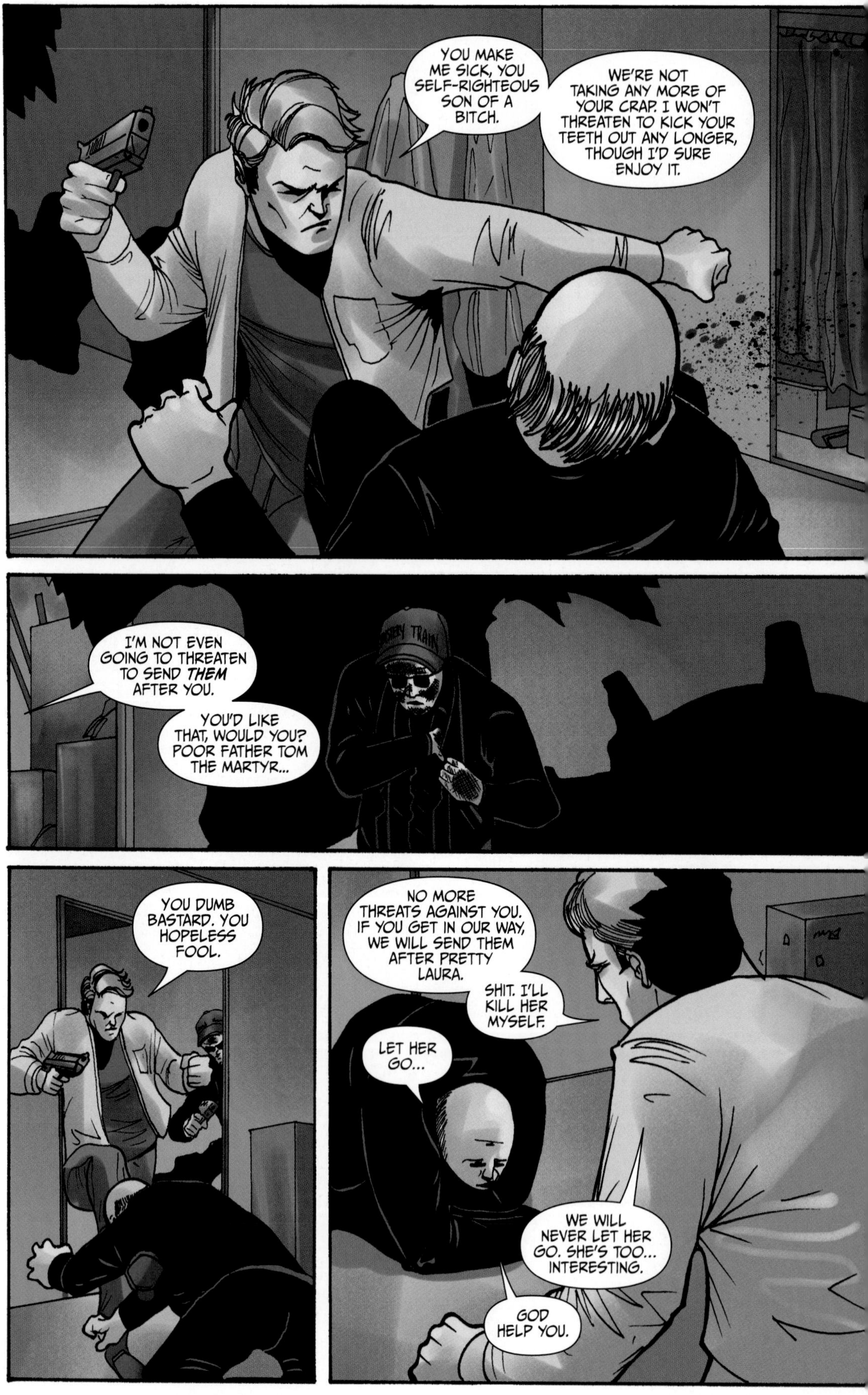
YOU MAKE ME SICK, YOU SELF-RIGHTEOUS SON OF A BITCH.
WE'RE NOT TAKING ANY MORE OF YOUR CRAP. I WON'T THREATEN TO KICK YOUR TEETH OUT ANY LONGER, THOUGH I'D SURE ENJOY IT.
I'M NOT EVEN GOING TO THREATEN TO SEND *THEM* AFTER YOU.
YOU'D LIKE THAT, WOULD YOU? POOR FATHER TOM THE MARTYR...
YOU DUMB BASTARD. YOU HOPELESS FOOL.
NO MORE THREATS AGAINST YOU. IF YOU GET IN OUR WAY, WE WILL SEND THEM AFTER PRETTY LAURA.
SHIT. I'LL KILL HER MYSELF.
LET HER GO...
WE WILL NEVER LET HER GO. SHE'S TOO... INTERESTING.
GOD HELP YOU.

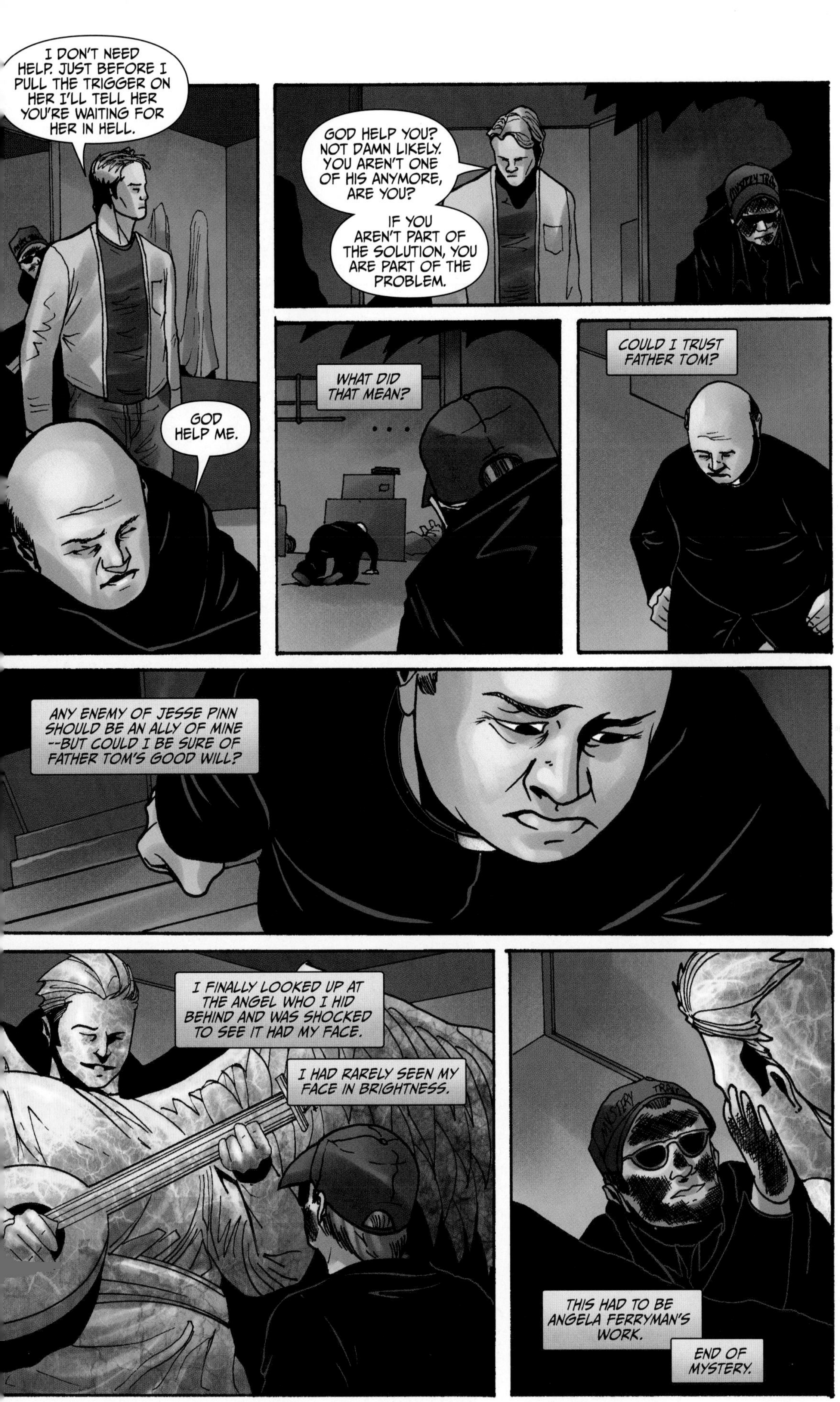

I DON'T NEED HELP. JUST BEFORE I PULL THE TRIGGER ON HER I'LL TELL HER YOU'RE WAITING FOR HER IN HELL.
GOD HELP ME.
GOD HELP YOU? NOT DAMN LIKELY. YOU AREN'T ONE OF HIS ANYMORE, ARE YOU?
IF YOU AREN'T PART OF THE SOLUTION, YOU ARE PART OF THE PROBLEM.
WHAT DID THAT MEAN?
. . .
COULD I TRUST FATHER TOM?
ANY ENEMY OF JESSE PINN SHOULD BE AN ALLY OF MINE --BUT COULD I BE SURE OF FATHER TOM'S GOOD WILL?
I FINALLY LOOKED UP AT THE ANGEL WHO I HID BEHIND AND WAS SHOCKED TO SEE IT HAD MY FACE.
I HAD RARELY SEEN MY FACE IN BRIGHTNESS.
THIS HAD TO BE ANGELA FERRYMAN'S WORK.
END OF MYSTERY.

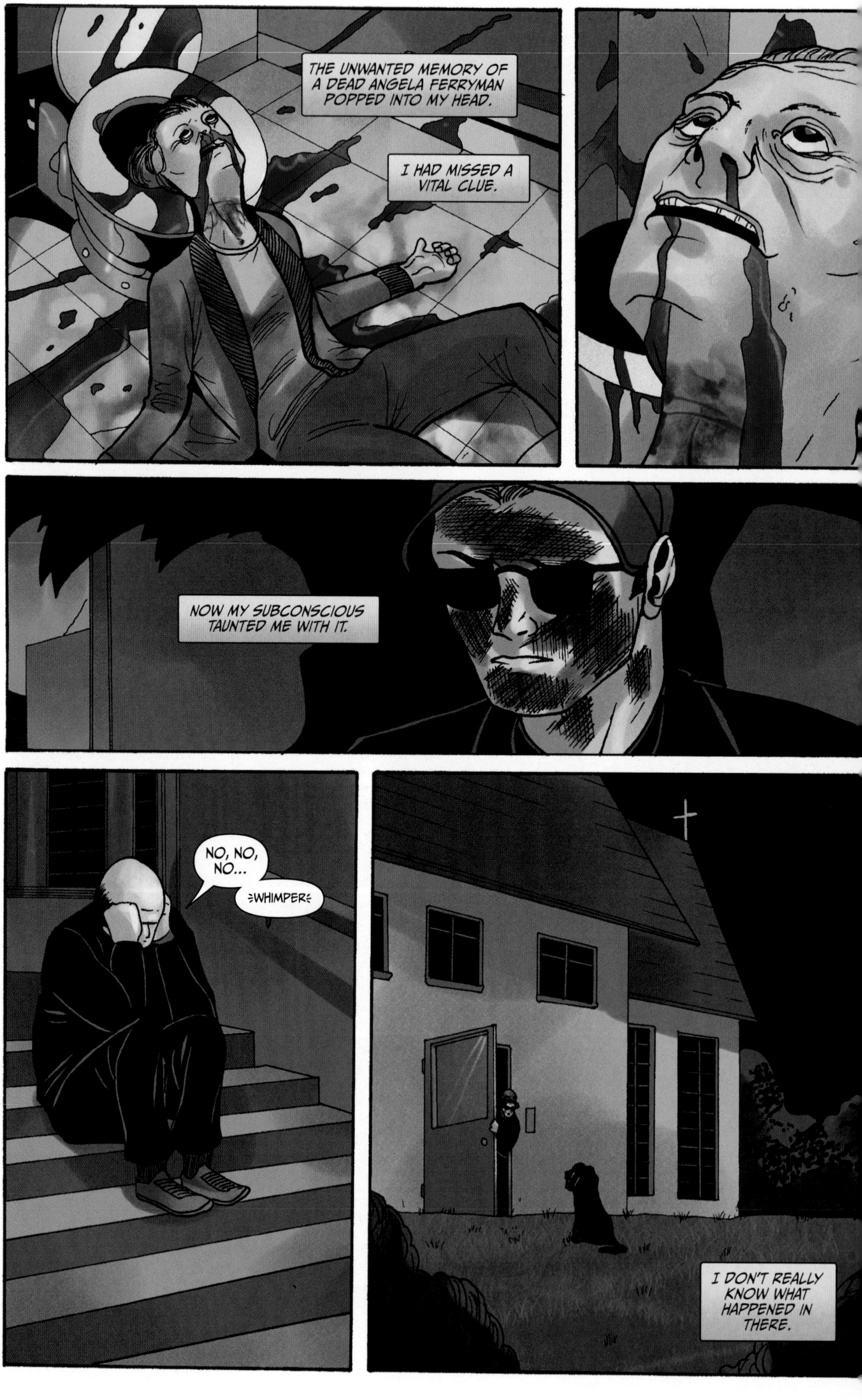
THE UNWANTED MEMORY OF A DEAD ANGELA FERRYMAN POPPED INTO MY HEAD.
I HAD MISSED A VITAL CLUE.
NOW MY SUBCONSCIOUS TAUNTED ME WITH IT.
NO, NO, NO...
WHIMPER
I DON'T REALLY KNOW WHAT HAPPENED IN THERE.

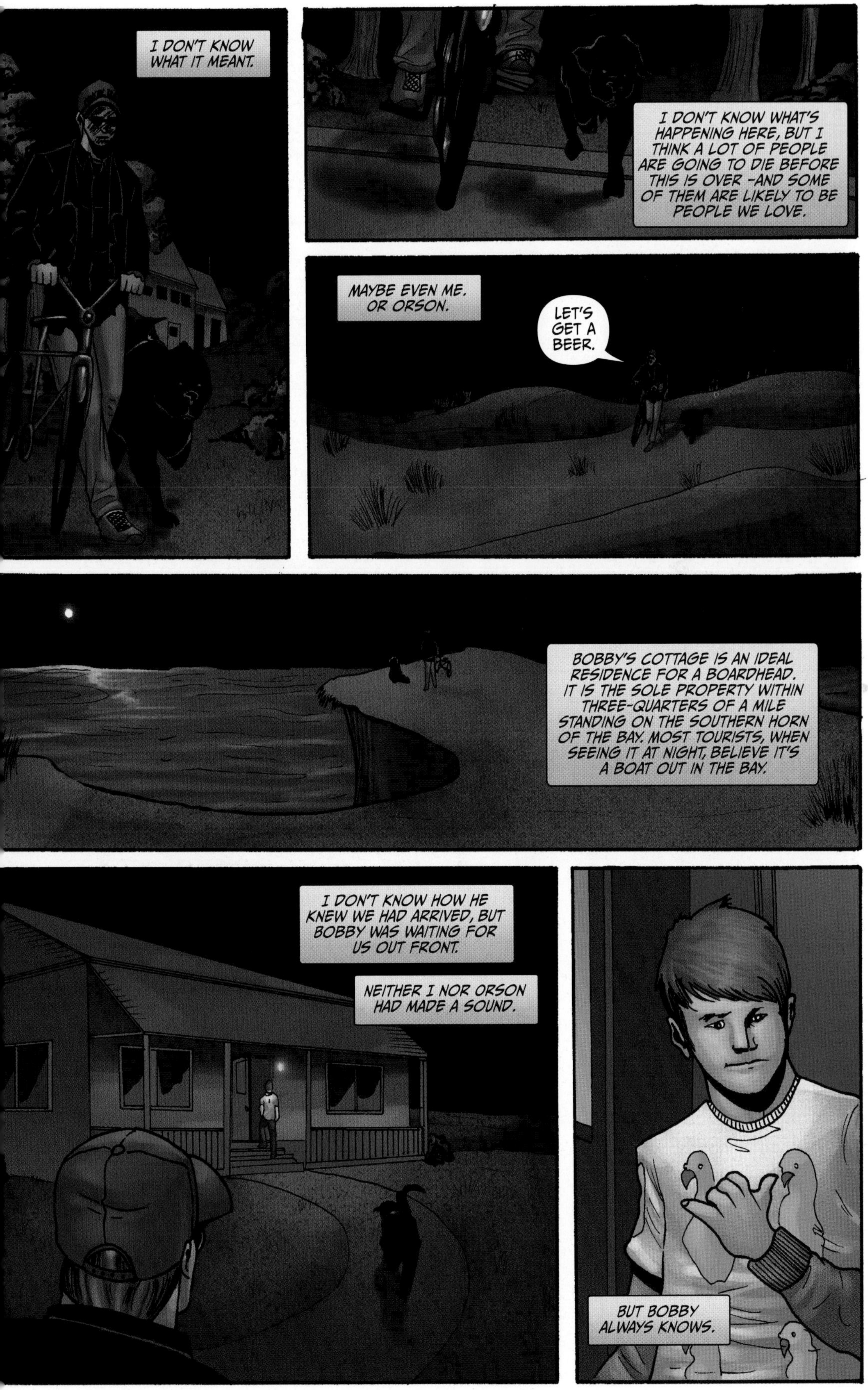
I DON'T KNOW WHAT IT MEANT.
I DON'T KNOW WHAT'S HAPPENING HERE, BUT I THINK A LOT OF PEOPLE ARE GOING TO DIE BEFORE THIS IS OVER -AND SOME OF THEM ARE LIKELY TO BE PEOPLE WE LOVE.
MAYBE EVEN ME. OR ORSON.
LET'S GET A BEER.
BOBBY'S COTTAGE IS AN IDEAL RESIDENCE FOR A BOARDHEAD. IT IS THE SOLE PROPERTY WITHIN THREE-QUARTERS OF A MILE STANDING ON THE SOUTHERN HORN OF THE BAY. MOST TOURISTS, WHEN SEEING IT AT NIGHT, BELIEVE IT'S A BOAT OUT IN THE BAY.
I DON'T KNOW HOW HE KNEW WE HAD ARRIVED, BUT BOBBY WAS WAITING FOR US OUT FRONT.
NEITHER I NOR ORSON HAD MADE A SOUND.
BUT BOBBY ALWAYS KNOWS.

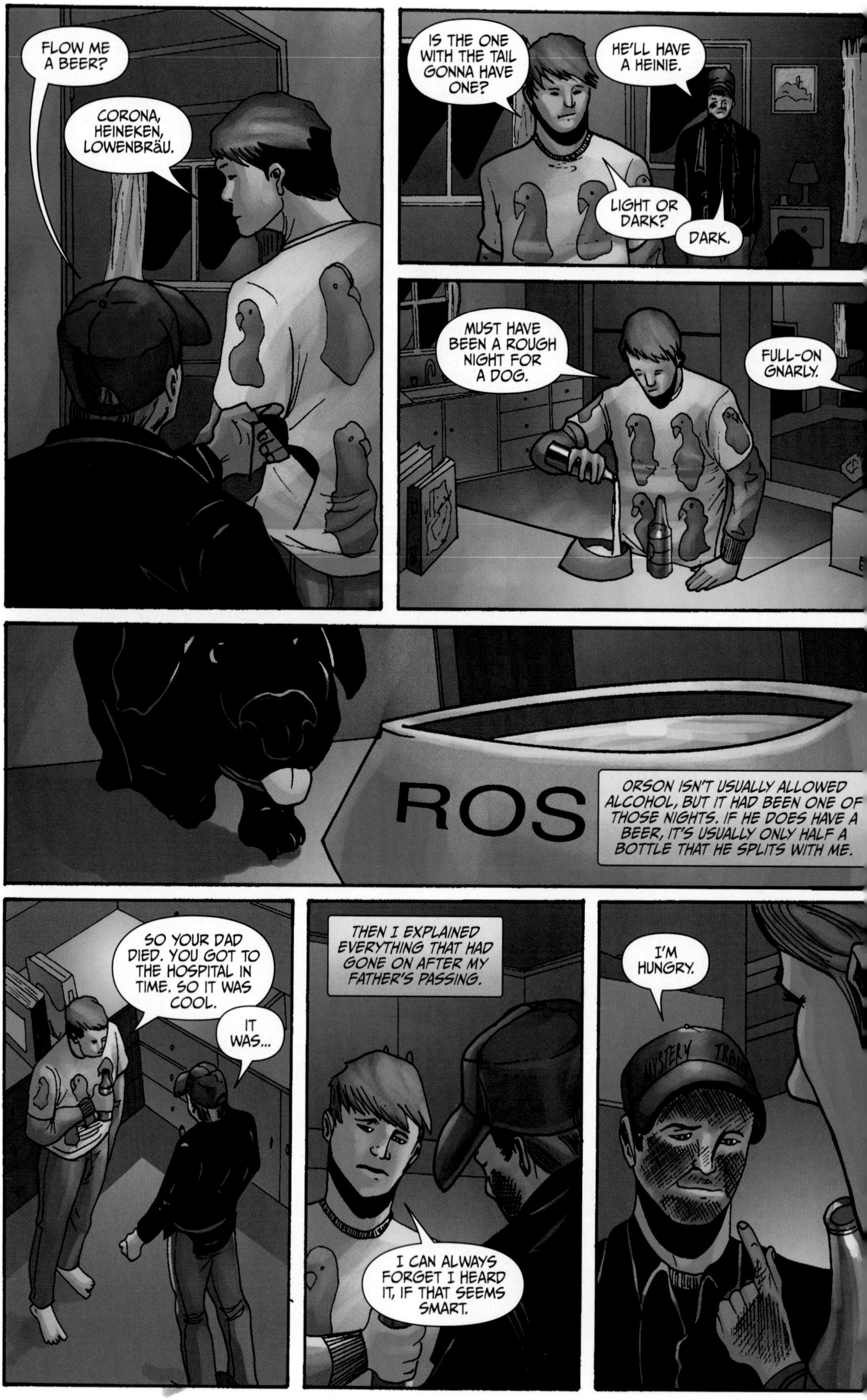
FLOW ME A BEER?
CORONA, HEINEKEN, LOWENBRÄU.
IS THE ONE WITH THE TAIL GONNA HAVE ONE?
HE'LL HAVE A HEINIE.
LIGHT OR DARK?
DARK.
MUST HAVE BEEN A ROUGH NIGHT FOR A DOG.
FULL-ON GNARLY.
ROS
ORSON ISN'T USUALLY ALLOWED ALCOHOL, BUT IT HAD BEEN ONE OF THOSE NIGHTS. IF HE DOES HAVE A BEER, IT'S USUALLY ONLY HALF A BOTTLE THAT HE SPLITS WITH ME.
SO YOUR DAD DIED. YOU GOT TO THE HOSPITAL IN TIME. SO IT WAS COOL.
IT WAS...
THEN I EXPLAINED EVERYTHING THAT HAD GONE ON AFTER MY FATHER'S PASSING.
I CAN ALWAYS FORGET I HEARD IT, IF THAT SEEMS SMART.
I'M HUNGRY.

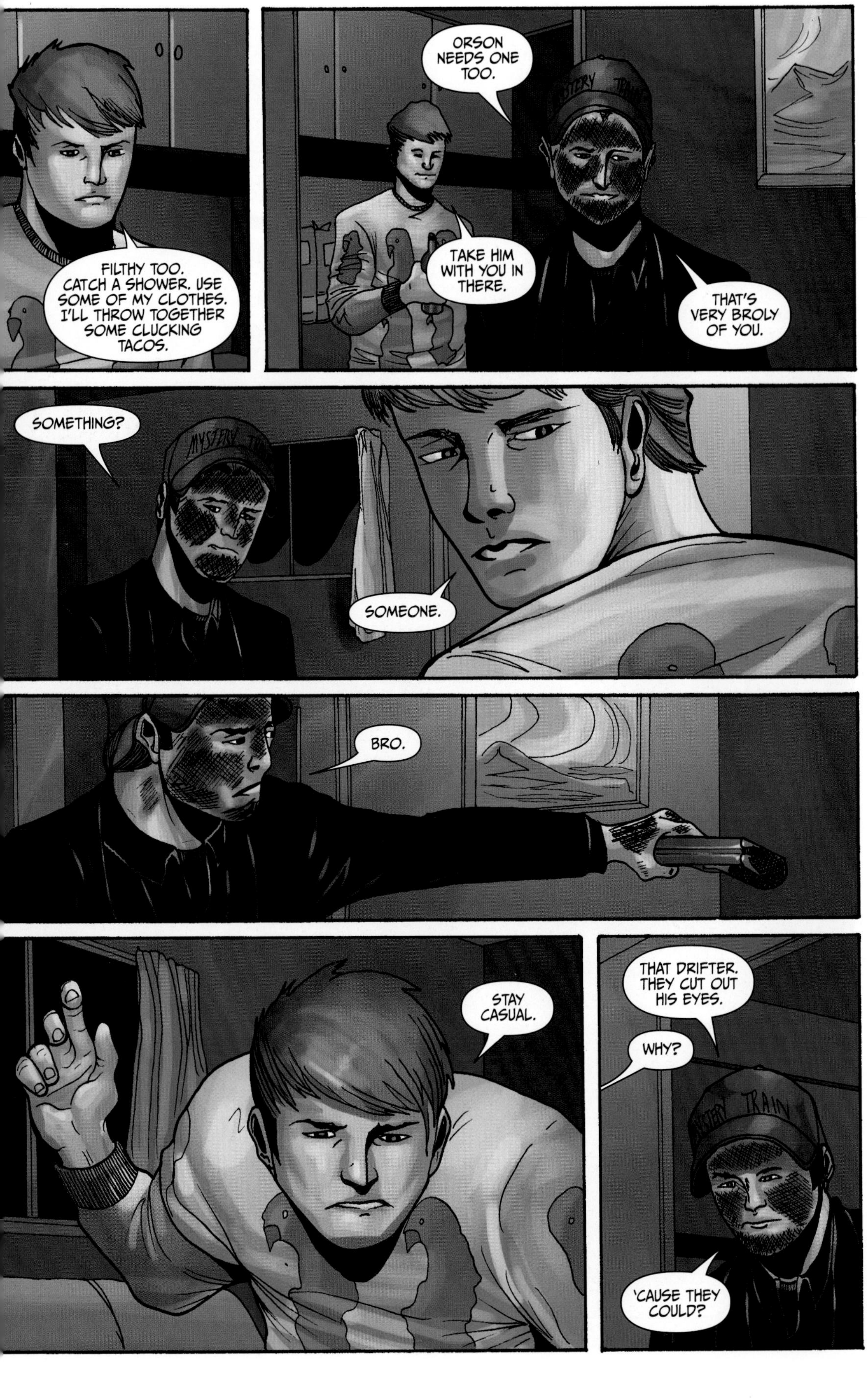
FILTHY TOO. CATCH A SHOWER. USE SOME OF MY CLOTHES. I'LL THROW TOGETHER SOME CLUCKING TACOS.
ORSON NEEDS ONE TOO.
TAKE HIM WITH YOU IN THERE.
THAT'S VERY BROLY OF YOU.
SOMETHING?
SOMEONE.
BRO.
STAY CASUAL.
THAT DRIFTER. THEY CUT OUT HIS EYES.
WHY?
'CAUSE THEY COULD?

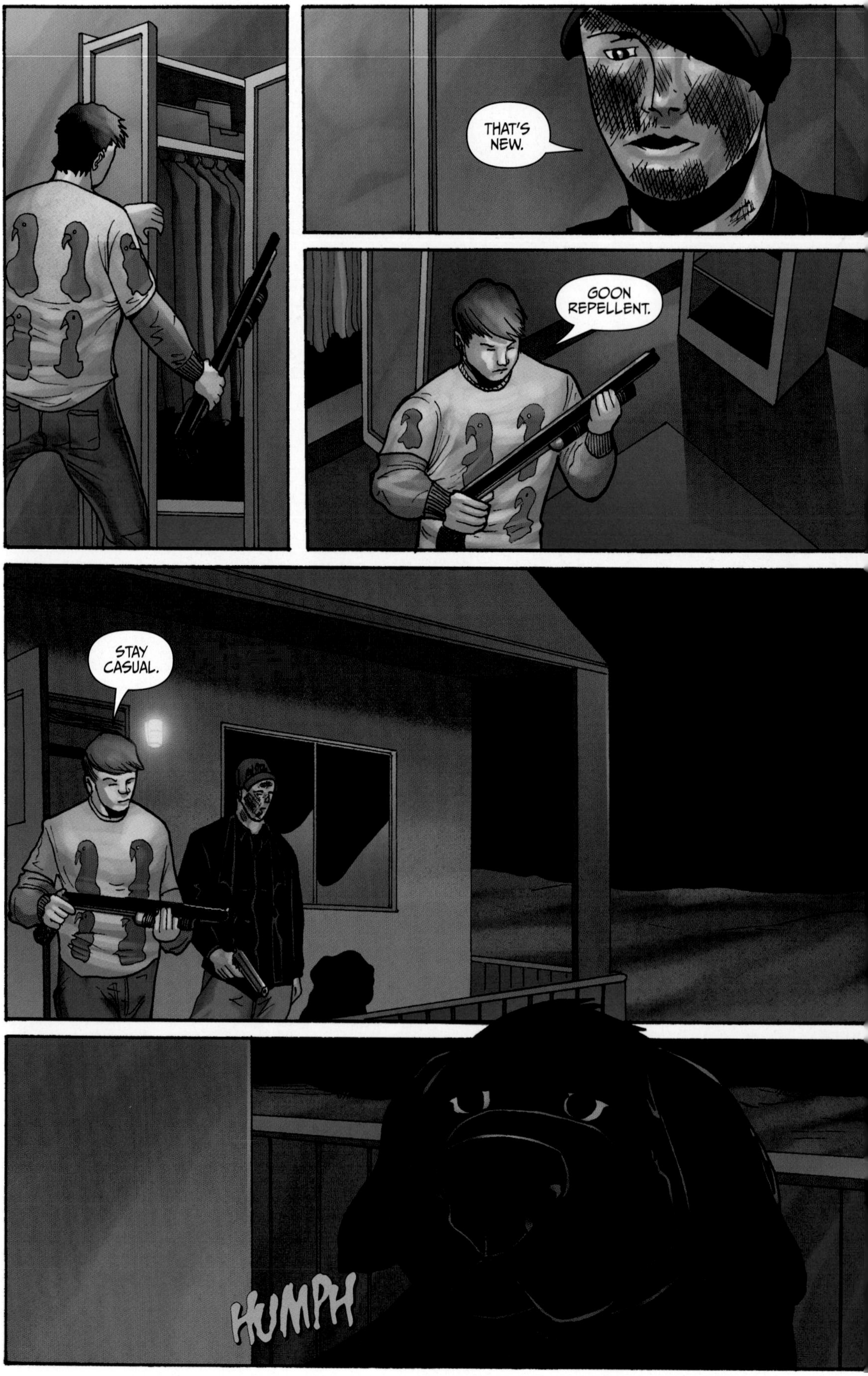
THAT'S NEW.
GOON REPELLENT.
STAY CASUAL.
HUMPH

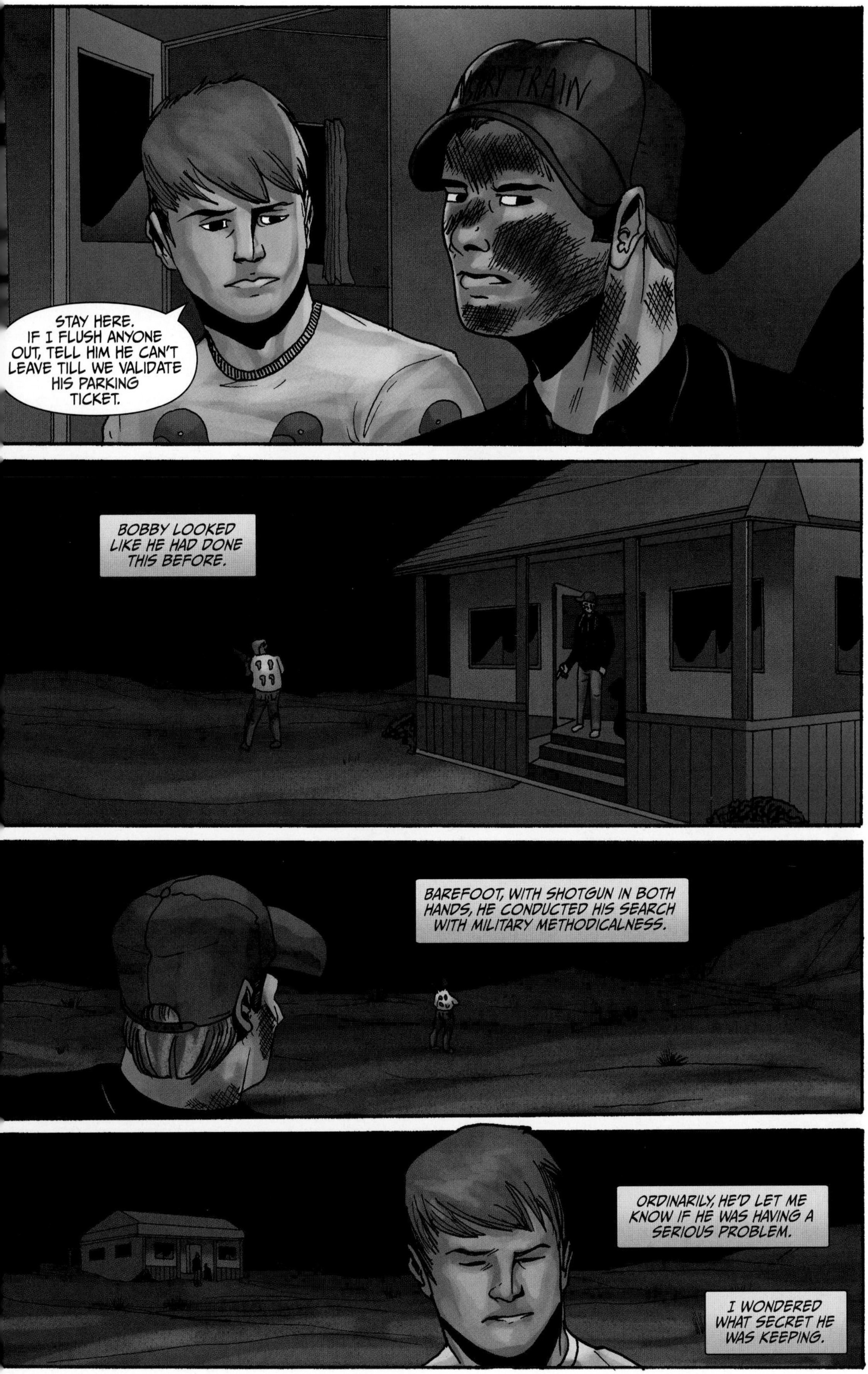
STAY HERE. IF I FLUSH ANYONE OUT, TELL HIM HE CAN'T LEAVE TILL WE VALIDATE HIS PARKING TICKET.
BOBBY LOOKED LIKE HE HAD DONE THIS BEFORE.
BAREFOOT, WITH SHOTGUN IN BOTH HANDS, HE CONDUCTED HIS SEARCH WITH MILITARY METHODICALNESS.
ORDINARILY, HE'D LET ME KNOW IF HE WAS HAVING A SERIOUS PROBLEM.
I WONDERED WHAT SECRET HE WAS KEEPING.

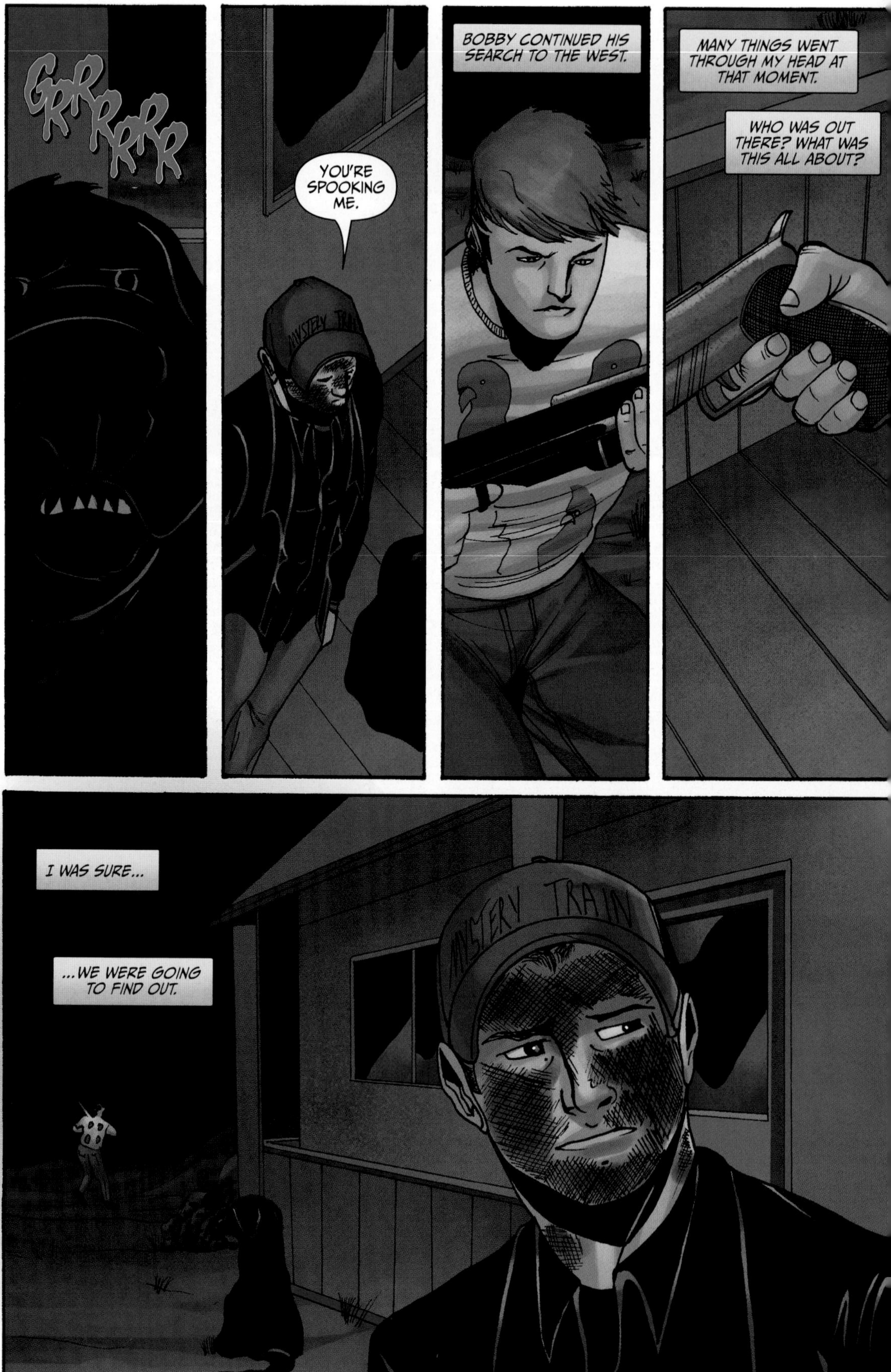
GRRRRRR
YOU'RE SPOOKING ME.
BOBBY CONTINUED HIS SEARCH TO THE WEST.
MANY THINGS WENT THROUGH MY HEAD AT THAT MOMENT.
WHO WAS OUT THERE? WHAT WAS THIS ALL ABOUT?
MYSTERY TRAIN
I WAS SURE...
...WE WERE GOING TO FIND OUT.
END BOOK ONE

SKETCHBOOK

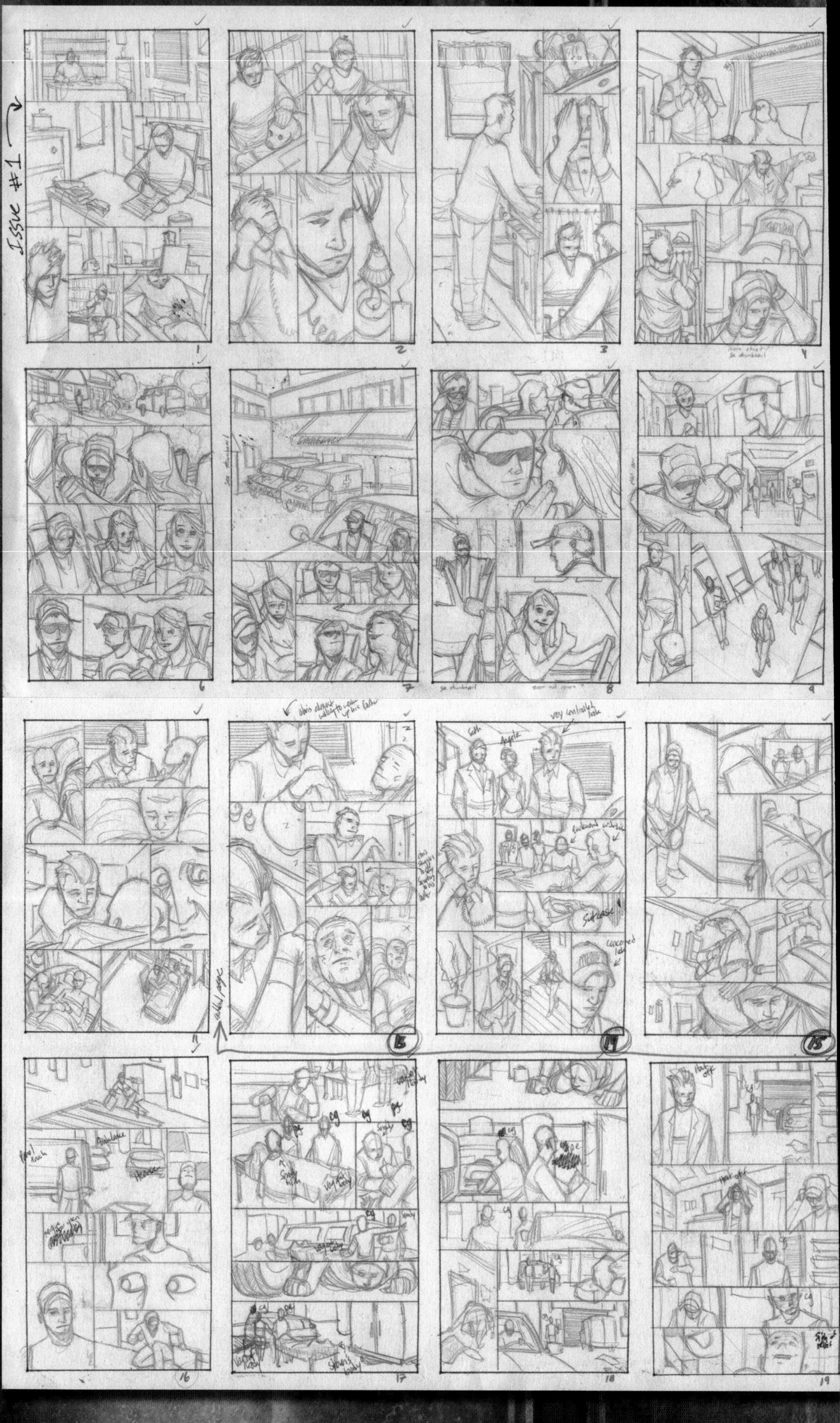
Issue #1

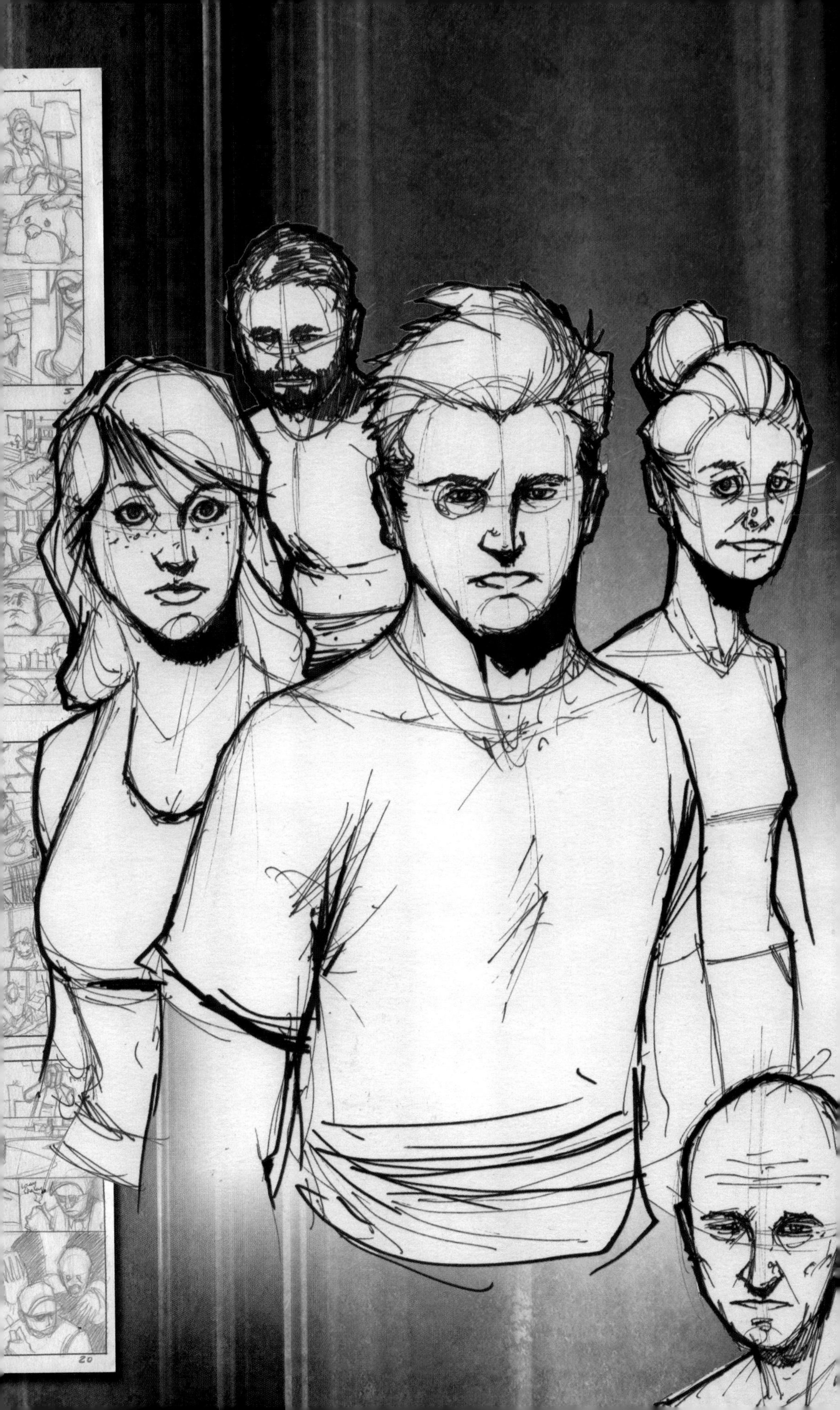

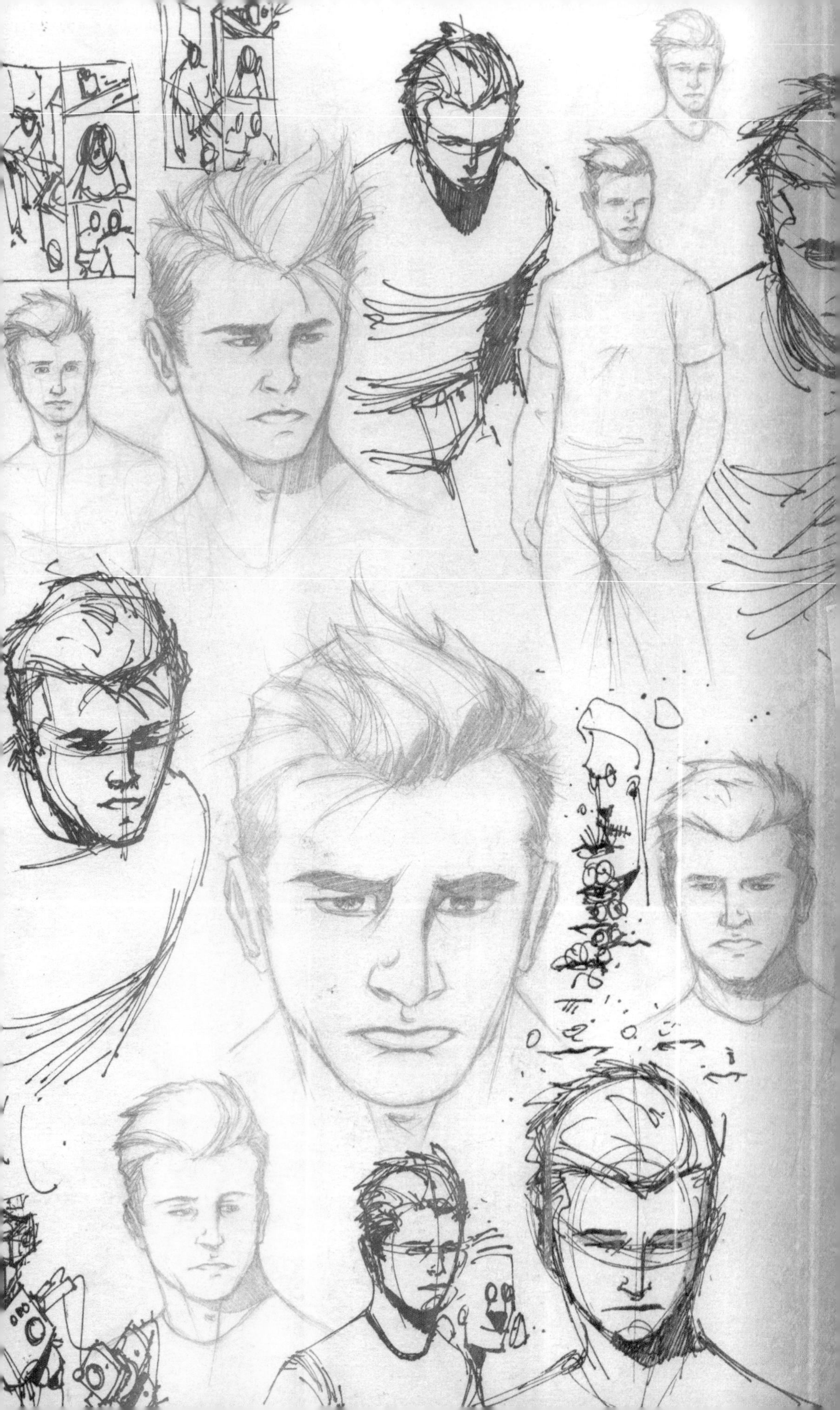

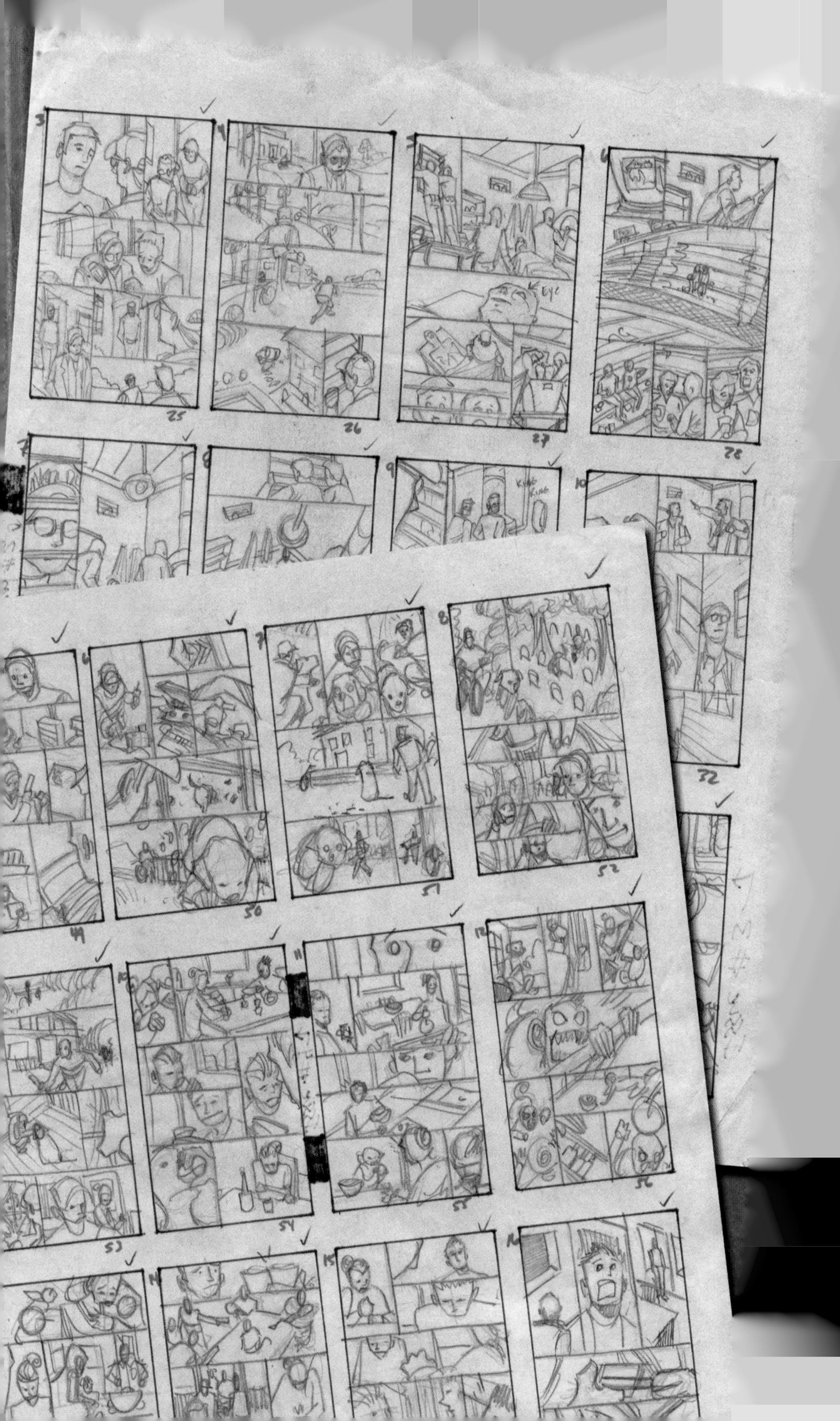

Eye
25
26
27
28
32
52
53
54
56

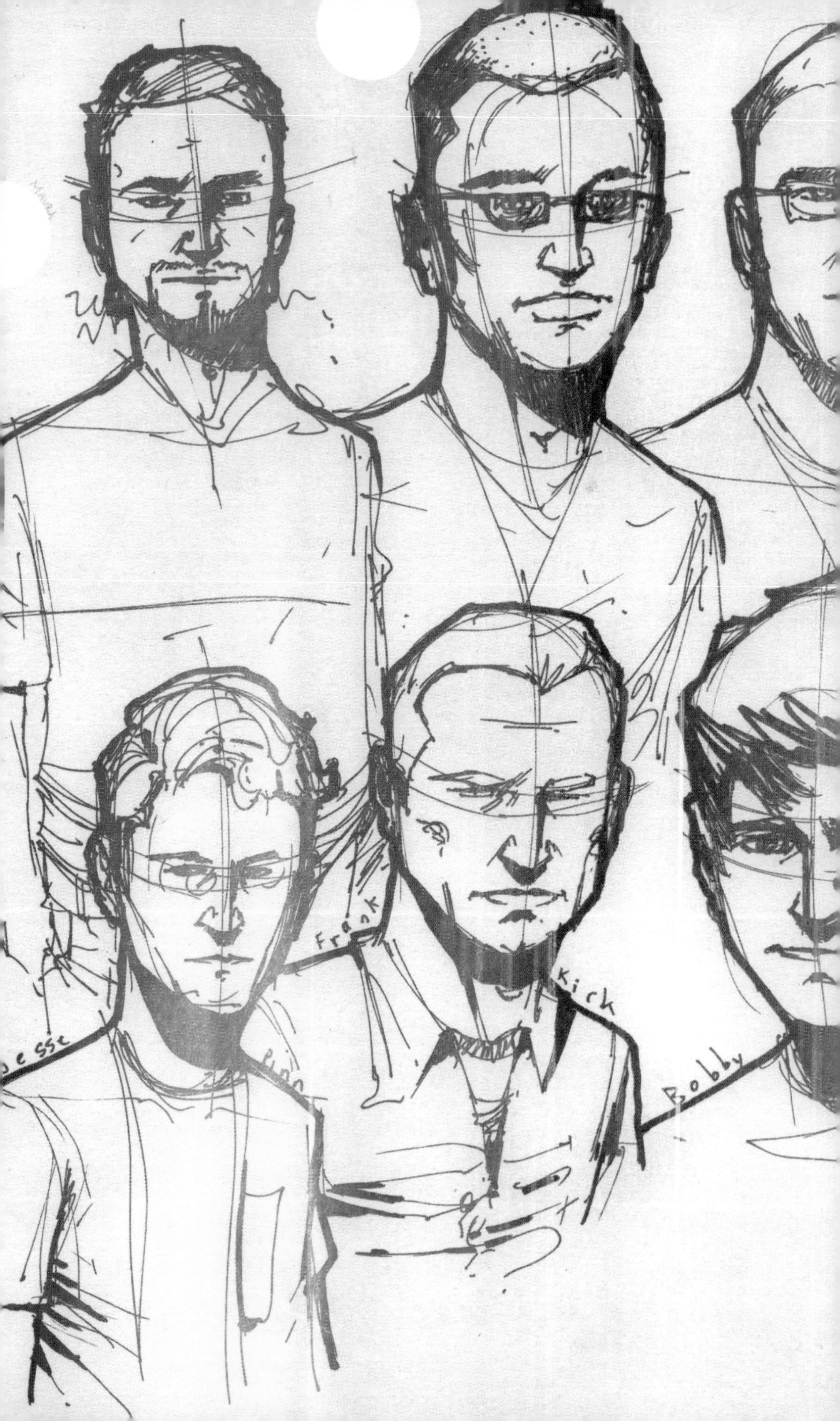

Frank
Kirk
Jesse
Bobby

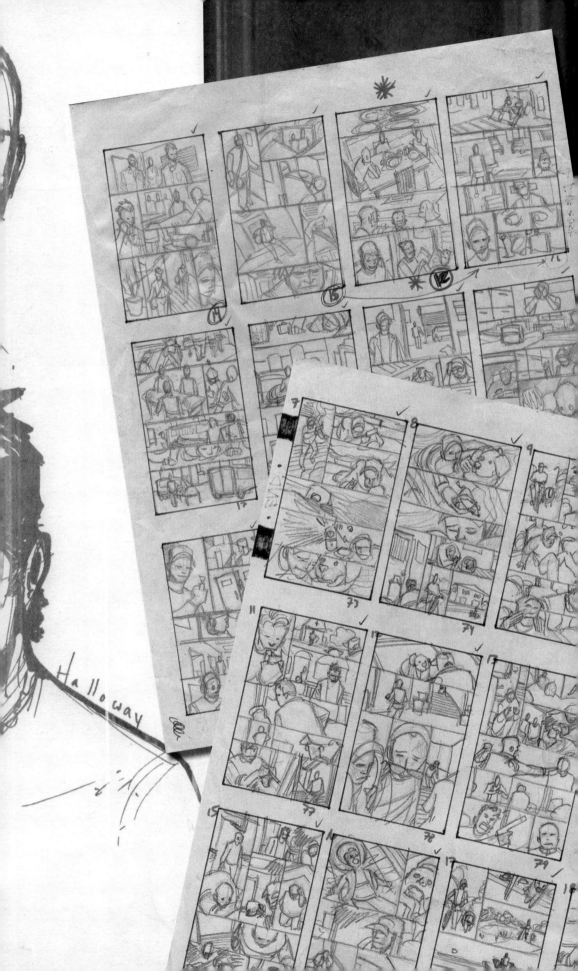

Halloway

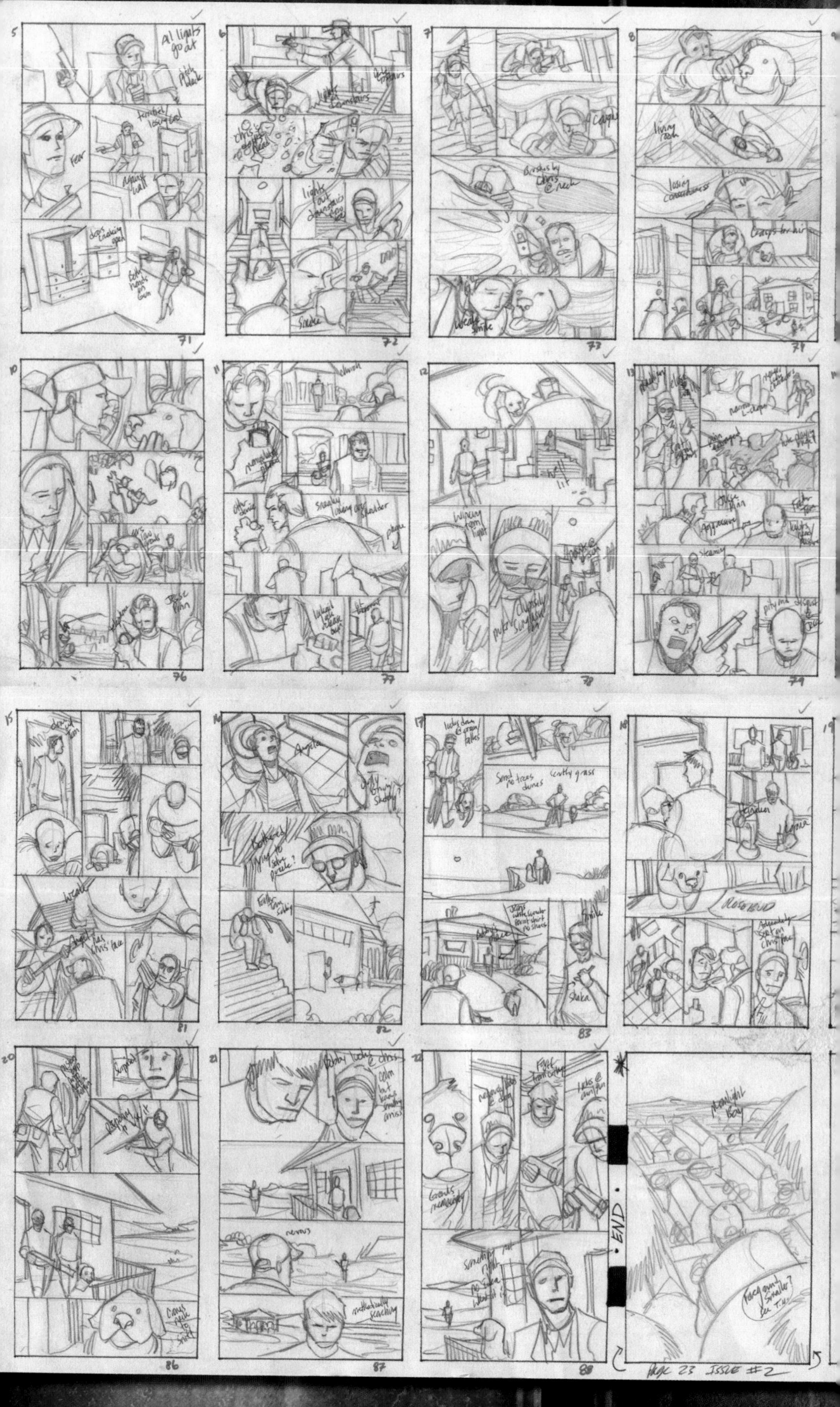

All lights go out
pitch black
Fear
light downstairs
Chris's
living room
losing consciousness
gasps for air
church
Sneaky
Angela
Sand
No trees
dunes
scrubby grass
Smile
nervous
Surprised
Greets neighbors
Calm
END
Page 23 ISSUE #2

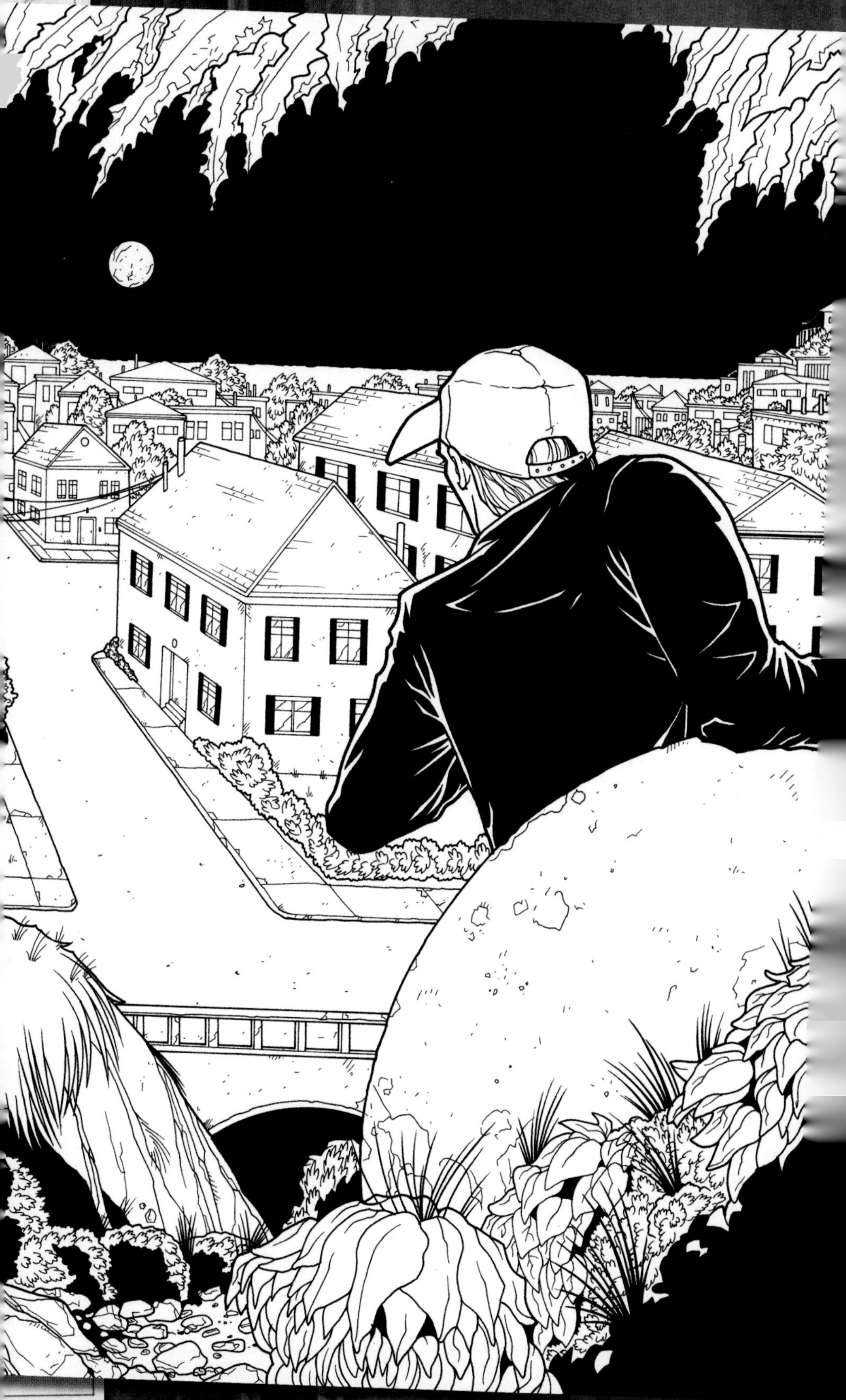

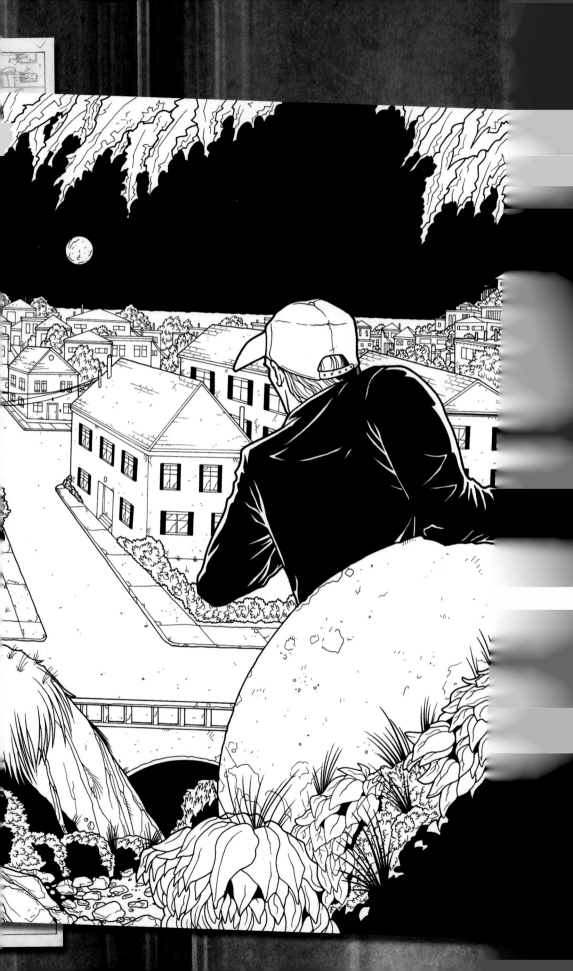

an interview with
grant alter & derek ruiz

Have you adapted any work for comics before?

Derek Ruiz (D): I have done it a couple of times. I've also been doing editor work on adapted works for the last six years. I enjoy writing these things more so than the editing though.

Grant Alter (G): I adapted a short Dresden Files story, but that is really the extent of the adapting work I have done. Primarily, I've written my own stories with my own characters. Though in that same book, I did get to write an original story featuring characters from the film, "The Warriors." That was a best of both worlds sort of situation.

What other sort of writing have you done in the past?

G: I've written tons of stuff that hasn't been published, as I think all writers have. Right? I mentioned my Free Comic Book Day short stories, but I have worked on a number of pitches and short stories for anthologies. With writing, so much of it is doing the work and putting the words on the pages and then, if you're lucky, people get to see what you've done.

Have you ever co-written a book before?

D: This was actually the first time I worked with a co-writer. I picked Grant myself since I knew the passion he had and the ability he would bring to the project. I also knew I was going to be too busy to work on the book alone so getting Grant to jump in and take some of the work load off my shoulders was great. I definitely would do it again on another project.

G: This was a first for me too. Naturally, comics are a collaborative medium, but this is the first time I shared the writing seat with another person officially. And yeah, I thought it worked well too. Though I could see how it could go horrifically awry.

Is the process changed by introducing another writer?

G: The way we handled it, the day to day writing work wasn't all that different than if we had worked solo.

D: Well, for me, writing comics is usually a somewhat solitary occupation but when you introduce another writer you have to take into account merging the two styles to fit

seamlessly. We had lots of discussions as to the best way to go about the adaptation. We decided to write our separate scenes and then really discuss the portions where we had to pull them together to make it seem like we were one guy doing all the work. I hope it ends up feeling that way in the final product.

G: Yeah, it was sort of like we worked on our own pieces and then edited each other until it fit together as seamlessly as we could get it. I think it would be harder if you were writing something original than it was using Dean's words the way we did. You don't have to take the writer's voice into account as greatly. But it helped a ton to have someone to bounce the planning parts off of.

How did you handle the fact that Derek lives in New York and Grant lives in St. Louis?

D: Lots of Emails, Lots of phone calls and con meet ups. We discussed this project a lot. Grant and I have been friends for a long while so I knew working with him would make the process go much quicker and be much easier. It was tough at first but we made ourselves very available to one another.

G: Yeah, the internet was a real godsend. It's changed the way comics are made across the board, but I know we wouldn't have been able to work nearly as efficiently without it. At one point, we were actually able to get pages approved by Dean's people as we finished them. It couldn't have worked smoother, really.

Was it easier or harder to write with someone else instead of alone?

D: I'd say at first it was tough meshing our styles and trying to figure out what to cut and what to leave in. But once we got into a groove, it became much easier. We broke the book up into sections and where they were supposed to connect we fused them together.

G: Hah. That's funny. I actually thought the beginning part was made tons easier by having another person to discuss it with. We knew how many pages we had to fill and where we needed to get in the story once we hit that limit, so it can be somewhat daunting to sit alone and have to map it all out like that. As for working on the actual script, we had to do that part by ourselves, so it didn't change much.

This volume contains the adaptation of the first half of the novel. Was it difficult to decide how to pace the comic adaptation?

G: Yeah, I think that's the hardest part. Especially if you like the source material. You really have to be ruthless in your choice of what to include and what to cut. That said, I had a pretty good idea how I wanted to leave the reader at the end of this volume. I wanted to end the volume at the beginning of what I knew was going to be an awesome sequence so as to really make you want to come back. And by the way, the next sequence is completely awesome.

D: I agree. Awesome.

Was this the first Koontz novel you'd read?

G: As much as I read, I am surprised to have to admit that yes, it was. I was aware of the name and that he was respected as an author, but the first time I was ever really exposed to his work was the Dabel Brothers adaptation of Frankenstein. After having read that, when I got an opportunity to adapt Dean myself, I was very excited.

D: For me, the answer is no. I had read Dean's Frankenstein series first and then I read both novels about Christopher Snow, which I really loved. After I found out I would be writing it I read it about 3 more times. I have since read about eight Koontz books, though Fear Nothing is my favorite.

Did you learn any tricks you plan to use to work on the next volume?

G: Yes, throughout the writing of volume 1, we figured out a much more efficient way to work than we had been using. Instead of thinking of the script as a whole, we started thinking about it in terms of 2 parts, the pictures and the dialogue. And we wrote those parts separately before lining them up and making them right.

D: Well we've had such a long break between volumes, I think we are more prepared than we were with the first volume. We will probably break down the rest of the story way in advance of putting in the dialogue. We will then go over the scenes with the editor to see what they think we should keep and what we should cut.

G: It'll certainly go smoother.

What was your favorite sequence to write in volume 1?

D: Anything with the crazy monkeys. How can you not like crazy monkey creatures?

G: Yes, I agree, the monkeys are great. I got to do the sequence where Angela tells Chris about them and I absolutely had a great time writing that.

What was the biggest challenge you faced in adapting this particular novel?

D: The biggest challenge for me was what to cut and what to keep. I always feel like if I cut the wrong scenes, it will hurt the overall product. So outlining a project beforehand becomes key. With an outline and the process of getting approvals from the author, the worry about what gets cut gets lifted from my shoulders somewhat. At least my choices are backed up anyway.

G: For me, it had to be how much of the beginning of the novel takes place within Chris's head, with him telling a story. In a novel, that works a lot better than it does in comics. It was tricky to come up with interesting visuals to fit with that monologue. That said, I am happy with the job we did and I think struggling through that process improved us as writers.

What other work do you have in the pipeline?

D: I actually can't talk about anything currently in the pipeline on my end except The Alchemist and to say I have a lot of cool things coming out next year.

G: I am working on my first novel and trying to get a few creator owned comics going. I also have a zombie short story that should be coming out soon in the Zombie Bomb anthology.

DEAN KOONTZ
FEAR NOTHING